Dearest Jean,

Blessings &

Love.

The Father's Heartbeat

*How Great the Father's Love for Us
How Rich and Beyond Measure!*

Divine Revelations From His Heart To Ours

Ella Jane Coley

**In Loving Memory
of
Ricky Martin Theriot**

*My only and dear son whom I was blessed with in this life
for fifteen very precious years, and who is now among
the great cloud of witnesses - cheering me on!*

authorHOUSE®

AuthorHouse™
1663 Liberty Drive
Bloomington, IN 47403
www.authorhouse.com
Phone: 1-800-839-8640

First published by AuthorHouse 12/1/2009

ISBN: 978-1-4389-9838-1 (sc)
ISBN: 978-1-4389-9841-1 (hc)

Printed in the United States of America
Bloomington, Indiana

This book is printed on acid-free paper.

All scriptures used are taken from The King James Bible, The Amplified Bible, The Message Bible, and The New King James Bible.

Acknowledgements

To My Lord and King, The Author and Finisher of my faith, who for the joy set before Him, endured the Cross, despised the shame, suffered affliction and has sat down at the right hand of the throne of God, who keeps me from being weary or exhausted, losing heart, and fainting in my mind.

Special Thanks

To my precious daughters and their spouses:

Crystal Theriot, who so faithfully, diligently and zealously labored untiringly, for so many hours. For her divinely inspired gifts and talents that was administered in these writings. Without her, these inspirations would not have been penned.

Marcy and her husband, Wayne Dowler, who stand by my side in ministry and hold up my hands.

Myra and her husband, Ronnie Wood, for their support and encouragement.

To my lovely grandchildren, Kristen, Marty, Haylee', Ashtin, Blaise' and Anisten, by whom I am so graciously blessed.

To my husband, Jim, for his encouragement to '*go for it*'.

To Passageway Ministries members and supporters, for their prayers and support.

To my co-laborers, friends, and relatives, who believe in me and in the ministry appointed unto me.

And to the many Ministers across this great nation and the globe who so faithfully cheer me on.

Dedication

To all the Family of Faith who desire the greatness of His Spirit.

Forewords

A devotional writer is a spiritual director - called and compelled to guide hearts hungering for holy communion with Father, Son, and Holy Spirit that buoys souls amid life's meanness, madness, and misery as trickles are turned into rivers of living water.

Only someone called and compelled into extraordinarily personal spiritual disciplines of prayer, fasting, and study can enable others to tap into His existential as well as eternal graces. The following pages witness to Ella Jane being a spiritual beggar telling other beggars where to find the food that has nourished her soul to nourish others.

As our Lord's friends allow Him to guide them through the wisdom and knowledge entrusted to her for them, a rare coupling of clarity, candor, courage, and gentleness will evoke praise and thanks as bravehearts are reborn if necessary and renewed as required.

Dr. Robert R. Kopp
Belvidere, Illinois
Pastor, Professor, and Iconoclast (www.koppdisclosure.com)
Author: <u>15 Secrets for Life and Ministry</u>
   <u>God's Top Ten List</u>
   <u>Golf in the Real Kingdom</u>
   <u>Don't Forget This</u>
   And soon to be released...<u>Cave Canem</u>

I have been privileged to receive the writings of Ella Jane Coley as part of my daily time with God. As Pastor Coley was developing these thoughts of exhortation, encouragement, wisdom and revelation from the Word of God, she shared them with a group of people daily and I can say that they were enriching and empowering to my daily walk of faith.

I have always said that the walk of faith in the seen world is a lonely one; others can only *"stand"* with us in faith. We need all the encouragement in the Word that we can get to walk this walk, then as the Word is opened in revelation to us, we come to the realization in the Spirit that our daily burdens are in fact carried by the Holy

Spirit. We are most certainly not alone. We then become sensitive to the Heartbeat of the Lord as it beats through the written and spoken Word, giving us strength as it pumps the abundant life of Christ into our very being. The heart of a true pastor does not beat of its own accord but rather resonates with the beat of the heart of the Father. It resonates with the love, wisdom, revelation and the empowerment of the Father.

The heart of Pastor Coley is such a heart, beating out the love of the Father for His people and ministering to the needs of His children. Our personal experience with Pastor Coley has proven this to be true in every way. She has been an encouragement to our family in the difficult times as well as the good. When anyone meets her she immediately assumes the role of a pastor for that is what she truly is. She has the gift of expressing the heart of God in words that touch the heart of the people of God. She ministers with a tender heart while she wars in the Spirit against the forces which oppress the beloved people of her almighty Jesus.

This book beats with the loving heart of the Father beating through the chest of His servant in the written word, encouraging us to always look unto Him, the source of our strength. As you read the words of this book, receive the words of revelation, encouragement, wisdom and power, but listen closely as you read. Listen beyond the words of this pastor's heartbeat, listen....yes, listen for the very heartbeat of God.

Buck Stephens
Advancing the Kingdom Ministries, Syracuse, New York
International Speaker / Evangelist
Author: The Coming Financial Revolution
And soon to be released...The Mudcake Rebellions

We are living in an age and time when we need each other to receive ministry, and be ministered to, concerning the things of the Kingdom. Those of us, especially in the pastoral ministry, need other mature brothers and sisters in the church to share with, fellowship together, and open our hearts to as we pray one for another to receive strength, direction, and encouragement in the Word. For over a period of twelve months, I have been receiving such spiritual strength from

Pastor Coley's daily devotionals, "Thought for the Day" of which this book is comprised. They have been such a rich and practical gospel message in our daily living. I recommend "The Father's Heartbeat" to all those who wish to daily sit at the feet of Jesus through the writings of my dear friend and fellow Minister.

Joseph Kingal
Papua New Guinea
Tele-Evangelist, World Evangelist & Pastor

This Book is a reflection of the love and encouragement Pastor Coley has so freely given, not only to me, but to all who are privileged and honored to know her. For the past twenty years it has been my great joy to have enjoyed loving Christian fellowship with Ella Jane.

She is an inspiration to me and to the many, many readers who receive her daily devotional, "Thought for the Day." One recent devotional, "Get Out of Neverland" states, *"It is heartbreaking to see Children of Light living in the Shadows of Neverland. They simply exist in life, and never experience the fullness of life with all its guts and glory."* She concludes by saying, *"He is a good God with precious promises of better things for us! The future begins now, and you never have to live in the Shadows of Neverland again!"* I know you will find this Book to be a constant source of encouragement and insight from your Heavenly Father's heart.

Bishop D. L. McLaughlin
Word Power Baptist Tabernacle
Forestville, Maryland

Preface

Having experienced the reality of my loving Father, I share portions of scriptures that have strengthened, sustained, guided and kept me through times of despair, when no hope could be found in any other. My prayer is that you may find comfort, strength and stability as you partake of the Manna from the Word of God.

The Psalmist writes a dear and favorite scripture, *"Unless your law had been my delight, I would have perished in my affliction. I will never forget your precepts (How can I?) for it is by them you have quickened me (granted me life)."* Psalms 119:92-93

Isaiah 43:2 speaks, *"When you pass through the waters, I will be with you, and through the rivers, they will not overwhelm you. When you walk through the fire, you will not be burned or scorched, nor will the flame kindle upon you."*

In times of testings and trials, may you be inspired and motivated to continue walking in Him, knowing there is victory in hope. May your experiences catapult you into a new dimension of God's Glory that can be attained only through these times. The Words of this Song has spoken to me over the years and I pray they will bless you also:

I've seen the lightning flashing, And heard the thunder roll
I've felt sin's breakers dashing, Trying to conquer my soul
I've heard the voice of my Savior, Telling me still to fight on
He promised never to leave me, Never to leave me alone
The world's fierce winds are blowing, Temptations sharp and keen
I feel a peace in knowing, My Savior stands between
He stands to shield me from danger, When earthly friends are gone
He promised never to leave me, Never to leave me along
When in affliction's valley, I'm treading the road of care
My Savior helps me to carry My cross when heavy to bear
My feet, entangled with briars, Ready to cast me down

My Savior whispers His promise, I never will leave thee alone
NO! NEVER ALONE! NO! NEVER ALONE
He promised never to leave me, Never to leave me alone!
Author Unknown

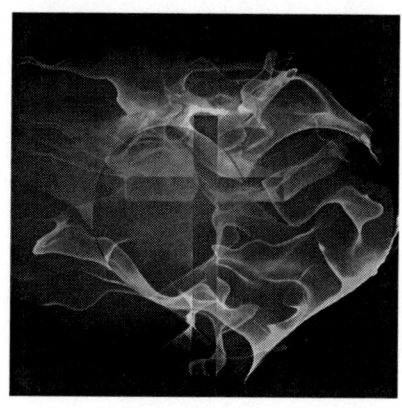

January

Leaving the old behind…
And stepping into our Future and Destiny!

January 1

A New Day is Dawning

Isaiah 43:18, 19 "Do not remember the former things, nor consider the things of old. Behold I will do a new thing. Now it shall spring forth..."

Can't you sense the undercurrents of change? Do you feel that something of great significance is about to happen? A new day is dawning for the Church...*and for you!*

A new day is dawning! God is doing a new thing and it shall spring forth *now*! *Now* is the set time of favor! He implores us to remember not the former things and to give no consideration to the things of old. The traditions we rely on and the methods we use to worship Him are of no relevance to the new things He is doing! The past glories of the church are not enough for today's necessities. It's important for us not to get weary in the work of the Lord, and to continue honoring Him with our very best. This is not the time to slack off, but to earnestly await the new wave of glory that is coming to the Church.

We must let go of the past so we can live in the present and prepare for the future! It's time for us to rise to new levels and reach for the things that belong to us. *We will never move forward while looking back.* We will never achieve greatness while being satisfied with mediocrity. We will never accomplish our mission if we have no motivation. We are ready for a new day to dawn upon us! We are positioning ourselves for the changes that are taking place, and for God to do an amazing and new thing! Let's prepare our hearts and embrace the new things, and let go of the old things that keeps us bound to the past! *A new day is dawning for you*!

January 2

Embracing the New

Isaiah 64:4 "For since the beginning of the world men have not heard, nor perceived by the ear, neither hath the eye seen, O God, beside thee, what he hath prepared for him that waiteth for Him."

Nothing ever stays the same, but time slowly changes things. Change is coming to the world, to the Church, and to us individually! We are in a great transition and must be prepared - ready and willing to move forward when the Spirit speaks to us to do so. We are in that all important transition that will impact our world as we know it. It is as though we have been pregnant, waiting and waiting during the gestation period, and now the heaviness of birth is coming upon us - *the time of travail is near so that sons and daughters can be birthed into the Kingdom. We are about to engage in labor - that moment before the birth!*

Do you feel it, too? There is a restlessness in the atmosphere, so we must be very careful to walk in the Spirit. Our hearts and attitudes must be in alignment with the Spirit, and *we must walk softly before the Holy One with clean hands and hearts.* There is peace in the transition, faith in His Word, and great promises to us as we walk with Him. Hold on, remain steadfast in the faith, and speak only what God says. Walk in forgiveness and love, refuse to hold on to anything that God is not in! God is doing a new thing in us, through us, and for us who are waiting on Him!

January 3

Significant Beginnings

Genesis 1:1 "In the beginning God…"
Psalm 102:25 "In the beginning You…"
John 1:1 "In the beginning was the Word…"

Christmas of 1968 there were 3 astronauts aboard Apollo 8, making their 9th orbit around the moon. At one point they turned their space craft into a chapel. As their cameras were turned on the moon, and 50 million people watched on TV, they took turns reading select passages from the first chapter of Genesis. It opens with four powerful words, *"In the beginning, God…"*

God is a God of Beginnings! He is described as the Author and Finisher of our Faith. We should always place God where He belongs - *in the beginning of everything!* When we do, God will be there! He will be there at the start of each new day. He will be there when we embark upon new journeys, and He will be there when we step into new and unfamiliar places. Oswald Chambers said, *"If in the first waking moment of the day you learn to fling the door back and let God in, every public thing will be stamped with the presence of God."* The single most important thing we can do is to find God in the beginning of our day. It will set the course and tone for all that will happen in the day. Burdens are lifted, loads are lighter, and we can walk in peace and with a spring in our steps, knowing that we have relinquished control to the One who controls everything!

He is a God of new beginnings! Maybe yesterday we had it all wrong and make terrible mistakes that left us feeling there was no hope for us. Be encouraged to know that even when we mess up… when we put God first, He will give us new beginnings!

January 4

Visions, Dreams and Purpose

Proverbs 29:18 "Where there is no vision, the people perish…"

There is nothing so sad than to see someone lose their way and give up on their vision. Numbness slowly replaces passion. The soul that was once sharp and vibrant becomes dull and lifeless. Life becomes nothing more than a routine. Today will be just like yesterday and tomorrow will be just like today. This loss of vision will affect every aspect of life, including worship and service to the Lord.

This is what happened to God's chosen people. They left Egypt, a place where they had once prospered but now had sons on the endangered list, to go into a dry wilderness that was their passage to the land of promise and blessings. Along the way they allowed their visions to perish and their dreams to die. *It was when they took their eyes off of the future and looked back at the past that they lost their way and died in the wilderness.* Only a handful of visionaries, dreamers and purpose-filled believers made it into the land of blessings. These few men of faith refused to let the vision perish. *They kept hope alive by daring to believe that God had set them up to inherit the place of abundance.*

Our future is determined by what we see and believe today! Are we looking at our yesterdays and yearning for them, or are we putting the past behind us and looking ahead with great anticipation? *God will meet us in our tomorrows to fulfill the dreams He gives us today!* Hold on to your visions, for in them we will find our passions, our dreams and our place of blessings! Setbacks are not failures and failures are not permanent when God is involved in our vision! The call is clear and the command is sure! Onward! Forward! March! Dream! Dare! Believe!

January 5

Filled With Purpose

I John 3:8 "...For this purpose the Son of God was manifested, that he might destroy the works of the devil."
Romans 8:19 "For all creation, gazing eagerly as if with outstretched neck, is waiting and longing to see the manifestation of the sons of God."

There are deep, intense longings that fill the heart and soul of every living person - longings and desires that, although hidden at times, give meaning and purpose to our lives. *It is how we pursue these desires and purposes, and **Who** we involve in our plans that determine our failures and successes.* Only the revelation and understanding of God's purposes for our lives will give us true joy and fulfillment.

It is so easy to get caught up with pursuing the wrong things in our thirst for success. We can easily be sidetracked by the "have to do's" instead of the *"what He wants me to do."* Our lives are programmed and our time with Him because another agenda in our buy schedule, fitting Him somewhere between "must do's", "have to do's" and "need to do's". But when our busy days are suddenly emptied and void, when the cloaks of titles, positions, power, and authority are stripped away leaving us uncovered, then we can stand before Him, honestly, vulnerable, and defenseless - and once again discover our true passion and purpose in Him! *We are never more alive and filled with purpose than when we are filled with Him, and His purposes and His plans!* When His purpose once again becomes alive and vibrant, **we suddenly know what it is we were born to do!** We are not measured by the world's standards of success, but only by His purposes and plans!

January 6

Live Life On Purpose

Romans 9:17 "...Even for this same purpose have I raised thee up, that I might show my power in thee, and that my name be declared throughout all the earth."

Have you ever had one of those days that was out of control? Do you sometimes feel that you have little control over what happens to you, leaving you feeling helpless and lost? I believe we all experience times like these, but let me encourage you to *live your life on purpose* today!

We are the children of a God of purpose that has destined us to overcome, overtake and overflow! Things may not go like we planned or hoped - *overcome it*! Maybe our hopes and dreams have been crushed by life's cruel fist - *it's time to pursue and overtake*! For some of us, life has emptied us out, leaving us wearied and worn, and we need to be filled up with hope, joy and overflow blessings. There is a purpose for the trials - *it is to make us overcomers*. There is a purpose for the tests - *they bring out the best of God in us*! There is a purpose in the sorrow and loneliness that brings deep aches and longing to our heart - *they are to empty us so Christ can fill us with peace and joy*. Securities are stripped away *so that we become dependent upon Him*. His Purposes are revealed when we walk the faith walk.

When life feels out of control, we can take the control back by giving everything to Him. Let's reclaim our promises and recapture our vision. Let's let Him restore us to full Sons and Daughters - walking in power, victory and purpose! We are not victims, but conquerors! Let Him organize our days and plan our futures! He is a Master Planner, equipped with every fact, hope and dream for our destinies! *Don't settle for mediocrity - Live life with Purpose!*

January 7

Trust Him With Your Destiny

Jeremiah 29:11 "For I know the plans I have for you, declares the LORD, plans to prosper you and not to harm you, plans to give you hope and a future."
Proverbs 19:21 "Many plans are in a man's mind, but it is the Lord's purpose for him that will stand."
John 6:38 "For I have come down from heaven not to do My own will and purpose but to do the will and purpose of Him Who sent Me."
Exodus 9:16 "But for this very purpose have I let you live, that I might show you My power, and that My name may be declared throughout all the earth."

You are set aside and chosen by God for His Divine purpose! Perhaps as a child you felt the call of God pulsing with every beat of your heart. At times you may have felt different, or even lonely because of a calling and purpose greater than your own. I know that in my own life there are choices I can make everyday, however sometimes the choice is not even mine to make. *It has already been made for me.* I simply must be accepting of His plan that has been tailor made for my life. Acceptance of His plans for my life brings peace, joy and anticipation that my life will not be lived in vain.

I am destined and ordained for a very specific purpose, and knowing this makes it my responsibility to do everything I can to fulfill His plans and surrender my will to His. Purpose. Destiny. Jesus knew at an early age that His life had already been mapped out for Him, that He was born to redeem the world. What an awesome responsibility. We know that at the tender age of twelve He was already very much aware of His destiny. He felt the calling of God pulsating through His body in every breath He took. He knew He was called out, separated and chosen from the beginning of time to be The Deliver. His choices had already been made for Him. *His responsibility was to accept the Father's plans and fulfill them.*

I encourage you to seek God for His plans for your life, and for your children's lives. God knew you in your mother's womb and designed you according to a plan He had in mind for your life. Destiny isn't a futuristic thing, but is already in process. Your destiny is found in His redemption and every step you take by faith as you follow Him, whether it seems grandiose or not. Your Savior is shaping you and marking your steps. He knows where the path diverges, and He knows every fork in the road. He planned your life for you...it's your responsibility to follow His plan by surrendering everything to Him...and *step into your destiny.*

January 8

The Place of There

Psalm 139:10 "Even there shall thy hand lead me, and thy right hand shall hold me."

Have you ever found yourself in a place and wondered how you got *"there"*? One day you were soaring with eagles only to wake up the next morning at the bottom of the barrel. You had a good beginning, a great start, but somewhere along the way, you ended up in a place called *"there"* - a place where you find yourself alone with God.

It is in the *"there"* places where we see God's greatness and provision, for *"there"* we find ourselves vulnerable and defenseless, helpless to even help ourselves. It is *"there"* we learn to depend upon Him and learn to hear His tender voice speaking to us, ***"Don't fear! I Am!"*** It is *"there"* we see His faithful provision and it is "there" we learn to trust in His goodness.

Don't despair if you find yourself in the place called *"there"*. *Your steps are ordered by the Lord,* and, even *"there"*, He will guide you! What may seem like a barren place could very well be the place of great things, the place where you see the faithfulness of God, the provision of God, and the place of new beginnings.

January 9

In Position

Habakkuk 2:1 "I will stand my watch and set myself on the rampart, and watch to see what He will say to me..."

There is a position you can get in where you can hear the voice of God!

Habakkuk knew this position very well. *It is the position of prayer...*it is attendance to the Lord! It is the position of *standing on your watch* and *staying there until He speaks*! I would say that the main reason most of us don't hear from God is because we are too impatient to wait upon Him, and are too easily removed from our positions of prayer! I love what Habakkuk said..."I will stand my watch...and I will set myself on rampart." The rampart was the bulwark set up to oppose assault or hostile entry. In other words, I will find a place before the Lord where I can see an assault of the enemy while I wait to hear from Him! I will find a position where I can hear Him clearly while standing on guard!

Are you in a position to hear from the Lord? Are you willing to wait and stand watch until He speaks? There is a position, a place, where we can stand watch as we wait to hear what God will say to us. A place that says, "I won't be moved until I hear from God! I won't leave this place until I hear what He has to say. I won't make a move or do anything without a word from Him." If we are determined enough, if we are desperate enough, if we are in a position of prayer, then we will hear from Heaven and will receive all that He has for us!

January 10

Positioned for Change

Philippians 3:13 "...Forgetting those things which are behind, and reaching forth unto those things which are before me."

God is positioning us for change! A new day is dawning as the Priests of the Lord step forth with great power and anointing to usher in the glory of the latter house! It's time for us to arise to new levels and reach for the things that belong to us. It's time for change!

Here are some things that will position us for change:

We must be desperate for God.

We must be alone with God in our desperation, not holding on to others.

We must be willing to fight for what we need.

We must have an encounter with God by coming into His presence.

We must be freed from the past - freed from rejections, fears, sins, failures, emotional abuse, deception, offenses and religious formalities.

We must be freed for the present and the future to live life to the fullest.

We must be willing to submit to God's plan and surrender our will to His.

Rise up today, shake off the old ways and walk in a new dimension that is filled with His glory and power! God is positioning us for change!

January 11

Positioned for Power

I Samuel 17:37 "...The Lord, who delivered me from the paw of the lion and from the paw of the bear, He will deliver me from the hand of this Philistine..."

The Spirit of the Lord is positioning us for change and for power! Are you ready?!

Most people are uncomfortable with change, and sometimes struggle with positions of power. How much easier it is sometimes to just sit back and let life run it's course. Of course, we never achieve much or stand in the company of greatness. Unwilling to take a risk, we often play it safe, never knowing defeats or victory. Are you willing to be positioned for power?!

The Armies of Israel were at a standstill while facing Goliath. They were ridiculed and shamed, afraid to engage with the giant. But there was one who dared - David, just a shepherd boy from the hills of Judea, stepped forth with courage and boldness in the Name of the One who held his trust. He dared to take a risk. He had been positioned for power while guarding the sheep. He had already been tested and tried when facing the bear and the lion. His time had come!

Child of God, the battles you have already fought have positioned you for power! Don't be afraid to face the giants in your future, for they are but a stepping stone into a place of power. The Spirit that kept you through yesterday's struggles will propel you into tomorrow's victories. Dare to be remarkable! Take the risk! Your time has come!

January 12

Positioned for Influence

Genesis 41:38-40 "And Pharaoh said to his servants, can we find such a one as this, a man in whom is the spirit of God? Then Pharaoh said to Joseph, Inasmuch as God has shown you all this, there is no one as discerning and wise as you. You shall rule over my house and all my people shall be ruled according to your word; only in regard to the throne will I be greater than you."

We are an influence to someone today. When we walk with the Lord in trust, faith, obedience and integrity, God will use us to be of great influence to others.

Joseph walked with God. He had complete faith in the Lord, that no matter what he had to go through, God was still in control. He maintained his integrity and was found to be trustworthy. Not once can we find where Joseph complained about the atrocities that had befallen him. He was hated and rejected by his brothers, sold into slavery, lied about when he wouldn't submit to the Captains lustful wife, thrown in prison and still trusted God with his life. Someone of great importance took notice of Joseph. God had positioned Joseph in prison to minister to the kings servants, who in turn dropped his name to Pharaoh. We know the end of the story...Pharaoh made Joseph ruler over his own household and all of the country - second only to Pharaoh! Joseph passed every test that was put before him and was positioned to influence two nations - Egypt and Israel! What a testimony.

Sadly, many Christians today loose the power of their influence. Slothfulness, laziness, a lack of integrity, and an unwillingness to submit to God's ways will cost us, and rob us of opportunities to influence leaders and governments. However, there are many Josephs' who are submitted to the Lord, who walk in integrity and chose the high paths over the wide paths. They are people in whom the Spirit of the Lord dwells! Allow God to position you for influence by standing for truth, integrity, and having a power walk of faith!

January 13

Positioned for Favor

Psalms 102:13 "Thou shall arise, and have mercy upon Zion: for the time to favor her, yea, the set time, is come."

Have you ever looked around and wondered why everyone was being blessed *except you*? It is a mysterious thing to those who walk uprightly before the Lord to see the prosperity of the wicked while you are struggling just to survive. A few days ago I went to two businesses. They were the same type of business and individually owned. One was chaotic and disorderly, the other was quiet, orderly and you could smell the success. One was struggling, the other was flourishing. Both businessmen were believers. But, as Paul Harvey would say, *"Now for the rest of the story..."*

Notice what the Psalmist wrote, *"God, you shall arise and have mercy on Zion, for the time to favor her has come."* I find it interesting that the author wrote that the favor would come upon the *place of worship*, or the house of God. This also tells me that Zion was going through some hard times and experiencing difficulties, maybe even felt forgotten by God, or overlooked when He was passing out the blessings. Sometimes we feel the same way - *overlooked and passed by*! But this man of God stood up and declared to the Lord... *"You will arise and have mercy on us, for now is the set time of favor."*

Perhaps the riches you have seen heaped upon the wicked are in a holding tank, waiting for the Lord to release them upon you at the set time of favor? God does nothing by chance. Joseph had to go to the pit before the palace and Jacob had to wrestle with the Lord before receiving the blessing. Just because we haven't seen it yet, doesn't mean it's not coming! Our persistence and faith will take us to the Land of Promise, releasing the favor and blessings of the Lord! Let us walk in confidence before God with a clean heart, and allow Him to position us for favor.

January 14

Expect a Miracle

Matthew 9:20-22 "And behold a woman who had been diseased with an issue of blood twelve years came behind him and touched the hem of his garment; for she said within herself, If I may but touch his garment, I shall be whole. Jesus turned to her and said, Daughter be of good comfort, thy faith has made thee whole."

Our expectation produces our miracles!

Faith activates the hand of God to produce miracles in our lives. And guess what…it doesn't take big faith…just faith the size of a mustard seed! God can take a little faith and create mighty miracles. One touch of His garment and the woman was healed instantly. One word spoken, one kindness given, one divine connection, one split second in time can produce your miracle. Expect something today from your Heavenly Father. He desires to bless you today. It is His good pleasure to prosper you in all your ways. When we extend our hands of faith towards Him, He extends His hand of miracles towards us!

January 15

Keep Sowing your Seed

Galatians 6:7 "...For whatsoever a man sows, that shall he also reap."

Each spring one of the elderly neighbors in our community plants a garden on a plot of land he owns next to my daughter's house. You'll see his white truck there every day, from early in the morning until later in the day. He is busily plowing the ground with an old hand held plow as he prepares the soil for planting. He is very diligent with his garden, making sure that the weeds are all plucked out before planting his seed. Later, as the garden begins to produce, my daughter will often come home to find fresh vegetables of tomatoes, squash, okra, watermelons or cucumbers on her doorsteps...all from this man's garden. It's heartening to see our neighbor so faithful to his garden. *He expects that his seeds will produce a harvest...and they always do*!

Everywhere the Apostle Paul went, he sowed seeds... in prison, before Kings, to the Jews and also to the Gentiles. He took every opportunity to sow seeds, knowing they would produce a harvest of souls. Ecclesiastics says to cast our bread upon the waters, and that it would return to us after many days! Sow seeds of Expectation for great Manifestations! Sow seeds of Anointing! Sow seeds of Miracles! Sow seeds of Financial Blessings and sow seeds of Kindness. Sow seeds for your needs. Never stop sowing seeds... they will produce a great breakthrough in due season!

January 16

Refuse to Give Up

Hebrews 10:35 "Do not therefore cast away your fearless confidence, for it carries a great and glorious compensation of reward. For you have need of patience and endurance so you may be able to perform and fully accomplish the will of God."

Your daybreak is coming!

Too often some of us give up just before our breakthrough and thereby forfeit our rewards. There is a great and glorious reward for us when we allow patience to have her perfect work. It is at that point that we are able to perform and fully accomplish what God has commissioned us to do. We must hold on to our confidence and put our trust in the One who holds our tomorrows. We don't know what tomorrow will bring, but we do know the One who has our tomorrows already planned for us. In Genesis 32, Jacob had an encounter with the Lord and wrestled with Him all night. Jacob would not let the angel go until He blessed him, and it was at the point of daybreak that Jacob received his blessing! No longer would he be called Jacob, but Israel, which means, *"You have struggled with God and with men, and have prevailed."* We, too, must prevail and refuse to give up until our daybreak comes!

January 17

There is a Due Season

Habakkuk 2:3 "For the vision is yet for an appointed time, but at the end it shall speak and not lie; though it tarry, wait for it, because it will surely come, it will not tarry."

Are you waiting for your due season?

When God births a dream or a vision into our spirit, we can be assured that it will surely happen. It may not come in the time frame that we'd like, but it will come at the appointed time. When God appoints the season, our vines will not cast their fruit before their time. When a vine bears fruit too early, the fruit is bitter and has not ripened into sweetness. Many times people will try to "hurry up" things, instead of allowing time to position them into perfection. But God's timing is perfect, sometimes requiring patience, and always requiring faith. When we wait for the end result, it will speak, every time, of the fullness of God's plans and declare His Glory! *There is a due season...daybreak is coming!*

January 18

Violent Faith

Numbers 33:52, 53 "Then shall ye drive out all the inhabitants of the land from before you, and destroy all their engraved stones, destroy all their molded images, and demolish all their high places, you shall dispossess the inhabitants of the land and dwell in it, for I have given you the land to possess."

Take by faith what God promised you!
We have beautiful and glorious promises the Lord gave us that we must not let the enemy take possession of. We should be violent in our faith, refusing to cower to the enemies that try to inhabit our dwelling places and our promises from God. If God promises us something, He will also give us the power to possess it! Many times we will see a person who is healed only to allow that sickness or disease back. We see some people who receive financial blessings that seem to lose it overnight. *Don't let the devil inhabit your blessing*! We do not back down, hunker down, sit down, fall down, or take a back seat to our enemies, but we have the power to dispossess them and claim our victory.

This is a powerful passage of scripture where God is saying that we must destroy the works of the flesh, take down every idol and resist every ungodly thought that tries to invade our territory! Resist the devil...he will flee from us! Let's possess our land and take by faith what has been promised to us.

January 19

The Right Attitude

Ephesians 5:19, 20 "Speaking to yourselves in song and making melody in your heart to the Lord, giving thanks always for all things unto God and the Father in the name of our Lord Jesus Christ."
2 Kings 4:26 "Run now I pray thee, to meet her and say unto her, is it well with thee? Is it well with thy husband? Is it well with the child? And she answered, It is well."

I love being around positive people! They are so refreshing and uplifting! As believers we should have positive attitudes and uplifting words, regardless of how things appear to be. We should never speak what we feel or see, but speak what God says. We must be determined to confess His Word in the midst of negative circumstances! The Word of God tells us that by our words we are justified and by our words we are condemned.

In this story, we know that Elisha prophesied to a Shunammite woman that God would give her a son, which He did. A few years later we find that the little boy died. His mother laid his little body upon the bed of the one who spoke him into existence! *We could say that she placed her dead promise upon the word!* She then went to the source who gave her the promise, Elisha. When Elisha asked her about her boy, she responded in faith, saying, *"It is well."* What amazing faith this woman had! When her son of promise died, her faith took her to a place of resurrection power! She refused to allow her circumstances to negate her promise from God. She refused to condemn her promise with negative speaking. She would not let go of the thing God said she could have, and held on till daybreak came. The end result was that her promise lived again! Her boy was restored to life!

We, too, can speak faith that will bring restoration into our lives. *Our words will produce miracle blessings when we align them with God's Word.* When questioned about our promise, let's respond, *"It is well, my daybreak is coming."* Praise is not dictated by circumstances, but rather who God is! Your weeping may endure for a night, but joy is coming to you in the morning. What was held up, held back and delayed is on its way. Hold your head up, God has heard! Daybreak is coming! Today, let's keep our attitude full of gratitude!

January 20

A Place Called Transition

Tran·si·tion - n. 1. Passage from one form, state, style, or place to another. 2. a. Passage connecting one subject to another in discourse. 5. Sports. The process of changing from defense to offense or offense to defense, as in basketball or hockey. 6. A period during childbirth that precedes the expulsive phase of labor, characterized by strong uterine contractions and nearly complete cervical dilation.

If you are like most of us, you are probably finding yourself in the place called transition. It is the place where we let go of our comfort zones and step forward into the unknowns! It is a place that we all will visit more than once in our lifetime. Transition always requires faith to trust that we are entering into something better than what we have now. Transition takes what we learned in our yesterdays and prepares us today for our tomorrows!

It's not easy being in the place called transition. *It means we have to let go of some of our old ways of doing thing and learn some new things.* Transition is the part of change that makes us uncomfortable and vulnerable, and will sometimes expose our weaknesses. It is important for us to cling to the arm of the Lord during our times of transition, and give no place for the enemy to come in and steer us in another direction! It is usually in our place of transition when the enemy can take us off course because of the vulnerable state we find ourselves in. But it is when we walk through the transitions that we can go from glory to glory, victory to victory! The place of transition will propel us into our victory, making us stronger, wiser and better!

January 21

Intersections, Detours & Roadblocks

Isaiah 30:21 "And thine ears shall hear a word behind thee, saying, this is the way, walk ye in it..."

It is most often in our place of transition that we will encounter some obstacles or wonder if we made the right decision. Often we will second guess ourselves, and sometimes God. Transition can be very unsettling, especially when Satan will place intersections, detours and roadblocks in our paths. It is during these moments when we must simply trust God to guide us through. Sometimes we must stand still and quiet while waiting for Him to speak in His still, small voice, *"This is the way, walk ye in it."*

The Children of Israel knew a lot about transitions as they came out of Egypt and into the wilderness. The saw a huge roadblock in front of the when they came to the Red Sea, but God cleared the path for them. Joseph encountered many detours on his journey to the palace, but God got him where he needed to be at the right time. Abraham faced lots of intersections on his journey to the promise land, *yet he trusted the kind voice of his Friend to guide him.* How much more important it is for us to trust God in our times of transition, especially when facing intersections, detours and roadblocks. Even more important, we must continue be quiet before Him so that He can guide us in the right direction. *Having the right attitude in transition will determine how far and how high we will go!*

January 22

Staying Grounded in the Change

Ephesians 3:17-19 "That Christ may dwell in your hearts by faith; that ye, being rooted and grounded in love, may be able to comprehend...the breadth, length, depth and height; and to know the love of Christ, which passes knowledge, that you might be filled with the fullness of God, now unto Him that is able to do exceeding abundantly above all that we ask or think..."

Lately the Lord has been speaking to me of new seasons, change and a stirring in the atmosphere...things that will define who we are in the earth. Change doesn't come easily for most of us, *even when the change is for our good!* We cling to that which is familiar and comfortable, but exciting things are coming our way! These are things we have waited for, prayed for, and believed for... so we need not be uneasy with what God is doing. We are entering into a new season, coming into the fullness of the Love of Christ, and will see the *"exceeding, abundantly, above all we ask"* things come to pass!

I grew up in the bayou country of South Louisiana where the only way to get to some of the remote places is by boat. While going into some of these rivers and bayous, one of the things you will see are great oak trees that grow along the river banks. Due to the erosion of these banks, you can see some of the roots of the trees growing in the soil of the river banks. It is an amazing sight to see both the roots and the outer part of these trees. These trees have withstood hurricanes, erosions and storms, and continue to be rooted and grounded in the soil. We are to be like trees planted by the rivers whose branches flourish and whose leaves wither not. *How high we go is determined by how deep our roots are!* Beloved, I am very excited about what I see coming upon the horizons... wonderful changes are coming to the Body of Christ.

It is important for us to be rooted and grounded so that when the winds of change blow, our faith will remain intact and trustworthy. It is during the seasons of change in our lives when we can start to feel lost, uprooted, and out of sync with the Spirit of the Lord. It is human nature to fear the unknown and to embrace these changes, so let us be mindful to stay rooted and grounded in the Word and the Spirit of prayer. They will keep us balanced as we enter into the new seasons in our lives.

January 23

Lifter of My Head

Psalm 3:1-4 "God! Look! Enemies past counting! Enemies sprouting like mushrooms, Mobs of them all around me, roaring their mockery: "Hah! No help for him from God!" But you, God, shield me on all sides; You ground my feet, you lift my head high; With all my might I shout up to God, His answers thunder from the holy mountain."

Just when you think you can't take another step God will be there to carry you. When it seems that the waters have overtaken you and your head is about to go under...He will lift your head and hold it high!

It was in the midst of his most devastating and desperate hour that David penned these remarkable words: *"O Lord, how many are my foes... But you, O Lord, are a shield about me, my glory, and the lifter of my head"* (Psalm 3:1-3). David's anguish was no doubt magnified by the fact that his adversaries were those once closest to him, those in whom he had once placed his confidence and trust, are now among those whose accusations are most bitter and hateful. If all the trials which come from heaven, all the temptations which ascend from hell, and all the crosses which arise from earth, could be mixed and pressed together, they would not make a trial so terrible as that which is contained in this verse. *The pain he felt was so great that strength failed him and he could not even hold his head up.* That's when He lifted up his eyes to the One who had never failed, and *who gently and tenderly lifted up the head of the giant slayer.*

Does it seem like you are surrounded by enemies who taunt you with their mocking cries of *"Where is your God now?"* My friend, *He is close, shielding you from the fiery darts of the enemy.* He is there, like a Mighty Standard to guard you from the floods of the enemy. *He is there to turn the weapons formed against you into failed missiles.* He thunders from His holy mountain as He stands to defend you. **He tenderly and gently lifts up the weary heads that have no strength left**, restoring us with His refreshing love, mercy and compassion. He is your shield, your glory...and the lifter of your head!

28

January 24

Whatever You Ask

John 14:13, 14 "And whatsoever ye shall ask in my name, that will I do, that the Father may be glorified in the Son. If ye shall ask anything in my name, I will do it."

If we have the faith, He has the means! There is nothing too hard for God to do! If He can calm a storm with His word, He can surely calm our troubled hearts. If He can touch a blind man's eyes and give him vision, He can remove the scales from our eyes so that we can see clearly. If He can stop a funeral procession and raise a dead boy to life, He can restore life to those that doctors have given up on. If He can speak resurrection to Lazarus, He can surely speak a future for us!

God has great plans for your future! When everyone has given up on you, God is there, *believing in you.* When we have lost all hope, *The God of Hope speaks hope to the hopeless.* When our vision has become cloudy and we have lost our way, *He touches our eyes and renews our sight*! When we are weary with trials and burdens, *He renews our strength so that we soar as eagles.* When we feel that we are all alone and no one seems to care, *He is there, gently cradling us in His arms.* When the darkness surrounds us, *the Lord of Light dispels fears and darkness.*

God can take nothing and make something! He can take broken dreams and turn them into bright futures. He makes our tears into jewels! He can give us songs in the night and joy in the morning! He can do anything!

January 25

Called to Soar

Isaiah 40:31 "But they that wait upon the LORD shall renew their strength; they shall mount up with wings as eagles; they shall run, and not be weary; and they shall walk, and not faint."

God is calling a remnant of eagle saints that will soar in the heavenlies. We are called to soar above the elements of this present darkness and into heavenly places as we wait upon Him!

Eagles are special to God. The eagle symbolizes God in His strength, beauty, solemnity, majesty, fearlessness, and freedom. He has keen vision and can see things with a pararamic view, seeing what others miss. The eagle's greatest gift is the ability to soar, using thermal currents of air to carry him when he is tired or fatigued. He soars through high places, and is lifted up by the currents that are underneath him that bring rest to his weary wings. *He lives in the realm of the supernatural and dwells in the high places of the earth.*

The Lord is teaching us to soar! He is teaching us to rest in in Him as He carries us high above the currents of distractions and troubles. He shows us how to rise above difficulties and hindrances in our life, and how to soar high enough to gain His perspective on what is below. It seems the hardest lesson in life is to learn to wait upon Him and not do something in our own strength. But *when we wait upon Him, we are assured of enough strength to finish the race and enough energy to enjoy our victory*! As we wait upon Him, our strength is renewed and we soar as the eagles! We can run without weariness and walk without fainting. We will see amazing things that others miss - the view from high places is breathtaking! Our perspective will change and our strength will be increased. It's time... to wait upon Him...and to soar!

January 26

Called To Peace

Ephesians 6:15 "And your feet shod with the preparation of the gospel of peace."
Colossians 3:15 "And let the peace of God rule in your hearts..."
1 Thessalonians 5:13 "...And be at peace among yourselves."

One of the greatest blessings in life is the peace of God. It is not our Father's will for us to live life in constant turmoil, anxiety, worry, and sorrow, but to be filled with all peace, to speak in peace, to walk in peace, and to be at peace with one another. Peace cannot be confused with complacency, *but peace is the fruit of trusting God.*

The peace of God assures us we are going to make it when things don't look so great. It is His peace that comforts us when our hearts are filled with sorrow and grief, and enables us to trust Him. It is peace that fills us with hope in those times when we don't understand what is going on. *This glorious Gospel of Jesus Christ is delivered by feet that have been prepared with the Gospel of Peace.* We are called to peace, and to allow His peace to rule our hearts! When our hearts are ruled by His peace, fears are dispelled, doubts are removed, and love and unity flow freely. *It is during the storms of our life and uncertain circumstances that God directs us to such peace that fails understanding...*peace like a river. We, who also experience the buffeting of Satan as did Horatio Spafford, are able to say with such assurance, *"I am at peace and it is well with my soul."*

Our God-ordained, Christ appointed path is always guided by peace.

January 27

Faith Will Take Us There

Habakkuk 2:4 "...The just shall live by faith."

Our walk with the Lord will always be a walk of faith. *Faith is what takes us through the battles and the trials,* and assures us that everything will work out for our good. *It is believing without seeing.* **Faith takes us beyond the unknown into God's reality...**one step at a time.

I really like what Patrick Overton says about faith..."*When you come to the edge of all the light you have, and are about to step off into the darkness of the unknown, faith is knowing one of two things will happen: There will be something solid to stand on, or you will be taught how to fly.*"

Faith in God produces the most solid foundation, even when all around us there is nothing but sinking sands. He is the Solid Rock upon whom we build all of our hopes and dreams. Faith empowers us to believe that when we step into the unknown, He is already there. Faith builds heroes who do exploits for God's kingdom.

By faith...we understand that this world and all that is in it was formed by the Word of God. By faith we can subdue kingdoms, bring righteousness, obtain promises and stop the mouths of lions. Faith quenches the violence of the fiery trials and makes our weaknesses strong. Faith teaches us how to fly!

January 28

His Anointed Ones

Psalm 20:6 "Now I know that the LORD saves His anointed; He will answer him from His holy heaven with the saving strength of His right hand."
2 Corinthians 1:21, 22 "Now He who establishes us with you in Christ and has anointed us is God, who also has sealed us and given us the Spirit in our hearts as a guarantee."

The line is drawn in the heavenlies as the souls of men choose which side they will be aligned with. There is a great interest in the heavenlies as God anoints His Church and sets apart them from the world, for God does not choose unwisely or as the world would choose. He seeks hearts that are pure, hands that are clean, and spirits that are consumed by the call! These are the men and women that God is raising up!

To be "anointed" is, among other things, to be made sacred (consecrated); to be set apart and dedicated to serve God; to be imparted with enabling gifts and grace; to be divinely designated, inaugurated, or chosen for some purpose. His anointed ones are sealed with His Holy Spirit and filled with destiny and purpose. They are the Daniels who pray, the Hebrew boys who won't bow! They are the Esthers who are called for such a time as this! They are the Ruths who won't turn back! They are the Marthas who serve Him faithfully, and the Marys who worship Him adoringly! They are the Lazarus' who come forth when He calls! They are the Peters who boldly proclaim His message, and the Pauls who spread the Gospel to Kings and servants!

*They are the ones who have God's ear...*the one whom He will save with His strong right hand! We are children of a Covenant God! Oh yes, He makes a difference between the children of the world and His children! He is faithful to hear us! He is mighty to save us, for we are His anointed ones!

January 29

Now Is The Time

1 Chronicles 12:32 "Of the Sons of Issachar who had understanding of the times, to know what Israel ought to do..."

Things have been very intense lately, almost as if there is a shift taking place in the unseen realms of this world. People are more driven, whether by fear, faith, or something else. There is an almost somber atmosphere as if the world is on the brink of something major happening. I believe God is positioning us and placing us spiritually, globally, geographically and financially. If we dare to believe and dare to obey, we will see and do the supernatural! We, *like the Sons of Issachar,* will also know what we ought to do! *We will understand the times and seasons, and will know when our time has come!*

Now is our time! It is time to build. It is time to grow. It is time to evangelize. It is time to preach the Good News of the Gospel of Jesus Christ to whosoever will let him come. It is time to stand firm, without compromise. It is time to love and forgive. It is time for exploits. It is time to step out in faith and on the Word. It is time to take authority over principalities, strongholds and spiritual wickedness in high places. It is time for the spirit man to dominate the flesh man. It is time to put on the whole armor of God and fight. It is time for breakthrough. It is time for blessings. It is time to separate ourselves and become the standard instead of the copy. It is a time for faith.

What holds us back from our time? Is it money? Do what you can with what you have. Is it fear? *Dare to step out in courage and faith and do what you are called to do.* Are you waiting for the Right Connection? You already have a Divine Connection with God. He has the power to promote, direct, and bless. God is giving us revelation, understanding, wisdom and knowledge of our times and seasons. *It is our time...don't let it slip away*!

January 30

There is a Right Season

Habakkuk 2:3 "For the vision is yet for an appointed time, but at the end it shall speak, and not lie: though it tarry, wait for it; because it will surely come, it will not tarry."

Have you, like so many of us, wondered when your right season would manifest? Many of us are still waiting for our season, causing us, at times, to question the path we are walking on. I know the enemy would like to tell us that this calling is *'something in our heads'*, and make us wonder about a lot of things. But, of course, deep down in our Spirit man, we know better! *There is a drive inside of us that keeps pushing us forward and a faith that remains unshakable!*

Different seasons come to our lives, seasons when we have the Midas touch and all is well. There are seasons when our next step is lit up like a neon light beckoning us onward. Then, there are those seasons of loss, uncertainty, and waiting that we walk through. *There are those seasons when our faith is tested to the utmost to believe what He has spoken.* So, how do we handle the uncertainties and unknowns that lie before us? How do we find the "perfect will of God" for our lives when all of Heaven is silent and our prayers seem to return unanswered? How do we wait when the pressures of time, energy and fellow mankind demand answers that we don't have? *Our natural instinct is to make something happen and to try to make our season of waiting come to an end.* Yet, when God says wait, we must wait! We can wait out a difficult season in rebellion and anger, or go through life disheartened and with a spirit of resignation. *Or, we can wait with anticipation, trusting, believing and knowing that a Right Season has been appointed for us!* An appointed time indicates that God has made an appointment with our future that can neither be rushed nor delayed. He orders a set time, in a specific place, with Divine connections, that result in a Right Season for us!

When you wait on that which God has promised, it is a promise that will surely come. The one who makes this promise is none other than God who cannot lie. Dry and difficult seasons *do not last forever,* and when our season of waiting is over, what has been dry and desolate shall blossom as a rose, and what has been so bitter to our soul shall be made sweet. Keep the faith and know that He is in control. He will guard over His chosen vessels who carry His anointing - for the right season will come!

January 31

Called to Heavenly Places

Ephesians 2:6, 7 "And hath raised us up together, and made us sit together in heavenly places in Christ Jesus: That in the ages to come he might shew the exceeding riches of his grace in his kindness toward us through Christ Jesus."

A few years back my daughter found great favor with the Lt. Governor of Louisiana and his staff. On one of her visits to Baton Rouge she brought with her a friend from Oklahoma. They went to visit the office of the Lt. Governor and were escorted by the LG's personal assistant and bodyguard who had made arrangements for the girls to visit the Governor's mansion. Upon arrival at the mansion they were greeted by the Butler who said, *"You must be Crystal! We have been waiting for you!"* and proceeded to show them around with an invitation to lunch. Her friend was speechless and awed by the honor and warm reception that was shown to my daughter.

That is only a shadow of the hospitality that God desires to show to His Bride! He has called us to sit with Him in heavenly places and desire to show the beauty and splendor of His kingdom! *His Holy Spirit welcomes us warmly and says to us, "We have been waiting for you! There is so much we want to show you!"* He has opened up His great treasury of grace and exceeding riches... and has made them available to us! We have been invited to dine at His table and feast in His Presence! He has shown us nothing but kindness and love, extending His hands of mercy and favor towards us. He took us from nothing and gave us everything! Like a Lover who adores His beloved, He is proud to call us His. He took us from the dark and gave us His light. He called us, who were living in the lowly elements of this world, into Heavenly Places with Him! *He did not step out of His holiness to come to us, but rather cleansed us from our unholiness and brought us into His domain*!

I am awed today...just as my daughter's friend was...by the hospitality and love that He shows me! I stand in awe of His holiness, His perfection and His Supremacy! *No King or Queen of this world could ever compare with His majesty and splendor.* But, mostly, I am awed that such a great and Holy God has chosen me... and you...to sit with Him in these Heavenly places!

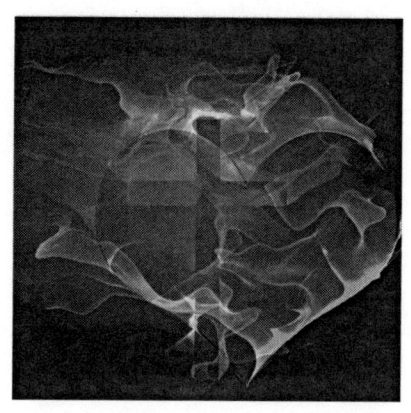

February

To fall in love with God is the
greatest of all romances;
To seek Him, the greatest adventure;
To find Him, the greatest human achievement!
-Raphael Simeon

February 1

You Have Something To Give

Isaiah 61:1-3 "The Spirit of the Lord is upon me because the Lord has anointed me to preach good tidings unto the meek; he has sent me to bind up the brokenhearted, to proclaim liberty to the captives, and the opening of the prison to them that are bound; To proclaim the acceptable year of the Lord, and the day of vengeance of our God; to comfort all that mourn; to appoint unto them that mourn in Zion, to give unto them beauty for ashes, the oil of joy for mourning, the garment of praise for the spirit of heaviness."

You have something to offer someone else - ***Jesus!*** He can do for us what no other can do. Remember how He brought you through your hard times and moments of despair! We, in turn, can minister that same grace and anointing to someone else who is walking where we once walked.

Jesus released His authority and power to us, and commissioned us to take His message to everyone we meet. *It is a great message of hope, redemption and grace!* Those who are brokenhearted need healing, and those who are captive in prisons of addictions and darkness need deliverance. He wants to bestow us the crown of beauty instead of ashes, give us the oil of gladness instead of mourning, and a garment of praise instead of despair.

My friend, if you know the Savior, then you can offer hope, truth and healing to those who need a Savior. Give them Jesus - the One who can restore, revive and renew crippled, wounded souls. Give them Jesus - the Master of the Storms! ***Give them Jesus - the One who can change their lives.***

February 2

Our Amazing God

Luke 9:43 "And they were all amazed at the mighty power of God…"
Mark 9:15 "All the people, when they beheld him, were greatly amazed, and running to him saluted him."

In this age of technology and knowledge there is little left that can still amaze us and inspire awe and wonder in our hearts. Things that were precious, sacred and rare have become common and ordinary, leaving little to be amazed us. Oh, but thankfully we serve an Amazing God who still has the power, the creativity and the ability to amaze us!

I am utterly amazed at the beauty of His holiness when I enter the sanctuary and experience the sweet Presence of the Lord. It amazes me to think that the Creator of heaven and earth desires to spend time with me, and longs to show ME His greatness and glory! I am humbled to be Chosen by Him, this Lord of Light, to be found worthy to serve in His house. It is my great honor to carry His Name and bear His banner of love. I am deeply touched to know that He, the Great Eternal One, hears me when I pray and swiftly acts to answer the petitions I bring before Him. He is an Amazing God and does things that are contrary to the ways of man! The power of His blood still amazes me with it's divine ability to transform a child of darkness into a child of Light, or to heal us of all our diseases! I stand in awe and amazement of this Great God that I know and love!

Beloved, *God is still in charge of this universe* and still amazes those who look for Him. He will be found by everyone who seeks Him and He will show Himself in Holiness and Majesty! He is doing amazing things for all who desire to see Him and who hunger for Him! The rain is falling on us and He is pouring out His Spirit upon all flesh, saturating us with amazing love and wonderment! He is still creating miracles as we enter the times of restoration and refreshment! We will see Him…and be completely amazed…as the hour of His visitation comes to us!

February 3

Wowed By God

Job 37:22 "Out of the north comes golden splendor; around God is awesome majesty."

Have you ever had one of those incredible moments when God just "*wows*" you? I'm not easily impressed by people or positions, however, I am constantly "wowed" by this Great One that I gave my heart to many years ago. I find that the Lover of my soul still loves to impress me, and enjoys taking the time to amaze me with His beauty and majesty.

One breathtaking sunrise, one clear, starry night with the moonlight falling softly upon me, or the glorious sound of a thunderstorm still amaze me. But even greater than these glorious sights and sounds that He uses to impress me are prayers that are answered in spectacular ways! Seeing God resurrect a body that was given a death sentence by physicians impresses me! Watching Him transform a hardened sinner into His child is awesome! Seeing baby Christians tentatively begin to take their first steps in faith brings great joy to my heart! Simply being in His Presence "wows" me!

I love being 'wowed' by God! His works are amazing! His love is unfathomable! *And...He loves showing off...just for me!*

February 4

Do You Love Me?

John 21:17 "He said unto him the third time, Simon, son of Jonah, lovest thou me?"

Perhaps we've all been here at some time or another...*the place of denial that left us living under a heavy cloud of self-condemnation.* The questions were asked, the accusations were made...*and we denied we knew Him.* Oh, maybe not in words, but surely our actions were not those of a true follower of Jesus, and we found ourselves doing what we vowed we would never do. Our love for Jesus was tested...and *we failed the test* and now taste the ashes of self-loathing and condemnation. If only we could just rewind.

Peter knew these feelings very well. After all*, if anyone should believe and stand for Jesus, it would surely be the sea-walking disciple*! Not once, not twice, but three times Peter denied that he knew Jesus. Oh the bitter thoughts that must have consumed him as he thought back to more glorious times...only for it to come to this cold, dark, empty night that echoed his denial over and over again in his ears. ***But, Jesus wasn't through with Peter, the denier***! He comes to him after His resurrection and asks, "*Peter, do you love me?" Not once, not twice, but three times! Coincidental? I think not!* Jesus sweetly offers Peter forgiveness and restitution, not once, not twice, but three times and gave Peter the chance to affirm to himself that he truly loved the Lord. Jesus, so tender and caring with Peter, was offering him forgiveness, acceptance, and trust! Trust that spoke volumes to Peter - trust that said, "*I believe in you, Peter!*"

We sometimes struggle to get beyond our mistakes and denials and find ourselves living a life that can only be described as "scraping the bottom." Yet, all the while we are condemning ourselves, He is offering forgiveness! Our hearts tell us that we blew it and we are not worthy to even speak His Name, yet ***He offers us His trust and faith...and the green light to go forward with Him!*** Tenderly and gently the Savior speaks to us..."*Do you love (agape) me?" "Do you love (phileo) me?"* Our hearts cry out,

"*Yes, Lord, I love You!*" He gently lifts the clouds of condemnation and the cloak of self-loathing, freeing us to walk into the Divine Destiny and Purpose He has called us into! Once again we hear that sweet voice compelling us..."*Leave the past behind and Follow Me!*"

February 5

The Proof of Love

2 Corinthians 3:9 "...That I might know the proof of you, whether ye be obedient in all things."

    "If you love me you'll do..." "If you love me you'll give..." These tactics are often used to manipulate and control someone, and take advantage of an infatuated heart, and often spoken from the heart of an immature and self-centered person. But real love will always give proof of its existence. It is a question that God will ask of every believer and every person who calls themselves a follower of Christ. *"How much do you love me?"*

    The proof of love is obedience. Your level of obedience is determined by your level of love. God is looking for obedience in the people who say they love Him. Why? *Because love for God has always been expressed through obedience.* Noah obeyed God by building an ark, and defying logic and facts. Abraham obeyed God by placing his son upon an altar of sacrifice, trusting that God knew what He was asking of him. Jesus was obedient to the Father's will when He prayed in the garden and allowed men to hang Him on a tree. He asked Peter, *"Do you love me?"*

    How much do we love Him? How does our obedience measure up? Can we trust Him enough to obey Him in everything that He asks of us? *We usually obey to the level of our comfort and commitment, but He is looking for people who will be radically obedient.* It might seem like we're stepping out on nothing, but we can trust the One who made everything out of nothing! He wants our obedience, not sacrifices, for *our obedience is the proof of our love for Him.*

February 6

The Agape' Way

I John 4:7 "Beloved, let us love one another: for love is of God; and every one that loveth is born of God, and knoweth God."

Years ago I entered into ministry with the specific purpose of ministering the grace, love, healing, and redemption of Christ Jesus to those who need Him the most. *My love for Him birthed in me a great love for* people, *a desire to see them grow in their faith, to live the life of an Overcomer, and to live the abundant life.* The greatest joys in life come when we can help someone else. *What matters in this life is more than winning for ourselves.*

I love the story that took place at the Seattle Special Olympics a few years ago. Nine physically or mentally disabled contestants assembled at the starting line for the 100 yard dash. As the gun sounded, they clumsily raced out with a relish to run the race to the finish and win. All except one boy, who stumbled and tumbled a few times, and began to cry. The other eight heard his crying. They slowed down and looked back. Then, the most remarkable thing happened! They all turned around and went back - every one of them! *All nine linked arms and walked across the finish line together.* The crowd went wild, the cheering went on for several minutes as people stood on their feet with a standing ovation for the nine! These little children taught us a lesson that day. *What matters in this life is more than winning for ourselves. What truly matters in this life is helping others win, even if it means slowing down and changing our course.*

We are held to a different standard of success. *It's about loving one another as Christ loves us.* It's about showing love when situations give us cause to judge. It's all about being kind when flesh wants to be harsh and strict. It's about forgiveness and mercy. It's about being there for each other...holding up hands that have grown weary....encouraging someone who is struggling....and letting His love flow through us in the Agape' way!

February 7

To Love and Be Loved

1 John 4:8, 10 "...God is love. Herein is love, not that we loved God, but that he loved us, and sent his Son to be the propitiation for our sins."

To be loved is the greatest of all human needs. We search for it, we hunger for it, and we sell out for it. It is not the things we accumulate nor the wealth we acquire that brings us the deep satisfaction of a life well lived - *but it is love*! *The great apostle had it right...the greatest of these is love!*

The majestic love of the Father was revealed in the magnificent gift of His Son. *Love stepped down from Heaven and walked among us!* Love saw worth in the sinful souls of men and redeemed them with His life. Love hung on a cruel cross and offered forgiveness to even the most vile and cruel soul. Love opened His back to stripes that cut it into ribbons of flesh for our healing. Love cried out for us who were guilty; and sinless, pure love wore the robe of shame, disgrace, and rejection so we could be made free. Love paid the price for our souls willingly and graciously. *Love calls out today, seeking those who are empty, lonely, and guilt-ridden.* Love offers hope, forgiveness and fulfillment. *Love will find you when you seek Him!*

To love and be loved is the greatest gift. Let Him bathe your heart in Love and restore your aching, searching soul. Let Love fill every empty part of your heart! Give Love the keys to the fears you have kept locked away so He can free your spirit to love! *Let us love as He loves - lavishly, nothing held back, and freely!*

February 8

The Love of a Lifetime

Jeremiah 31:3 "...I have loved you with an everlasting love..."

We all have an unquenchable need to be loved unconditionally and to be understood. This aching need does not discriminate...the wealthy need it as much as the poor, the famed desire it as much as the unknowns. This deep, gnawing need drives many people down wrong paths in their search to be loved, accepted and understood. Nothing hurts as much as feeling unloved. No rejection is as painful as having your love returned unaccepted. No frustration is greater than that of being misunderstood. There are many lonely people who walk around with smiles pasted on their faces, but inside are hurting with pain that cannot be put into words.

Yet, all of these things that our soul hungers for is just a whisper away. *"Jesus!"* He loves us unconditionally and cares about us. He takes the time to listen when we make the time to talk to Him. He understands us when no one else does. He's never to busy to spend time with us. He loves us, not for our money, influence or great abilities, but because we are His. No one can love us like Jesus does, nor can anyone fill the gut-wrenching loneliness like He can. Precious One, He loves us so much that He poured His life's blood out for us, and purchased us with His life.

We will have a spiritual awakening when we understand God's great love for us as He reveals His Father's heart to us and shows us His everlasting love. Oh how He loves you today. Let Him clothe you with His love and peace. He cares and He understands.

February 9

Look Again

I Samuel 16:7 "...For the Lord seeth not as man seeth; for man looks on the outward appearance, but the Lord looks on the heart."

I am so glad that God sees us differently than others do!

Years ago after my youngest sister passed away, her baby boy came to stay with us for a while. He was only three and was very fond of his oldest brother who was in his early twenties. My husband would often tease him about his older brother (you've got to know Jim) by saying that he wasn't very much to look at. My little nephew would swell out his chest and open his little mouth and say, "*Look again, Uncle Jim, look again.*" He wanted everyone to see his big brother the way he did - someone who had a big heart and who was heroic in his little eyes.

Our Father sees what others cannot see in us. He looks beyond our faults and sees our needs and uniqueness. He sees hearts of gold where others might only see a rough exterior. He sees hurts where others only see smiles. He sees beauty in us when others see only ordinary. He sees greatness when others see only smallness. He sees something worthwhile in us while others might not give us a second glance.

He desires for us to see others in the same way that He does. The next time we see someone whose appearance is less than pleasing to us, *look again! People are worth taking a second look at*! The person whose demeanor is hard and cold might very well have the heart of a child, just waiting for someone to bring it out. The one who seems unapproachable may just be shy and misunderstood, longing to talk to someone - *look again!* The girl who goes around with a smile might be hiding tears and hurts - *look again! You were worth a second look - so are others! Look Again!*

February 10

The Miracle of Love

Romans 5:8 "...While we were yet sinners, Christ died for us."
1 Peter 4:8 "...Love covers a multitude of sins."

He was dirty and his clothes were ragged and torn. He smelled. The young mother, holding her baby close to her, hoped that she could conduct her business quickly and get away from this fellow who was attracting the attention of her young child. The old man winked and giggled at the baby. The baby responded with a wide mouthed, one-toothed smile. His eyes glistened as pure joy flowed from the little one. The little one reached his clean, innocent baby hands towards the old man. The old man hesitated, but the baby was insistent that the old man hold him. Finally, the mother placed the baby in the old man's arms and the baby cackled with glee. He plastered the old man's cheeks with wet, sloppy baby kisses before going back to his mothers' arms. She saw tears in the old man's eyes, as he quietly thanked her for the gift she had just given him. Her heart pricked her as she made her way to the car. Where she saw filth, her innocent little boy saw a heart. Where she had seen ragged and torn clothing, her baby had seen into the soul of the man. *That's what love does...it looks beyond the faults and sees the needs.*

How like the mother we are and how like the baby God is. He sees the soul and the heart of mankind, looking past our stench and unworthiness, and gives us the gift of unconditional love. Who doesn't want to be loved unconditionally? We, like the old man, will often feel unworthy of that kind of love, yet, God is there, loving us in spite of our sins and failures. Love...that Divine Nature of God! *Someone once said where there is an abundance of love there will always be miracles.* Maybe the reason we don't see more miracles is because we hold back the love that works the miracles!

May God give you great big, wet, sloppy kisses today as He looks upon you with glee and delight! May the Miracle of Love fill your heart and your day, taking you out of the "ho-hum" routine into the Divine Atmosphere that is abundant with Love!

February 11

Demonstrations of Love

I John 3:17 "If anyone has material possessions and sees his brother in need but has no pity on him, how can the love of God be in him?"
Galatians 6:10 "As we have therefore opportunity, let us do good unto all men, especially unto them who are of the household of faith."

How very easy it is for us to tell others we love them, but showing love will often inconvenience us. Let's be honest, most of us don't like to be inconvenienced. We don't mind doing for others if it is an easy thing and doesn't take up too much of our very busy time.

God tells us to *do good* unto all, ***especially unto them who are of the household of faith. We are to take care of each other,*** extending helping hands and rolling up our sleeves to get involved! Love is demonstrated when we make time to visit someone who is in the hospital or prepare a meal for someone who is sick. Love is demonstrated when we offer to serve in our church, taking on roles that no one else wants. Love sees the needs...and does something about them! The path of love will always take us the extra mile! *Romans 15:1 "We then that are strong ought to bear the infirmities of the weak, and not to please ourselves."* Love eases burdens and pain. *Philippians 2:3 "Let nothing be done through strife or vainglory; but in lowliness of mind [humbleness] let each esteem other better than themselves."* Our attitudes and actions are to be taking care of one another unselfishly, without a desire for recognition.

Real love compels us to help other believers in need. If we turn or look away, deliberately neglecting the need, showing no pity or compassion for the believer, then we demonstrate a lack of God's love in our life. Love is not only expressed in words, but **love is demonstrated in the things one does.** *Love demands action* and often sacrifices to meet the needs of others. I John tells us to love one another, whereby the world will know that we are His disciples. Isn't it about time that we let our love be demonstrative? It's time for the world to take notice that we are His disciples because we have love for each other! Let our love be demonstrative!

February 12

Motivated By Love

1 Corinthians 13:8 "Love never fails..."

    The greatest people in the world to be around are not dignitaries or great musicians or famous stars...*but people who are full of God's love.* They freely share their blessings with others and have no wrong motives or hidden agendas for doing so! Great people do great things that often go unnoticed, unrewarded, and unacknowledged, but they do it anyway because *they are motivated by love!*

    It's not hard to spot them, for they are filled with a rare, but beautiful attribute of love that defines them as His! This is what the great Apostle Paul wrote about love...

Love never gives up.
Love cares more for others than for self.
Love doesn't want what it doesn't have.
Love doesn't strut,
Doesn't have a swelled head,
Doesn't force itself on others,
Isn't always "me first,"
Doesn't fly off the handle,
Doesn't keep score of the sins of others,
Doesn't revel when others grovel,
Takes pleasure in the flowering of truth,
Puts up with anything,
Trusts God always,
Always looks for the best,
Never looks back, but keeps going to the end.

    If what we do isn't motivated by love, then it is in vain. If what we say or preach isn't spoken in love, it is only noise! We can have all the "right" ingredients, a winning personality, a voice like an angel, and the bank account that would cause Midas to envy, but if love is lacking, these things don't matter. What really, truly matters is that we are filled with His love...and that we love each other!

February 13

The Greatest Thing

1 John 4:8 "...God is Love."

I read a story about a little boy who, one morning before school, broke off a small branch from her prized Azalea bush and took it with him to school. The mother, having an already difficult day, was late in picking up her six year old son. Arriving, she found her son and a couple of other students in the classroom coloring and drawing. The teacher pulled her into the hall and said she needed to talk to her about her son. The mother, fearing the worst, listened intently as the teacher began speaking. *"See that little girl over there,"* said the teacher, pointing to a little girl who was busily coloring. *"Her parents are going through a horrific divorce. Yesterday she came to school very upset and crying. Although she whispered these words, everyone in the class heard what she said. 'No one loves me' she cried."* The teacher continued, *"This morning I watched your son go up to her, hand her the flowers and whisper in her ear, "I love you."'*

Simple little words, yet what an impact they have when spoken to a heart that is hurting. The Apostle Paul was right, the greatest thing is love. After all, God is love and we know there is nothing greater than God. Where there is love there will always be hope and faith. We are so blessed, not only to be so divinely loved, but to have love to give. This is our commission for it is the hope for mankind. As Emmet Fox so eloquently put it, *"There is no difficulty that enough love will not conquer; No disease that enough love will not heal; No door that enough love will not open; No gulf that enough love will not bridge; No wall that enough love will not throw down; No sin that enough love will not redeem."* Want to make a difference in someone's life? Love them.

"Love one another as I have loved you" - Jesus.

February 14

A Love Note

Jeremiah 31:3 "The Lord of old appeared unto me, saying, Yes I have loved you with an everlasting love: therefore with lovingkindness have I drawn you."
Ephesians 3:19 "And to know the love of Christ, which passes knowledge, that you might be filled with all the fullness of God."

Today is a reminder of how much the Father loves you. As we reflect upon certain moments in our lives, we can't deny that the Great Jehovah was there with us, cradling us from harm, protecting us, guiding us and loving on us. You have had amazing experiences that confirmed and reaffirmed that you are so loved by the Father. Times when death should have overtaken you, but God said no! Times when He was simply saying to you, *"I am here...and I love you eternally!"*

You are important to Him! You have great worth and are valuable, needed and wanted. He loves you deeply...passionately. He loves you for who you are...and what He sees that you will become. His presence fills the empty places in your heart. His presence fills you with great joy and peace. He is like a beautiful, sweet lingering aroma to remind you He is there...lingering in the shadows and present when you awaken from slumber. He is there during the troubled moments that try to harass you...just relax and breath Him in. He calms the storms that blow our way and clears away cobwebs that would cloud our minds. Oh how He loves you! How mindful He is of all that touches you.

This great Prince...King of all that is Holy...desires to meet with you today. His scepter is extended towards you, bidding you to come into His presence and find all that your souls longs for. Give yourself a great big hug from your Father...and tell yourself..."*I am greatly, deeply and unashamedly loved by my Father."*

February 15

Love Lavishly

John 15:12, 13 "This is my commandment, that you love one another as I have loved you. Greater love has no one than this, than to lay down one's life for his friends."

We are recipients of love lavished on us by the Father! We can see His love displayed each morning when the sun peeks over the horizon, ushering in the mercies of the Lord. His love shines in the twinkling stars that merrily dance in the heavenly night skies. One day, we will see with our eyes the nail prints in the hands and feet of our Savior - the marks of His great love for us. As I meditate upon the love He lavishes on me, I can't help but believe that He is worthy of so much more from us than we give Him!

Jesus said that all of the law was fulfilled upon these two commandments - to love the Lord with all our hearts, and to love our neighbor as ourselves. Do we really lavish our love on Him? I believe that when we love Him our actions will show it. It will be seen and heard in every deed and word! Our thoughts will always be upon Him - the Lover of our souls! Have we fallen in love with Him, or are we serving Him out of mere obligation? Do we get excited about spending time with Him? Are we looking forward to His return? Do we love our neighbor as ourselves? Do we consider the feelings of others, even in our moments of distress? Jesus said that they (the world) will know we are His by the love we have for one another! I want His love branded upon me so that everyone who sees me will know that I am His! I belong to Him! When we love lavishly, we might think we are putting our hearts at risk, but dear one, we lose nothing and gain all for Him! Love makes sacrifices! Love endures! Love is kind...and patient!

Love thinks more of others than of self! This world needs more genuine love...and *we are the carriers of lavish love*! Let's love lavishly!

February 16

Love in the Right Places

Romans 5:8 "But God demonstrates His own love toward us, in that while we were yet sinners, Christ died for us."

The deepest, most profound desire of every human being is to be loved, to feel that they matter to someone. Everything else is secondary to the need to be loved. Sadly, many seek love in all the wrong places with illicit love affairs, the bottom of the bottle, or though drugs that numb their pain. Deep with the heart of every woman is the desire for someone to be her champion and find her worth fighting for. She is looking for that knight in shining armor to rescue her, and if necessary, to die for her. In the most closed chamber of a man's heart beats the desire that someone will love him for who is he and will stand and defend him to the world.

The greatest news I can give you today is this - *Jesus Christ is that someone we are looking for, and has already declared His eternal and everlasting love to us.* He is that Champion that believes we are worth fighting for, He is the One who will defend us against every accusation of the enemy. He found us worth dying for, and has rescued us from the clutches of sin, shame and damnation. Oh, how He loves us! I John 3:1 tells us, *"Behold what manner of love the Father hath bestowed upon us, that we should be called the **sons of God**".* Being a child of God is the highest privilege of our salvation, and as His children, we are heirs and joint-heirs with Christ Jesus. John 3:16 says, *"For God so loved the world (you) that He gave His only begotten Son."* What a great gift and what an honor it is to have His love shed abroad in our hearts. He loves us with an everlasting love.

Comfort yourself with this knowledge, *"Nothing can separate us from the love of Christ".* Romans 8:35. You are special to Him! You matter greatly to the Great Someone who formed you in your mother's womb. You are important to the Creator of the universe. Oh how He loves you!

February 17

I Delight In Him

Isaiah 58:14 "Then shalt thou delight in the Lord; and I will cause thee to ride upon the high places of the earth..."

The Lord delights in us today...and in our prosperity! We bring Him great pleasure and satisfaction. He finds us highly pleasing! Can we say the same about Him?!

I went to a church conference where all of the speakers were sitting on stage looking as though they had swallowed lemons. It didn't appear that they found God delightful at all. Then, a young minister came in and sat with this group of prune faces - but he was different! *He stood out from the rest.* His face was shining with love and he wore the biggest smile I have ever seen. Joy oozed from him and love for Jesus radiated from him.

David delighted himself in the Lord...and in His laws! We, too, can delight ourselves in Him, knowing that He is with us. Let's not wear Him like a worn old shoe, but give Him the highest honor, and the highest praise. Let's bring joy to His heart and give Him a reason to delight in us! All that we long for is found in Him! The beauty we yearn for is woven into His presence! At His right hand are pleasures that surpass our desires! In His presence is joy forevermore!

February 18

Love Them Anyway

Matthew 5:44, 45 "But I say unto you, Love your enemies, bless them that curse you, do good to them that hate you, and pray for them which despitefully use you, and persecute you; That ye may be the children of your Father which is in heaven..."

It takes a big hearted person to be kind to those who have been unkind, *yet it is what God expects from those who follow Christ.* It takes a lot of mercy and grace to pray for someone who has mistreated us, *yet God expects nothing less than for us to love them anyway.* It takes a lot of courage to forgive someone who has hurt us deeply, *but we can do it because of Christ.*

Beloved, we do not carry the spirit of the world...but we have been liberated to love as Christ loves us! Our betrayals and wounds will make us want to react in like manner, executing revenge and exhibiting bitterness and malice towards the offender. But *Christ who lives in us will give us the power and strength to put to rest those feelings so that His love can manifest in us.* Christ in us will forgive the offender and heal our hurt. Greater is He who lives in us! He is greater than the hurt, greater than the pain, and greater than the offense. It takes Christ in us, the Hope of Glory, to forgive...*but we can do it*! How? Allow His love that has been shed abroad in our hearts to love them, to forgive them, to heal us! It doesn't mean that we become a mat for them to wipe their feet on, but it does mean that we pray for them, forgive them...and love them.

People will treat us unkindly...love them anyway! People will betray us...love them anyway! People will be hateful and malicious... love them anyway. People will walk away from us...love them anyway. *Never, never, never, ever stop loving people, for it is by showing His love that we manifest who Christ is*!

February 19

The Art of Serving

John 13:14 "If I, then, your Lord and Master, have washed your feet; ye also ought to wash one another's feet."

In today's world *it is often hard to find someone with a true servant's heart, even among Christians.* Everyone wants to be served instead of serving. You will usually find the servant's heart in someone who is gifted in the social skill of hosting. A great hostess always serves with grace, tact and dignity, ever alert to the needs of her guests, and quick to respond to that need.

Jesus knew the art of serving others. After all, He came to serve, didn't He? He served the 5000, He served the sick, He served the despondent and cast outs. He washed the disciples' feet - a very dirty task since they walked everywhere they went! He was all about servanthood, putting the needs of others above His own. That is indeed a rare quality in many of God's ministers today. No wonder the world doesn't understand the value of servanthood! Jesus taught us that in order to be great, we must first serve. As we serve others, be mindful that we will not always be thanked or appreciated, but *we must serve anyway because this is the heart of Christ Jesus.* We can be gracious in serving others, without murmuring and complaining, because it is what Jesus would do and He expects no less from us. As we serve, let it be unto Him and we will find that the task of serving can be beautiful and joyous.

February 20

Thinking Good Things

Philippians 4:8 "Finally, brethren, whatsoever things are true, whatsoever things are honest, whatsoever things are just, whatsoever things are pure, whatsoever things are lovely, whatsoever things are of good report: if there be any virtue, and if there be any praise, think on these things."

As we read this passage of scripture, we find that Paul was exhorting the saints to think upon the things that bring praise to God. Think about your blessings instead of your troubles! If we were to count all the blessings we have, they would far exceed any problems or troubles. *We can walk the high road today by simply thinking upon things that are uplifting and freeing.* Thinking wrong thoughts, negative thoughts or depressing thoughts only pull us down. Paul said to think upon the things that are true. Many times we look at the "facts" and think that they must be true. However, when we think upon the truth, which is what God says, our thoughts will become uplifting and victorious, causing us to soar as the eagles.

Paul encourages us to think upon things that are lovely and pure. I want to challenge you today to begin thinking lovely things about the people around you today, or maybe someone who you are struggling with. You will find that your attitude will completely change towards that person when you begin to think of them in a different light. Look for the good things in them. Accentuate the positive. *Refuse to let negative thoughts keep you from the best things that God has for you.*

February 21

See The Good

Psalm 31:19 "Oh, How great is Thy goodness, which Thou hast stored up for those who fear Thee, which Thou hast wrought for those who take refuge in Thee, before the sons of men!"

Some people think that God's goodness means the absence of pain, difficulty, sorrow, sickness, poverty or trouble; however, I find that His goodness means something far better than just physical blessings. His goodness is found all around us in the every day things.

I am convinced that there is far more good in this world than we realize! The sun still shines, there is still enough air to go around, the world is still turning, and *God is upon His throne*! We love and are loved. The miracles of life fill our days and sustain us through the nights. Pure innocence can still be found in the eyes of a new born babe and heard in the laughter of our children. If we have one person we can call a true friend, then we are rich! I believe there is more good than bad in most people, and even the vilest person is offered redemption through Christ. *There is still hope, there is still love, and there is always God!* He is good all the time.

Today, *I will spend my time looking for good in people.* I know I will find it...in a smile or embrace, in a kind word, or in the generous gift of one sharing the burden of another soul. Instead of looking at the bad, I will give thanks to God for His goodness, His unfailing love, and His blessings!

February 22

He Fulfills

Psalms 63:1 "Oh God, thou art my God; early will I seek thee: my soul thirsts for thee, my flesh longs for thee in a dry and thirsty land, where no water is."

We live in a generation that is always looking, always wanting, always desiring something, never satisfied and never fulfilled. It seems like they are always searching for the new high, the better and bigger toys, and the latest thrill. They are unquenchable in their need to be entertained and thrilled, and have an insatiable appetite for more.

Oh but we have something that remains constant and fulfilling! God always fulfills! He satisfies the longing soul and fills us with His goodness, mercy and abounding love. There is nothing that can satisfy us like Jesus, and we have an encounter with Him, He gives us water to drink that quenches our thirst. We never have to be lonely again when we have Jesus - *He fulfills every longing*! Peace and contentment that can never be found anywhere else is ours today because we walk with God! When we find ourselves becoming dissatisfied and empty, we can call on Him and He gives refills! Let us not walk another moment in loneliness, discontentment or searching, but we can call on Jesus and He will fulfill every time!

February 23

Who We Are

II Corinthians 3:2 "Ye are our epistle written in our hearts, known and read of all men."

"Who are you?" I've had this question asked of me...you probably have too. Usually it was a Christian who felt a connection with me. Sometimes, the questions came from someone who didn't know Christ, but sensed there was something different about me. *May I remind us today who we are?!*

We are children of destiny, filled with purpose and created for His pleasure. We are lights in the darkness and shining truth to those around us. We are temples of the Lord filled with His Holy Presence. We are strong warriors, made for battles and destined to overcome. We are gentle and kind, gracious and loving. *We are seed sowers of mercy and reapers of love.* We are faith walkers and word talkers. We were chosen before time and space, and are deeply loved. We are dangerous to the enemy and a threat to Satan. We are ransomed and redeemed chosen children of the Most High! We are recipients of God's mercy and compassion. We are image bearers of God and reflections of Christ. We are needed and we are wanted. We are the Church...we are the Bride!

February 24

Reflections of Him

Galatians 1:15, 16 "...But when it pleased God...to reveal His Son in me..."

We learn early in life to wear masks that hide who we really are because to be genuine is to be vulnerable. It's socially incorrect to reveal what you really believe.

But God wants to remove the masks and reveal who we are! His Beloved! It is so refreshing to be with someone who is real and genuine! I remember years ago we sang a song that said, *"To be like Jesus, To be like Jesus, All I ask is to be like Him."* An amazing thing occurs when we spend time in His presence - our old man decreases and He increases! The more time we spend with Him, the more we become like Him. He yearns to impart His most precious thoughts to us as a lover would to His sweetheart. He desires for us to know His heart and become intimate with all of His ways. Remember the saying, "Your life is the only Bible some people see?"

How important it is for us to spend time in the presence of Jesus so that we can rightly reflect who He really is. *People need to see real love and feel real peace.* We can offer that to them by reflecting who Christ really is! We are His reflections!

February 25

My 'I Am'

John 8:58 "Jesus said to them, Most assuredly, I say to you, before Abraham was, I AM."
Exodus 3:14 "And God said to Moses, I AM WHO I AM. And He said, Thus you shall say to the children of Israel, I AM has sent me to you."

I feel I am getting to know Him all over again! Each day I catch a glimpse of Who He is...and I am awed by His Greatness, His Strength, and His Divine Love. He is my "I Am"...my "More Than Enough"...and my "All That I Need."

The I Am In the Old Testament was everything to His people. *Provider, Rock, Shelter, Tower of Strength, Cloud by Day, Fire by Night, Healer, Everlasting Father...He was everything!* He was "*I Am*", the Uncreated Creator, needing nothing else to be added. Jesus in the New Testament is everything to man and the only way to God. He is *Counselor, Comforter, Healer, Redeemer, Deliverer, Peace, Lion of Judah, Prince of Peace, and Savior of the World. He reassures us that before there was a Moses, He was "I Am."*

Perhaps today you can take heart in knowing and believing that this Uncreated Creator, this great "*I Am*" cares deeply for you and is on your side. He is everything we need, and in Him we find the longings of our souls satisfied. He still guides, He still provides, He still heals, and He still saves the souls of men.

February 26

A Personal Savior

Luke 10:33 "But a certain Samaritan...had compassion."

I am so thankful to have a personal Savior! One who cares deeply for me and is concerned about everything that I am touched with. The most beautiful relationship we can have is an intimate one with our Savior. He graces our lives with His special touch and beautifies us with His salvation. He promises to be with us always, and never takes His eyes off of us. He has imprinted us in the palm of His hands. We are the apples of His eye!

He is in the valleys that I walk through, for He is the Lily of the Valley! He is the beautiful rose found amongst the thorns that prick at me. He hears the silent prayers that arise from the depths of my heart when words cannot be uttered. When I am wounded He gently pours in oil and wine to restore me. He is the Good Samaritan, doing for us what the law (the priest) could not do. Religion and law offers us no mercy, but He is compassionate towards us. He doesn't only look at us in our fallen condition and walk on by (like the Levite whose sacrifices would only cover us for a while), but saw our fallen condition and paid the ultimate price so that we could be redeemed from the curses of sin and the law. When we are so weak that we can't walk on our own, He gives us His strength...and carries us! He provides a place of refuge and safety for us - a place of provision to meet all of our spiritual needs (the inn), known today as the Church. He places caretakers over us in the persons of Pastors and Teachers. And...He has promised that He will come back for us! We have a wonderful, marvelous and loving Personal Savior who is always there!

February 27

One Gentle Touch

Matthew 17:7 "And Jesus came and touched him, and said, Arise, and be not afraid."

Everywhere I look I see people who need to be touched with kindness, gentleness and love. This week has been a week of trials and adversities for many of the people that I know and love. My nature and my role as Pastor makes me want to take care of every one of them, but alas, I have limitations that hinder me from "fixing" all of their problems. However, I can allow Christ in me to touch them with gentleness and kindness, and pour His healing balm on their battered spirits to soothe and encourage them.

We don't have to search far to find people who are hurting. The news is full of events that portray hurting people - people who need a kind voice and a gentle touch to carry them through. We are shown mercy every day - why not show that same mercy to others? We are recipients of His kindness - why not bestow that same kindness to others? One gentle touch can lift a soul from despair and one kind word can bring healing to a heart that is hurting. One act of generosity can make the difference if a person will eat today.

One tender touch could be all it takes for a sin-wearied soul to come to a loving Savior. We all need kindness and gentleness - things that if withheld would make life just an existence. Reach out to someone today and touch them with tenderness. Speak words of kindness that will bring healing, hope and salvation. One Gentle Touch...may change One Life today.

February 28

Only The Best For Him

Luke 21:3, 4 "...This poor widow has cast in more than they all... but she has cast in all the living that she had."

The Spirit of the Lord has been so sweet and tender to me during the past few days. I have found myself wanting to weep in His Presence and worship Him in His beauty and Holiness. Only He is so worthy of my tears, my praise and the best gifts my heart can give...that of my purest and sincerest worship.

He deserves our best gifts...*those that are given from our hearts*! It is these simple, yet priceless gifts that gain His attention and favor. We may not have great riches to lay at His feet, but we can give Him our all, much like the little widow who gave two mites. How small and insignificant it seemed to be in comparison with the wealth that was placed in the offering that day, *yet it touched the heart of Jesus like no other gift did, for you see, she gave her all!* It is when we give Him our all that we give Him the honor, the glory, the respect and the trust that He is worthy of. He takes to heart those things that are given from the heart!

Let us not give our gifts to Him lightly. It's more than just dropping a check in the offering or coming to the House of Worship on a Sunday morning. He is worthy of our best gifts - *gifts that are given with heartfelt worship and adoration*! Only the best will do for Him!

February 29

Keep Jesus Close

James 4:8 "Draw near to God and He will draw near to you..."
James 5:8 "...Stablish your hearts: for the coming of the Lord draws near."

"*Keep Jesus close and take Him with you every where you go.*" I awaken each morning with these words racing through my mind. I can't help but think how critical it is to us to stay close to Jesus.

Many voices clamor for our attention...voices that are seductive and appealing, and voices that rant and rage, which if we listen to, will bring deceit, anger, strife and sorrow. Their purpose is to distract us from walking in God's divine will and to prevent us from fulfilling our purpose. Their mission is to bring confusion and disorder, rebellion and doubt, fear and failure, sickness and death. Beloved, *He will keep us in perfect peace if our minds are stayed on Him!*

The old hymn says, "*Jesus keep me near the cross...*" As long as we stay close to Him we need not fear, for under the shadow of the cross there is safe ground. As long as we stay close to Him, we will not be deceived by other voices that tempt and deceive. As long as we stay under the blood, we have Divine protection. Stay near the cross and close to the Savior, for His ways are perfect and His will Divine. When our vision is clouded by fears and tears, and when our way is unknown, as long as we stay close to Him, Jesus will guide us in peace, grace and tender mercy. He is our Comfort, Shelter and great Redemption! Keep Jesus close to You, and never let Him go!

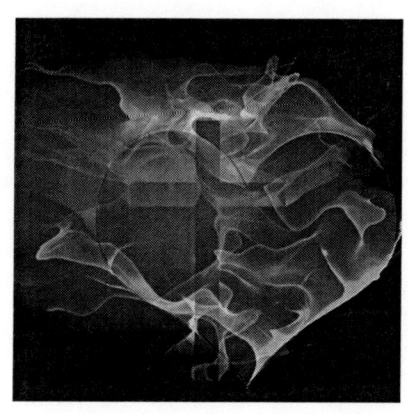

March

Anticipate Him…
Feel the Winds of Hope blowing again!

March 1

His Strength - My Weakness

2 Corinthians 12:9, 10 "...For My strength is made perfect in weakness...for when I am weak then am I strong."

If we are human, we are sure to have some weak areas! There are things that we simply can't do, whether they are physical, financial, emotional or relational. Even the great Apostle Paul had things that he had to deal with. In Romans 7:19, he tells us, *"For the good that I would, I do not: but the evil which I would not, that I do."* All of us have things we would love to do, but are limited because of resources, finances or physical restraints. We all battle with something that we wish was eliminated from our lives! It might be temper, anger, jealousy, quickness of speech, or perhaps it is a sickness or financial distress. Let's face it - the flesh has some weaknesses!

However, there is hope for our weaknesses! Paul said that God's strength was made perfect in the weak areas of Paul's life! We think that God can only use the strong, the mature, the smart ones, the beautiful ones or the wealthy folks. We think, *"How can God use me when I have this weak area in my life?"* Well, He can and He will! God is not impressed with strength, or charisma, or silver tongues, or great numbers - we are! God doesn't get much glory when only our strengths are used in our work for Him, but, oh how He gets the glory when He uses weak vessels! Years ago I had the beautiful privilege of meeting a woman who was bound to a wheelchair, but gave her all to preaching the Gospel! I remember seeing her roll that chair up and down the aisles as she ministered the Word of God. She refused to let her physical limitations hold her back!

What are we going to do with our weaknesses? Most of us excuse, defend, deny, or hide our weaknesses, but God says, *"I want to use them! I want to work through your weakness!"* God works through weak people on purpose so that He can show His great strength!!

March 2

God Loves Impossibilities

Exodus 6:1 "...Now shalt thou see what I will do..."

We've all been there...faced with impossible circumstances. I have learned through the years that God's best work is in impossibilities!

We've battled fears and doubts, and we have vanquished pride. We have encountered resentments, bitterness and self-pity. We have walked through deserts of overwhelming loneliness. We have risen above valleys of humiliation. We found ourselves in the land of Egypt facing fires of affliction. At times the only companions to be found were sorrow and suffering. But...we are on the upward climb! Psalms 30:5 says *"Weeping may endure for a night but joy comes in the morning!"*

It is in the place of impossibilities that God gives us glorious promises! It is in the fires of affliction that God fashions His best works, transforming our imperfections into His perfection. Through our trials we learn how to surrender completely to His will and realize these things:

Through the Change - God will lead us
Relax and Rest in Him - He is in control
Rejoice - God is Faithful

It is when we face the mountain of impossibility that God shines brightest. He gives us hinds feet to get us up this mountain and into the high places with Him. We are rising to new heights, seeing the splendor and beauty of the Lord! God loves impossibilities and loves to show off through them. Whatever impossible situation you are facing today, know that it is a splendid opportunity for God to show off! Accept the change for God is in control of it! It's time now to see what God will do!

March 3

"I Will" Promises

Exodus 23:22-31 "If you obey His voice and do all that I speak, then, I will be an enemy to your enemies and an adversary to your adversaries. For My Angel will go before you...you shall serve the Lord your God, and He will bless your bread and your water. And I will take sickness away from the midst of you.....I will fulfill the number of your days...I will send My fear before you, I will cause confusion among all the people to whom you come, and will make all your enemies turn their backs to you...I will drive them out from before you, until you have increased, and you inherit the land...and I will set your bounds from the Red Sea to the Sea, Philistia...For I will deliver the inhabitants of the land into your hand..."

Wow! What wonderful reasons we have to be on God's team! He has these awesome promises if we will serve Him! Why should we listen to that voice that tells us we are giving up so much to serve the Lord, or God does great things for others, but not me. Look at all of these tremendous promises He gives to those who serve Him...He will be an enemy to our enemies...His Angel shall go with us...He shall bless our bread and water, and take sickness from our midst. Cast down the voice of doubt and unbelief. Let your expectation level rise to believe that God will fulfill each and every promise He has given you!

We can hold God to His Word – He tells us in Isaiah to put Him in remembrance of His Word! So...Step out on the Word! The God that watches over His Word will perform it. He rules creation with the power of His Word. His laws govern the universe – His testimonies are sure (Psalm 93:5). David said in other words, your laws are irrevocable, and utterly reliable. They are the same yesterday, today and forever. *His word is his constitution, containing all the legal degrees.* He has bound himself to his Word – come boldly, ask, make your petition known. We can bind God to His Word... remind Him of His covenant promises and unbreakable pledges to bless and protect and answer prayers of the believers! Expect His "I Will" Promises.

March 4

"Can Do" Faith

Habakkuk 2:3 "For the vision is yet for an appointed time, but at the end it shall speak, and not lie, though it tarry, wait for it; because it will surely come, it will not tarry."

If we can believe, then we can achieve it!

Our dreams are unique, and we are the only ones that can make them happen. We cannot do it alone, but we need help, both human and divine. But we must first see the dream, then believe in the dream, and most importantly, believe in the One who gives us the dreams. We, by faith, must see ourselves as God sees us, successful and completing the paths He chooses for us. For some of us, our dreams can happen quickly and suddenly, but for the most part, it requires a lifetime dedication and perseverance to see our dreams fulfilled. Discouragement and silence will often beset us when the going is slow and tedious, but we must have a *"can do"* faith that will get us to where we desire to be.

If necessary, take tiny steps towards your dream and goal, and don't waver in your course. If you stay with it, you will get there. Don't despise what is in your hands, because it could be the seed that grows the dream. A leaking faucet can fill the bathtub, if you plug the drain. It is a matter of time. A journey of a thousand miles begins with a small step. Develop the *"Can Do"* Faith, believe in yourself, and believe God to complete what He starts!

March 5

Great Potential

Jeremiah 29:11 "For I know the plans I have for you, says the Lord...to give you a future and a hope."

My daughter and I were shopping for her a new car. In speaking with a young salesman who was very laid back, we wondered if he was even interested in making a sale (wow)! Later, we went back to this dealership after deciding this was the right car and went into the young man's office. On his desk was a calendar where he had written down the names of potential clients. We saw my daughter's name there with these words written next to it...***Great Potential!*** It was somewhat of a surprise to us that he viewed us in that way, considering how low key he had been. Appearances can be deceiving!

Beloved, God sees Great Potential in you! You may sometimes wonder if His eyes are even upon you and if He is interested in what is going on in your life. At times it may appear that He is very uninvolved with your dreams and desires, but don't be fooled! He knows what is inside of each one of us, and will sometimes allow us to figure it out without pressuring us. He is quite the Gentleman... and will never force something on us, but will allow time, design and patience to bring out those qualities in us that are our best features! He sees all the potential that is laying dormant in us, and with exact precision and timing, will bring it to the forefront, exposing the greatness that is within us. He has great and wonderful plans for us. Don't ever doubt that God sees and knows what is on the inside! God has a plan for you, and it is a great one!

March 6

Tests Produce Testimonies

I Peter 1:7 "That the trial of your faith, being much more precious than of gold that perisheth, though it be tried with fire, might be found unto praise and honor and glory at the appearing of Jesus Christ."

"Why me, Lord?" Does this sound like you? Why must we go through another trial? Why another test? Why me? These are questions that most of us have asked ourselves, and have even questioned the Lord about. My friend, there is purpose in the tests that we go through. Each test is meant to give us a testimony!

We must never forget that nothing can touch us without God's permission. Each encounter with distress is full of purpose and promise. Often we can't see beyond our trouble, but that's where our faith grows stronger. It's believing without seeing that brings victory.

My heart hurts for those who are going through sadness, loneliness and despair. God wants us victorious in all things. He is a mighty God and wants mighty sons and daughters! He is a Conqueror and desires that we also be conquerors. We are to be reflections of Him! He is not defeated, nor is He cast down. He cradles our grief stricken hearts and longs to take us to the place of peace. Joy surrounds Him and He dwells in praise. It may feel as though you'll never experience joy again, or wonder when will you taste victory, but hold on, dear one! Whatever struggles we encounter today, know that there is strength in the struggle! Our most defining moments are in the times of distress! We can face every conflict with confidence knowing that God is with us and for us! Remember this...it's just a test and *God believes you won't flunk the test!*

March 7

Come Boldly

Hebrews 4:16 "Let us therefore come boldly to the throne of grace, that we may obtain mercy and find grace to help in time of need."

My children and grandchildren know that if they are ever in need they can always come to me, and if it is in my power, I will not deny them anything. They have unconditional favor and boundless love, *because they are mine.* They *expect results,* and most of the time, they get them.

God desires that we come into His presence with boldness. He is our Heavenly Father in whom we have unconditional favor and unmerited love! He loves us, and will not deny our requests! James 6:16 tells us, *"The effectual fervent prayer of a righteous man avails much."* *Effectual* means fixed position and suggests an unmoveable, unshakable mindset. *Fervency* speaks of boldness, built on solid evidence, absolute proof, that supports your petitions. *Effectual fervency means coming into God's court, fully convinced, that you have a well prepared case.* This confidence to come into His Courts is beyond emotions, loudness or pumped up enthusiasm. How do we obtain this confidence to come boldly? *By knowing and standing on His word.* Jesus said that all things are possible if we believe!

We can bind God to His Word...remind Him of precious covenant promises and unbreakable pledges to bless and protect. His Word is all the documentation we'll ever need to present our requests to Him! It means we can come into God's house and into His presence, and boldly remind Him of HIS Word...to bless us, protect us, and heal us! God always honors His Word!

March 8

Great Expectations

Matthew 9:29 "...According to your faith, so be it unto you."

God will never disappoint! *If we have the faith, He has the means!* God operates through expectations and is moved by faith! Believers must stand steadfast in faith and trust in God even when we cannot see all of the promises of God fulfilled. The faith that God approves of is faith that is able to surrender God's promise back to Him for their fulfillment according His word!

Two blind men followed Jesus and were asked, *"Do you believe that I am able to do this?" "Yes, Lord."* He told them, *"According to your faith (or expectation), so be it unto you. And their eyes were opened."* Jarius, whose daughter was dying, told Jesus, *"Lay your hand upon her and she shall live."* His level of expectation was high! I love the story of Blind Bartimeaus. He had great expectations! When Jesus called his name, he threw away his garment that he had worn all of his life that labeled him a blind beggar*! He got rid of the garment of bondage* and received what he had dreamed about and had longed for all of his life. His expectation level was so high that nothing nor no one could keep him quiet. When the Word came walking by him, he reached forward, called out and got a miracle! His expectation made him whole!

It's according to my earnest expectation...that I receive! Paul said, *"My expectation and my hope will be found in Jesus."* Let's get rid of the garments of bondage and get a higher level of expectancy. Dare to have great expectations!

March 9

Keep Believing

Ephesians 6:13 "Wherefore take unto you the whole armor of God, that ye may be able to withstand the evil day, and having done all, to stand."

There comes a pivotal point in the storm when the circumstances will change!

The storms will not last forever. There will be a defining moment in the storm when things begin to change. We must have faith that outlasts our storms! There is a great recompense of reward awaiting us. Paul said there would come times when we must stand against the wiles of the devil, and having done all, to keep standing!

I love the story of the little boy who was aboard a boat that shipwrecked in the middle of a storm. He found his way to a huge rock and clung to it with all his might. Finally the rescuers came, and when asked how he survived, he replied, *"Those winds blew really hard, and at times almost blew me off this rock. The waters were rough and choppy, and it seemed like everything was shaking...except this rock. I shivered and I shook, and I was afraid, but not one time did this ole rock move or shake. I knew that as long as I held on to this rock, I would be okay."*

We may be in the midst of a storm, but just know this...we can cling to the Rock of safety and we will survive the storm intact! Satan would love to blow us off, but he can't! He would love to take us out, but he can't! The enemy would love to veer us off our course, but he can't! We will hold on to the Rock, to the Word, and to the Promise, and see the circumstances change!

March 10

The Eye of the Storm

Acts 2:2, 16 "And suddenly there came a sound from heaven as of a rushing mighty wind, and it filled all the house where they were sitting...But this is that which was spoke by the prophet Joel..."

Several weeks ago the Lord spoke to me and said that a *new wave of glory is coming to the Church*. Within a week or so after that He spoke again and said that we are in the *eye of the storm*. Many of us have sensed that a great change is coming and that we are in a transition. As we wait upon the Lord during this transition time, we have God's assurance that He is with us and in charge!

We are in the eye of the storm. A hurricane's strongest winds are in the eye wall, dense clouds surrounding the center of the storm. Hurricane hunters break through this wall of clouds that are the most dangerous and closest to the center of the storm and enter into the eye of the hurricane. There they can track the pressure and intensity of the storm.

Winds are blowing - the winds of adversity are blowing stronger each day, demanding and fierce. But the winds of God are blowing even stronger! They are blowing throughout the world today as prophesied in Joel and Acts, pouring out His Spirit upon all flesh. We have been positioned by God to be able to track the intensity of the storms! We have been given power to break through the intense winds and dense clouds of the storm to enter into the eye of the storm! We are hidden in the secret place with the Most High God, who reveals His secrets to His servants. The storms may blow fiercely around us, but we are held by His Word! We may feel the effects of the change that is coming, but we can trust the One who brings the change. I encourage you today to be open, willing and obedient, and receive the power and authority Christ transferred to us so that we can face every adverse wind and be a part of that great wind of God that is blowing upon the earth!

March 11

Safety In The Storm

Psalms 91:1 "He that dwells in the secret place of the Most High shall abide under the shadow of the Almighty."

I remember the day John F. Kennedy Jr.'s plane went down. Trying to navigate through a storm, his instruments failed and the plane was flying upside down in the storm.

It's hard to see when you're in a storm. Visibility is diminished and we can't rely upon what we see. Most drivers will pull over to the side of the road when visibility fails. However, if we are in a plane or boat, we must learn to rely upon our instruments to get us to safety. We all go through storms in our lives. Storms of adversity blow against us to dash our faith and conqueror us. Conflicts arise to try to consume us. One of my favorite hymns is *Never Alone*. It says:

I've seen the lightning flashing, I've heard the thunder roll.
I've felt sins breakers dashing, trying to conquer my soul.
I've heard the voice of my Savior, telling me still to fight on.
He promised never to leave me, never to leave me alone!

There is safety in the storms for us. Psalms 91 speaks of a secret hiding place where we can dwell in safety under the shadow of His wings! There is a place of refuge for the Children of God! He can see what we can't. He knows how to keep us when we are buffeted and in distress. We can rely upon Him to guide us safely through. The storms will pass, leaving in their wake strong, secure believers, who trust in their God! I will say of the Lord, He is My Rock, my Mighty Fortress, my Safe Place! He is calling to us today to press on, keep fighting, and keep going! He is with us and *we are never alone!*

March 12

Dancing in the Storm

John 16:33 "...In this world ye shall have tribulations, but be of good cheer; I have overcome the world."

There is an old Gene Kelly film that almost everyone is familiar with, especially the scene where he dances in the rain. He has reason to dance for he found out that he is loved. The rain could not stop him from singing and dancing, and it was this scene that endeared this movie to so many people.

How much more reason do we have to dance and sing, for we are dearly loved by the greatest One of all! Life will bring many storms to us, but we can learn to dance through them because His love is *consistent*, *unchanging* and *eternal*. Our Father is not a fair-weather Friend, but is the kind of Friend that sticks closer than a brother! Jesus warned us that in this life we would have many trials, but we can *be of good cheer*, for He overcame the world! In essence, He was telling us to *"learn how to sing and dance through the storms"*, for they will pass, but He will remain!

We can dance in the storms! We can still sing in the rain! We can still give Him Praise, for we are all safe, we are intact, and we are still loved by the Father. As W. E. Timmons said, *"Life is not about waiting for the storm to pass. It is about learning to dance in the rain."*

March 13

Times of Refreshing

Isaiah 28:12 "...This is the rest wherewith ye may cause the weary to rest; and this is the refreshing..."

God always comes through! Just when it seems we are about to languish in the dry seasons of life He sends us times of refreshing!

God knows we need these times of refreshing that restores our souls! He understands that we need to taste of His goodness and see His mighty works! There is rest for the weary and hope for the hopeless! There is joy for those who have walked in great sorrow! He sends blessings that often come in disguises to strengthen our faith and renew our minds. He gives us "Wow" moments to remind us of His majestic power!

The times of refreshing come to us after great battles, valleys of sorrow, and wearisome walks. *Yes! It's our time of refreshing!* Time to be refreshed. Time to be restored. Time for joy. Time for laughter. Time for strength. Time for hope. Time for blessings. Time for restitution. Time for healing. Time for wholeness. Time...for the Church!

March 14

Seize the Day

John 9:4 "I must work the works of him that sent me, while it is day: the night cometh, when no man can work."

What opportunities presented themselves to us today that were ignored, unacknowledged, overlooked or rejected? A missed call, an unspoken message, and the belief that tomorrow we'll do what we didn't do today will overshadow our dreams and goals, and will eventually dim what was once a bright neon light that was lit up with passion, desire and a 'go getter' attitude. Duties, cares of life and business keep most well meaning Christians from ever becoming all that God intended for them to be.

I have waited a lifetime to preach the Gospel of Jesus Christ on foreign soil. I have held the dream deep in my heart for over thirty years. I recently received invitations (all within days of each other) to go to Nepal, India, and New Guinea to preach, and ***now I am living my dream!*** I am seizing my opportunity and living a dream I have longed to see all of my life.

We have this moment, this day, this opportunity to do something and to take one step toward our goal. I am strongly persuaded that if we are going to do anything for the Lord, we must do it now! *What are we waiting for?* If we can hear one voice calling out in desperation and answer that call...if we can give a little bit more of our money to farther the cause of the Gospel...if we can offer what we have to be used by God...if we can use our own two hands, our skills and our talents to build God's kingdom...if we can spend some alone time with the Lord...then we must seize this day, for now is the time to do something. How sad it would be to die before we ever really lived, really dreamed, really did something great for Jesus. What are we waiting for?

March 15

There is a Reward!

Hebrews 6:10 "For God is not unrighteous to forget your work and labor of love which you have shown toward His Name…"

God is not unfaithful to forget your labor of love!

The Preacher (Solomon) spoke eloquently to us of a season and a time for everything. There is a time to plant and a time to reap, a time of sowing and a time of harvest. Many days, weeks and months go by when a farmer plants seed into the soil before seeing anything happen. Yet he continues to water that seed and labors to remove weeds from his garden. He has faith that one day a tiny little sprout will shoot up from the ground that will bring him the harvest he has waited so patiently for. And so it is with us. Many times we cannot see what is going on with the seeds that we sow, but it is still there, waiting to come forth at the appointed time. *Hebrews 10:35, "Cast not away therefore your confidence which hath great recompence of reward. For ye have need of patience that after ye have done the will of God, ye might receive the promise."* Be not weary in well doing for ye shall reap if you faint not!

There is a harvest time for you, dear one, *so hold on to your promise and don't quit!* Keep Believing… Keep Trusting… Keep Planting… Keep Praying… Keep Holding On! God doesn't forget! His timing is not our timing, but His ways are perfect! It's not over, it's not dead, it's not forgotten, but God is the Author and Finisher of all things! It's never too late for Him! Your time has not come and gone - it's just begun! Enjoy your journey into your destiny and put your trust in the one who numbers your steps.

March 16

God Is My Help

Hebrews 4:16 "Let us therefore come boldly unto the throne of grace, that we may obtain mercy, and find grace to help in time of need."
2 Chronicles 14:11, 12 "And Asa cried out to the LORD his God, and said, "LORD, it is nothing for You to help, whether with many or with those who have no power; help us, O LORD our God, for we rest on You, and in Your name we go against this multitude. O LORD, You are our God; do not let man prevail against You!"
Psalms 54:4 "Behold, God is my helper..!"

Are you prepared to trust God? Can you withstand the intimidating cries that fill your ears with these words, *"Where is your God now?"* Can your faith stand the tests of unanswered prayers and delayed answers? Is your walk of faith only talk, or does it have staying power that will keep you grounded when everything is shaken? Are you fighting battles that seem to go on forever with no end in sight and you wonder if you'll ever win? Have you put you faith out there only to be left hanging and wondering if you made a mistake? **Let me assure you that God is your Helper** and it is only a matter of time until He renders your enemies helpless and defeated... if you will stand firmly in faith.

Spurgeon said this, *"It is the most bitter of all afflictions to be led to fear that there is no help for us in God."* Don't buy the lie that says God will not help you! Said Tozer: *"What we need very badly these days is a company of Christians who are prepared to trust God as completely now as they know they must do at the last day. For each of us the time is coming when we shall have nothing but God. Health and wealth and friends and hiding places will be swept away and we shall have only God. To the man of pseudo faith that is a terrifying thought, but to real faith it is one of the most comforting thoughts the heart can entertain."*

Perhaps you, like me, have poured yourself into something or someone and just have not seen the results you long to see. Don't loose hope, for God is your Helper! Don't allow doubt and fear to make you think there is no help for you, but stand firmly in faith and boldly enter into the throne room to find the help you need. Faith will stand the tests, the defeats, the humiliation and intimidation of the enemy. Faith will remind you in your lowest, most vulnerable moment that God is your help and He will not fail you!

March 17

The Power of the Word

Psalm 107:20 "He sent his word and healed them..."

I stand amazed at the power of God's Word. Oh, how He loves His Word and watches over it to perform the things that He spoke. David wrote in Psalm 119:154, *"Plead my cause, quicken me with thy Word."* He said in Psalm 119:162, *"I rejoice at thy Word as one that findeth great treasure."* Psalm 119:81, *"I hope in thy Word."* Psalm 89:34, *"My covenant will I not break, nor alter the thing that is gone out of my lips."* Psalm 119:89, *"Forever, O Lord, they Word is settled in Heaven."* David was acknowledging and accepting that God's Word was the ultimate authority. Whatever need He had could be met in the Word.

Then David did something that we should do sometimes, he reminded God of His Word. Psalm 119:49, *"Remember thy Word unto thy servant, upon which thou has caused me to hope."* We, too, should speak God's Word back to Him, reminding Him of His promises to heal us, to save us, to redeem us, to bless us for our faithfulness.

In Matthew 8:5-13 is the story of the centurion whose servant was sick. He came to Jesus asking that his servant be healed. Jesus answered the man saying, *"I will come and heal him."* The centurion said it wasn't necessary for Jesus to come to the servant, *"Speak thy Word only and my servant will be healed."* He recognized the authority of the spoken word - it was all that was needed to heal his servant. Jesus, amazed at his great faith, sent His Word and in that very hour the servant was healed.

Today, I place my faith in the Word, reminding God of all of His promises for you.

> *If you are sick...He sends His words of divine healing to you.*
> *If you are discouraged...He sends His words of encouragement to you.*
> *If you are sad...He sends His words of joy and peace to you.*

If you are in need of financial blessings...He sends His words of prosperity to you.
If you are lonely...He sends His word that He is a present help.

God is not limited by time or distance, but is quick to hear, and hastens to perform His Word to you today. Stand on His Word! Cast off sickness, disease, discouragement, torment and walk in the fullness of His Joy. *Today God has something special for you that can be found in His Word.*

March 18

Be Still And Know

Psalm 46:10 "Be still, and know that I am God; I will be exalted among the nations, I will be exalted in the earth!"

Then, there is God! In the stillness of the night and in the quiet rising of the sun, God is there, bringing peace to a heart that is hurting. He can be found in the wee hours of the morning writing a song upon the lips of a saint who has known suffering and sorrow. He is there in the busy hours of the day guiding one lost soul back to safe shores.

He is there, when all other help is reduced to nothing and we've reached the limitations of what man can do. He steps into the stillness...and *we suddenly know He is God!* When our glory has faded and our power has become useless, He shows us what a loving, caring God can do. His wisdom supersedes our understanding and knowledge, and we learn to trust Him even when it looks hopeless. And, when our steps falter and become a little slower under the weight of heavy cares, He gently scoops us up and carries us until we are strong again. He exalts Himself among the nations and declares Himself to those who search for Him.

Then, there is God! You are not alone, *but you are accompanied by One who is greater than any mountain in your path.* He fights for you and defends you against your enemies. He vindicates His little ones and empowers His people to rise up from the ashes of defeat and to step into His glory! Yes, when man has reached his limits, and all that can be done has been done...there is God! Be still...and know!

March 19

It's Already Done

John 1:1 "In the beginning was the Word..."
Psalms 89:34 "My covenant will I not break, nor alter the thing that is gone out of my lips."

We all believe that there is none like our God and that nothing is impossible with Him. However, there is a higher level that we can take our faith to! Not only do we believe that we serve a mighty God who is able to do the miraculous, but we also believe that *He is the very Word that He speaks*! He and His Word are entwined with each other...and are one!

When God speaks something, *in His mind it is already done*! He spoke this world into existence with His Word! He spoke and all that is now was created! In the beginning was the Word!

When He spoke His Word of healing to you, in His eyes you are already healed! When He spoke His Word of destiny to you, as far as God is concerned, it is already a reality! When He spoke a promise to you, to God it is already done! You may still feel sick, but in God's thoughts you are already healed! You might be caught up in the heat of a battle, but God has secured your victory with His Word! It may look like you are going under, but His Word has taken you to the realm of *Over* -- Overcomer, blessed abundantly, above and over all that we ask or think! It may appear that your promises are unraveling, but by His Word restoration is already assured!

It is when we step out by faith on His Word that all these things become reality to us! They are already real and completed to God, but we must take ourselves into that realm where God exists and obtain the very promises that He spoke to us! He has not changed His mind about His promises to us, nor has He altered what He promised to us. He is already dwelling in our promises, now it is up to us to move in and let the Word be alive and real to us...seeing it as He sees it...Already Done!

March 20

He Believes In You

Hebrews 13:6 "...The LORD is my helper; I will not fear..."

There is One who will walk every step with you, even when those steps are slow and faltering! Perhaps you feel alone in your struggle or pain. You wonder, *"Is there anyone who cares about me and what I am going through? Is there anyone who has a little time to hear what I have to say? I just need someone to talk to,...someone who believes in me."*

There is <u>One</u> who believes in you! He has all the time in the world to listen to you and has inclined His ear to hear what you need to say. He waits for you to turn to Him. He is anxious to hear all about your day, your dreams, your desires. He is troubled by what troubles you, and has made your enemies His enemies. He believes in you...and in your dreams. *After all, He is the One who breathed those dreams and visions into your being. He believes you will make it, you will endure, and you will overcome triumphantly!* He sees the hurting wounds inflicted by life's harsh blows, and His healing touch will ease your pain. He sees the attacks that left you crippled and broken, and extends kind hands of mercy and compassion to you. He sees your struggles and has already purchased your victory. He sees your weakness...and longs passionately to hold you until you are strengthened. *He believes in you, even when you falter, and will pick you up and carry you until you can walk again.*

If you need reminding today of how much He loves you and believes in you, just remember the cross! *After all, He loved you to death!*

March 21

He Hears

Psalm 116:2 "Because he hath inclined his ear unto me, therefore will I call upon Him as long as I live."

God hears each time we call out to Him!

I find it frustrating to talk to someone who is not listening. They may go through the appearance of hearing, but they just aren't tuned in to what I'm saying. It's evident that their thoughts are somewhere else by the response they give.

David said the Lord inclined His ear to me. This meant that he had God's full attention, that God was bending down towards David to capture every word that was being spoken. When someone is interested in what you have to say they will give you their undivided attention. Their posture is turned towards you, and if they are really engrossed in what you are saying, they will bend their heads toward you. When we call upon the Father, He is interested in everything we have to say. His ear is bent towards us to capture every word that we speak. How reassuring it is to know that God cares so much about us that He hears and understands the language of our hearts. We can talk to Jesus about anything and everything, knowing that He takes great interest in what we have to say.

March 22

You Are One of a Kind

1 John 3:1 "Behold, what manner of love the Father hath bestowed upon us..."

In this very busy and congested world *it is so easy to feel alone and unloved,* even by those closest to you. But, you are very important and you matter to someone who loves you more than life itself...God!

He took great care and time to specifically design you to be who you are. He gave detailed attention to your personality, your laugh, the color of your eyes, and even those secret things are hidden in the depths of your soul! There is no one else in this whole wide world that is exactly like you - you are an original designed by an Artist whose brush was filled with colors he took from the rainbow and put in your dreams. He sees you as He created you to be, the person you are becoming. Others may see flaws, imperfections, or an incomplete being, **but He looks at you through the red blood of Jesus and sees...perfection**! He handpicks your talents, your skills, and your creative abilities, and deposits them deep in the treasure box of your heart. He alone holds the key to your treasure box, and when He is given access to your box, the treasures that are overlooked or flawed become holy and spectacular!

You matter to Him! *Your dreams, your hopes, your aspirations are all important to Him.* He cares deeply for you and desires to be so intimately involved with you that all that really matters to you...is Him! You can trust Him and you can believe in His love for you. *In this busy, crazy world...you matter!*

March 23

Tenderly He Watches Over You

Matthew 28:20 "...I am with you always..."

  You are on His mind today. He tenderly watches over you, even when you feel all alone with your burdens and your sorrows. He is there to comfort your heart and ease your mind. Can you hear Him as He tenderly whispers into your ear, *"I love you"* ? See the price that He paid as He stretches out His loving hands towards you... hands that are marred by scars. If only you could look into His eyes.... there you would find everything that your heart longs for and desires - *unconditional love, unfathomable favor, and unmerited grace.*

  He already knows what is on your heart. He knows and understands the concerns there. He is quite aware of the problems you face, problems that seem to great for you to handle. He is waiting for you to ask Him. *Just ask - He will do it.* If you are His, and you abide in Him, He says you can have whatsoever you ask. Don't think for a moment that He doesn't care or understand. He is the only One who fully and completely loves and understands you. Reach out to Him...Call His Name...He will come to you. Lift up your hands that have grown heavy and weary...and praise Him though this storm!

  Let Him love you. Let Him show you His way. He is tenderly watching over you. He knows how to care for His own, and will give you His very best...just ask!

March 24

Is There Anyone...I Can Show Kindness To

2 Samuel 9:1, 3 "And David said, Is there yet any that is left of the house of Saul, that I may show him kindness for Jonathan's sake?... The king said, Is there not yet anyone of the house of Saul to whom I may show the kindness of God? And Ziba said to the king, There is still a son of Jonathan who is crippled in both feet."

*The kindness you show someone today may be the last kindness they will ever know...*it may be the only kindness they have ever known. Life can be cruel and harsh for many, and if we will take a moment to really see those around us, we will see a great need for kindness.

She came back into my life just a couple of years ago. My niece had moved away from her family years ago, married and raised her family...a family that knew us only through stories she shared. She was lonely and life had not been kind to her, and she wanted to reconnect with her family. We talked almost daily by phone, for she still lived far away. I saw her last October when I was in her area... and saw the frail condition she was in. I met her little girl and one of her sons, and spent a few happy hours with her. She called me, all excited because her husband had gone to Church with her last Sunday and gave his life to the Lord. A few hours later, I received the news that she was no longer with us, but was now in that eternal city, renewing old acquaintances and singing around the throne. Shocked at the news because I had just spoken with her, I was also very, very glad that I had shown her kindness while she was here.

Is there anyone that you can show kindness to today? I am sure that if you look, you will find someone in need of kindness. Look beyond the crippled feet, the unappealing appearance, and see the need. You have the power to show kindness to a heart that is hurting. Look at society's "throw away" people who fall beneath the social acceptances because they are poor, or not very educated, and are treated with terrible unkindness by those who can't see the heart of gold underneath the brokenness. Find the "cripple" who once sat at a fine table and enjoyed better days, but now is resigned to just existing in life because of circumstances beyond his control. Our world is not very kind to such folks, but thankfully, we are not of this world, but have a different nature! He has entrusted some neglected soul into your hands that you, like King David, can show kindness and favor to for Jesus' sake. Today could be the last opportunity you have to show them love and kindness.

March 25

Leave the Shadows of Silence

Psalm 94:17 "Unless the LORD had been my help, My soul would soon have settled in silence."

Nature is slowly awakening from her silent slumber. Her songs are heard throughout the trees in the melodies of songbirds. Trees are beginning to bud and the gray, dismal earth will soon be ablaze with color as spring approaches. Winter is retreating and life is returning. The shadows of silence is replaced with the harmonious sounds of the joys of life.

We, too, know what it's like to emerge from the slumber of the cold, dismal winter seasons. *Wounded hearts that retreated into the shadows of silence can now feel the spark of hope of a new day dawning.* Voices that have been silenced by mistakes, failures, disappointments, and defeats are finding new strength and will be silent no more! Songs that have lain dormant from hearts that have known the deafening sound of despair are bursting forth in joy and gladness. *The prophetic voice of the Spirit is emerging loud and strong to declare the way of the Lord!* The shadows that have bound us to the past are slithering away as the King of Glory breaks through the clouds of hopeless captivity. The shadows of silence can no longer keep us quiet, but the voices of praise and victory are rising in momentum and power to slay the voices of the past. The silence is fleeing...as a new day of glory emerges from the shadows and the Lord Himself declares He is our help and our strength!

Today is a new day for you...a day of hope, a day of joy, and a day of victory. Leave behind the shadows of mistakes, disappointments, and shame...and step into a day of rejoicing and victory.

March 26

A Child's Greatest Hope

Malachi 4:6 "And he shall turn the heart of the fathers to the children, and the heart of the children to their fathers, lest I come and smite the earth with a curse."

I enjoyed seeing the involvement of my grandson-in-law as he and my granddaughter prepared for the arrival of their first child. He was very involved in everything...the doctors appointments, the baby showers, and even choosing the theme of the baby room. I knew in my heart that Scott would be a good daddy to Baby Anisten, and would be very involved in her life. I believe he will always be there for her and will do everything in his power to meet all of her needs throughout her life. *The greatest gift he can offer her is to be a godly father and to show her that real men love Jesus.*

What is a child's greatest need? To know Jesus loves them. *What is a child's greatest hope?* To have Godly parents who guard over their souls, point them to the Cross, and instill in their hearts a faith that will never be shaken and a love that will endure. The greatest hope for our Children can be found in these three things...*A Godly Mother, a God-loving Father, and a Church that loves Jesus.*

The World wants our children...and wants them badly. Oh, how blessed are the children who have a Mom who guards over their hearts. Blessed are the children who have found a family of faith in a Church who loves Jesus passionately through word and deed. Secure and safe are those who have a Dad that guards their souls against the enemies of the cross and the predators of this world. Give your children hope, give them love, and give them Jesus. That is their greatest hope!

March 27

Divine Appointments

John 4:4, 7 "And He must needs go through Samaria...and there came a woman of Samaria to draw water..."

The Lord has appointed this to be a day of divine connections, interruptions, interventions, and purpose for us! *We may think our day is going to go a certain way, but He has other plans for it!* He will take us out of our way so that His purpose can be done in our lives, or in the life of someone who needs a divine appointment with us!

Jesus went out of His way to meet a woman by a well. The disciples couldn't understand this interruption in their schedule, but Jesus knew there was someone who needed a drink of living water... so *He paused in His busy schedule to meet her need.* She had a Divine Appointment with Destiny - and met a man who changed her way of life! Paul was on his way to Damascus and had a Divine Intervention with the Savior, who transformed his way of thinking! Zacheaus had a Divine Purpose for climbing up a tree - he needed a Divine Appointment with the One who forgave sins!

Sometimes we, like the disciples, may not understand some of the interruptions in our schedules, but Jesus has a purpose for them. Some of us are in line for a Divine Connection - that one person, one meeting or one contact that can propel us into the reality of our visions! God has set up Divine Appointments for us that will literally transform our lives - taking us into positions of authority and supernatural blessings! He has made a Divine Appointment for those of us who need a Great Physician, and has already set in motion Divine Healing for us. God knows who to send, when to send them, and how to send the right people into our lives that will produce blessings, overflow and divine purpose! Remember, if He went out of His way to bless a woman by a well, He will also go to great lengths to make a Divine Appointment with you!

March 28

Give Me The Anointing

Isaiah 10:27 "And it shall come to pass in that day, That his burden shall be taken away from off thy shoulder, And his yoke from off thy neck, And the yoke shall be destroyed because of the anointing."

The Church has had it all! We've enjoyed beautiful worship and talented musicians! We've heard teaching on every subject known to man! The Church has created programs designed to help, aide, assist and lift the suffering from people. Programs have their place, but I'm looking for a solution to our problems that will transform lives, free addicts and change a persons heart! Sadly, these things have replaced the precious anointing of the Holy Ghost by putting band aids on the problems. Without the anointing, we are useless for the work of God. We can talk about leadership skills and we can teach courses and all that is good but the greatest leader cannot lead properly without the anointing.

The anointing is being *set apart for the service of God.* The anointing is the *empowerment from the Holy Spirit for service.* The anointing is the difference between a great singer who performs flawlessly and entertains our flesh, and the voice of one who, although untrained but anointed, can make a sinner weep over his sins, and minister peace to the hurting heart. The anointing is the difference between a minister who can deliver a five-point sermon with charisma that tickles the ears, and a minister who preaches the gospel in simplicity and truth that penetrates into the soul of man, and makes hell tremble!

Upon the beginning of His ministry, Jesus announced to the world that He was the Anointed One, sent to preach the gospel, to set captives free, to deliver all those in bondage and to *destroy every yoke!* Give me that same anointing that will not just put a temporary fix to our problems, but the anointing to destroy yokes and free captives! Give me the anointing that ushers in the Holy Presence of the Living God! Give me the anointing that brings the power back! Give me the anointing that defines the Chosen from the Called, and separates the Church from the religious! The anointing gets the job done - every time!

March 29

Make Me Willing

Daniel 10:12, 13 "Then said he unto me, Fear not, Daniel: for from the first day that thou didst set thine heart to understand, and to chasten thyself before thy God, thy words were heard, and I am come for thy words. But the prince of the kingdom of Persia withstood me one and twenty days: but, lo, Michael, one of the chief princes, came to help me..."
2 Corinthians 10:4 "For the weapons of our warfare are not carnal, but mighty through God to the pulling down of strong holds."

"Lord, make me willing!" Unable to sleep last night, I lay before the Lord in prayer for family and friends who are going through some pretty tough situations. I questioned Him, *"Lord, why haven't we seen our prayers answered as quickly as we have in days past?"* The desperate situations are framed by time, and time is running out for some. The answer came..."*Who is willing to intercede in prayers that pull down the strongholds? Who is willing to dedicate themselves to fasting for these precious ones?"* I cried out, *"Make me willing, Lord, to do what You require me to do."*

Daniel prayed fervently...but still the answer had not yet come. Being a man willing to do what is sometimes necessary, he fasted and prayed diligently for 21 days. At the end of those 21 days the Lord gave him the answer, not only to his prayers, but also why it had taken so long! *There was a great war fought in the heavenlies as Satan attempted to intercept the answer to Daniel's prayers.* Daniel did what was necessary to get results and answers. Can we say the same?

The Holy Spirit has equipped us with great and mighty weapons of warfare, yet we treat them casually and often they go unused. Why? Because *to engage in warfare means we must get involved. Unwilling to commit ourselves to the warfare, we offer up paltry, lifeless prayers that deceive us into thinking they will move the Hand of God.*

God wants prayers that are fervent from righteous lips and willing hearts that burn with passion, compassion, and love. He honors the prayers of those who are willing to spend some time on their knees for others. He uses those who are willing to get involved with His works and who agree with His methods. I can no longer participate in half-hearted prayer attempts to get God to move, but cry out to Him to make me willing to pray effective, powerful prayers that can pull down the strongholds! *"Make me willing, Lord, and I'll do what You require! Make me willing Lord, to be inconvenienced when You ask me to stop everything and pray! Make me willing Lord, and anoint these lips of clay and heart of flesh so that I can be a channel for You to flow through!"*

March 30

Who Is On First

1 John 4:19 "We love Him, because He first loved us."
Luke 10:27, 28 "And he answering said, Thou shalt love the Lord
thy God with all thy heart, and with all thy soul, and with all thy
strength, and with all thy mind; and thy neighbour as thyself. And
he said unto him, Thou hast answered right: this do, and thou
shalt live."

    "Don't hold on too tightly to the things of this world..." The sweet voice of the young woman who had lost her younger sister echoes in my mind, and I know too well what she is talking about. *She was reminding us to keep Jesus first, for everything else can be taken from us in a split second.*

    Hold on to Him tightly and never let Him go! It is He who holds our future in His hands, and *a future with Him is a future worth believing in.* He holds the key to our success and to our joy. Our money and possessions are poor substitutes for the success that can be found only in Him. Spouses and children cannot fulfill us like He can. Aspirations, goals and dreams are but temporal and fleeting achievements unless placed in His hands. Who or what sits on the throne of our hearts could easily be displaced tomorrow unless that Someone Is Jesus! There is only One who deserves to be First - the One who said, *"Not my will, but Thine!"* The One who *"first loved us, even when we were in sin!"* The One Man who said, *"I'll put You First!"*

    God demands to be first, and the first things belong to God! There is only one place that is worthy enough of Jesus in our lives - First! He refuses to be second place, second string, second fiddle...or copilot! It is said, *"If He is not Lord of all in our lives, then He is not Lord at all in our lives."* Let's not hold on too tightly to the things of this world, for in the end, they will all pass away. Put Jesus first! *He alone is worthy of First Place in our lives!*

March 31

Get Up!

I John 4:4 "Ye are of God, little children, and have overcome them: because greater is he that is in you, than he that is in the world."

Get up! These are the Words I hear in my spirit today! Get back on your feet, you are better than the blow that struck you! You are bigger than the hand that is against you. *Greater is He that is in you than he that is in the world!*

Be determined to stand! Purpose in your heart that you will stay the course! Don't quit, don't stop, and don't give up! Stay the course and don't waver in your faith! You will make it! You will keep going! You may have fallen, but you will get up!

If you have taken some hits that seem to have knocked you down, The Lord would say *"get up!"* Don't stay down for a minute longer, but encourage yourself in the Lord to get up! You have too much going for you, and you have come too far to give up now! Too many are cheering you on! The calling on your life is too great! There is too much to gain! You are not "down for the count", *but you will rise again...this time in the strength and power of the Lord that will slay your foes and defeat your despair!*

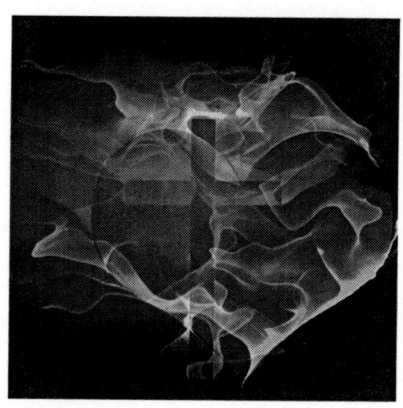

April

The submission of the Lamb
And the roar of the Lion
Won my victory!

April 1

Costly Worship

John 12:3 "Then took Mary a pound of ointment of spikenard, very costly, and anointed the feet of Jesus, and wiped his feet with her hair; and the house was filled with the odor of the ointment."

Have you ever just gone through the motions of worship? We sing and clap our hands, but our hearts just aren't in it. We find ourselves acting out our worship when we have grown cold or distant, or perhaps when our minds are consumed with other things rather than Him. We often present a dressed up version of praise, but keep the worship locked up inside of us. We offer Him worship that doesn't cost us anything. *David said that he would not offer the Lord anything that had not cost him something.*

Mary had something that she paid a dear price for, something that wasn't common or ordinary, and she lavished it on Jesus. I'm sure the box that it came in was beautiful and also pricey, but what was in it was far more valuable. She broke open her beautiful alabaster box so that what was inside could be showered on Jesus. Her worship was costly and dear to her. Some did not like it and suggested that the money could have been used for better purposes. *What better reason is there than Jesus to break open extravagant worship?*

The most beautiful worship we can bestow upon our Savior is worship from our hearts - *extravagant, uncommon and costly worship from adoring hearts*. We must break open our boxes, releasing the aroma of our worship to the One who is most worthy. Notice that when Mary broke open her box, the aroma of the perfume filled the house. When we offer Jesus worship that is from our hearts, worship that sometimes comes from brokenness, *the aroma of our worship will fill our homes and our place of worship.* The next time we start to offer Him worship that is a motion only, let's break open our alabaster boxes and offer Him worship that He is worthy of - worship that has cost us something, worship that comes from our hearts, worship that says we appreciate what Jesus has done for us.

April 2

Expressions of Love

John 3:16 "For God so loved the world that He gave His only Begotten Son..."

Love will always express itself! Someone recently posed this question, "*If the love of God has been shed abroad in our hearts, why aren't more people expressing that love.*" I wonder, too, why love isn't demonstrated more among the Body of Christ.

I look at the price that Jesus paid for our salvation. It is free, but it sure isn't cheap. He loves us so much that He endured Gethsemane, praying so hard that the blood vessels broke and He sweated blood. He loves us so much that He endured the scorn and mockery of the religious world who spat upon His dear face. He loves us so much that He was beaten by angry soldiers who opened up His back...the back that carried our sins...and exposed it to torture beyond imagination. He loves us so much that He allowed them to drive nails in His hands and feet, pinning Him to a cruel cross and suspended between heaven and earth. He loves us so much that for one dark moment in time, He was forsaken by God and filled with loneliness that was unbearable. Love expressed itself that day that split time in half and opened up the way to the Father to all who will come. You and I are recipients of His demonstration of love. It was not just words that He mouthed, but it was love in action that forever changed who we are.

How do we demonstrate our love for Him? Do we lavish our love on Him through extravagant worship? Do we give Him our very best gifts and not the left-overs? Do we truly love His Church and enact that love through expressions of devotion and commitment? We cannot love Him without loving each other! Love will express itself! Love gives! Love demonstrates! Love gets involved!

April 3

Yes, Jesus Loves You

Jeremiah 31:3 "...Yea, I have loved thee with an everlasting love; therefore with loving kindness have I drawn thee."

Jesus loves you...oh, how He loves you! He adores you and is deeply, passionately in love with you.

He created you for His Divine pleasure and for His purpose. You are created in His image, fashioned by His own hand, and washed in His precious blood. Your past is redeemed, your present has purpose, and your future is secure. He purchased you from the auction block of sin, delivered you from bondage, and wrote His love for you in red. It is a perfect love. He gives all, and holds nothing back.

There is safety in His love. There is security in His love. He will keep you until that glorious day of His appearing. Don't be afraid! Don't lose hope! Don't be discouraged! Everything that touches you touches Him. He sees everything you are going through, feels every hurt and disappointment with you, and walks through every dark valley with you. He will get you through this valley, too. He sees the fears, the concerns and the turmoil, and asks that you simply trust Him. *He understands the times that we are living in, but wants you to know that these times are in His hands* and He has already provided a place of safety and security for you. He whispers through the dark and unknown..."*Fear Not, I am with You! Be Not afraid, for I am your God!*"

Yes...Jesus loves you...so very, very, very much.

April 4

What Label Do You Wear?

John 19:22 "Pilate answered, What I have written, I have written."

Have you ever been labeled? I would guess that we all have at one time or another in our lives. We are labeled because of our parentage or family name, or by our social standing. Most of us have been labeled as being a good person, or by our success in life or by our career. We are even classified by the label of the clothes we wear.

There is One who was labeled the Miracle Worker, The Son of God, and Wonderful Counselor. At times He was even called a devil by those who hated Him. It was the custom of the day when crucifying someone that their crimes would be written on a board and posted at the top of their cross. However, as Jesus stood before Pilate, there was something about Him that was different. Pilate gave the command to write *King of the Jews* on His sign. In response to the protests of the people, Pilate responded, *"What I have written, I have written."*

Satan likes to label us and reminds us of the things we have done, the mistakes we have made and the sins we have committed. He is good at accusing us and taking us on long guilt trips. But, the King of the Jews has a written response to Satan that declares us as Children of the Most High, Heirs of God, and Priests of the Lord. It is forever sealed, written in the red blood of the Savior. He labels us as forgiven, loved, redeemed, and (I love this one) MINE! We are called Overcomers, More than Conquerors, and Winners. I am honored to be labeled Christian by the world, and wear my label with joy and thankfulness, grateful that my name is written in the Lamb's Book of Life. What label are you wearing?

April 5

Hosanna!

Matthew 21:9 "...Blessed is He that cometh in the name of the Lord; Hosanna in the highest."

I wonder if we see the King of Glory for who He is? Could that be Him riding on a lowly donkey? Jesus rode into Jerusalem on the Jericho Road just days before His crucifixion. It was a triumphant entry that was filled with loud shouts of praises of the people who had seen His miracles. Palm leaves (representing victory) were spread before Him and waved into the air as He made His way past the people. Hosannas were heard throughout the city as Jesus made His way in.

The encyclopedia describes Hosanna as this: Hosanna (hozan) [Hebrew: save now, an intensified imperative, a cry, addressed to God. The dictionary defines it as this: ho·san·na (ho-zan) interj, *used to express praise, or, adoration to God. n. A cry of "Hosanna." A shout of fervent and worshipful praise.*

When Jesus enters a place, victory comes with Him! He will hear our cries of "Hosanna" (God save us now or victory now). Some of will cry Hosanna to the Lord to say *"God save us now"*. Some of us will cry Hosanna meaning *'victory has come'*! As we worship Him today, worship Him with Hosanna's ringing out our praise. Victory will surely come! He will hear and save us!

April 6

Nothing, But Nothing, Can Stop the Miracle

John 12:10 "But the chief priests consulted that they might put Lazarus also to death."

Nothing or no one can undo what God does! Conspiracies cannot kill your miracle! Adversity cannot annihilate your promise! Evil plans cannot eliminate your resurrection!

Godless leaders hated Jesus and despised the miracles that He performed. Far too many believed upon Him when Lazarus was resurrected, causing these back-slidden religious men to feel intimidated and threatened by Jesus! Even Lazarus became a target of hate because of his miracle. Yet, these mortal men could not destroy resurrection power! They could not undo what Christ had done! All the evil and the hatred in their hearts could not defeat the power of the Life that was now in Lazarus!

No weapon formed against you can prosper! They will try to silence the miracle in your life, for they know the power of your testimony will bring glory to Him! But they cannot prevail! Conspiracies against you will come to naught! Destructive words against you cannot destroy your miracle! Evil plans designed to take you out will fail, because what God breaths life into will live! Nothing can stop the miracle that God has ordained for you!

April 7

It Wasn't 'Normal'

Luke 2:7 "And she brought forth her firstborn son, and wrapped Him in swaddling clothes, and laid Him in a manger; because there was no room for them in the inn."
Matthew 27:29 "And when they had platted a crown of thorns, they put it upon his head, and a reed in His right hand, and they bowed the knee before Him, and mocked Him, saying, Hail, King of the Jews!"

One of the things most people struggle with is feeling *"different"* and not like everyone else. Teens are really challenged by this, but also many Christians wrestle with not being like everyone else. As Children of God, we can expect to live lives that are *"not normal."* We can expect to feel *"different"*, *"set apart"*, *"separated"* from those around us. Some of us don't quite understand what it is that makes us different from everyone else, but it is the mark of God upon our lives, the infilling of His Holy Presence, and the plan that He has for us. We are called to a walk of faith that will present challenges to us that others don't face. *But...it is who we are in Christ that really makes us "not normal".*

Jesus was not like any other king. He was not born in a royal palace with a silver spoon in His mouth, but in a humble stable. He did not live in fine estate homes, but in the home of a carpenter who made a living using his hands. As a young boy growing up, He surely felt very different from all His friends. Yet, He knew Who He was and *that was enough.* He grew up to become the most talked about, written about figure in History. His impact upon the world and mankind is still felt today. He was King of Heaven and Earth, yet they savagely put a crown of thorns upon His royal head and gave Him a reed for a scepter. Mockingly, they called Him "King." They spat upon Him and tore into His flesh with their anger and sin. No, He was not a normal King. He did not live a normal life of a King. He, the King of glory, came into the lives of ordinary people and did extraordinary things, and still they refused to acknowledge His Sovereignty.

Don't be discouraged when you feel *"not normal"*. Don't feel forsaken because you feel "set apart and separated" from others around you. *We are not called to live "normal" lives, but to live* above *the elements around us.* We can never be satisfied living in darkness, but *are called to bring light to the darkness.* We, too, must go through our Garden's of Gethsemane and pick up our crosses on the way to the palace! One day we will reign with Him. We are heirs and joint-heirs with Christ Jesus...we can never be "normal". We know WHO we are in Christ...and that is enough for me!

April 8

Sweet Surrender

Matthew 26:39 "...Oh My Father, if it is possible, let this cup pass from Me; nevertheless, not My will be done, but Your will be done."

I wonder how many of us can truthfully say that we have surrendered all to Jesus. Is there something we are holding on to that we just haven't been able to surrender to Him? It is part of our human nature to want to control certain things, especially those things that are most important to us. *Dear one...there will be a test on our submission!* When we completely surrender to His will, peace will completely envelop us. Perhaps some of us have been hurt by others and can't let it go. Or, maybe some have suffered tremendous loss in life and bitterness has tried to set in. Some have heard the Lord calling us into ministry but haven't surrendered our wills to His yet. We may not understand why we must go through some of the things that are appointed to us, but know this...*there is peace in submission!*

Jesus passed His test in the Garden of Gethsemane. His flesh cried out and fought against the path that was appointed for Him. He cried out in anguish for the bitter cup to pass from Him, yet in that same breath released full control to the Will of God and said, "*Nevertheless, not my will but Thine be done.*" Peace that comes only through submission then strengthened Him to accomplish the hard task that was set before Him. Hebrews tells us that Jesus, for the joy that was set before Him, endured the suffering of the cross. *We were the prize that He focused on*!

I pray that today the Sweet Holy Spirit will gently, but firmly deal with us in the areas that we have not surrendered to Him. May the power of the Holy Ghost give us the strength to sever ties that need to be broken, to release all our heartaches and pain to Him, and to surrender our wills to His! May His peace overtake us as we surrender ALL to Him.

April 9

The Cost of Love

John 15:13 "Greater love has no man than this, that a man lay down his life for his friends."

My heart was deeply touched as I listened to the words that were being spoken at Bible Study this past Wednesday night. I looked around and saw tears flowing down the faces of others. Some had bowed their heads as the words washed over us, *taking us to a place that time will never forget* - the place called Golgotha where Jesus endured unspeakable torture and pain, indescribable humiliation and utter disgrace.

The Innocent Lamb was judged guilty, condemned without a cause, and was crucified for the sins of another. *Yet, He endured it all like the King He was...without complaint and without bitterne*ss. He was gracious and loving to the unkind and unlovely. We learned some things that night in Bible Study - things that we take lightly and for granted. Things such as *it cost Jesus a terrible price to love us.* I wish you could have been there, I know you would have been touched, too, and you would have left having a keener appreciation for everything the Savior went through for us. The loss of blood, the gut wrenching pain and agony, the strain upon His heart and body was too much for one man to endure, yet endure it He did. ***It cost Him to love us.*** It cost Him every drop of blood in His body. It cost Him for our healing - His flesh ripped and torn into ribbons from lashes that exposed His organs to the wooden splinters of a cruel cross. It cost Him the pain of separation from His Father at the moment He needed Him the most. Our mistakes, our sins, our failures, our sorrows and grief cost the Savior a broken heart, a lonely death and a cruel cross. He paid the price willingly and submissive to the end to the Father's plan of salvation for us.

Dear One, You are so greatly loved by the Savior and the Father. He loves you with an eternal and everlasting love and did everything humanly and Godly possible to prove it to you. Never forget just how much it cost Jesus to love you!

April 10

It Wasn't A Good Day

Luke 23:33 "And when they were come to the place, which is called Calvary, there they crucified Him..."
Mark 15:34 "And at the ninth hour Jesus cried with a loud voice, saying...My God, My God, why has thou forsaken me?"

So we think we're having a bad day! Things just aren't working out the way we had anticipated. A friend betrayed us or maybe we had to sacrifice something we didn't want to give up. No one understands us...seems like no one really cares. Nothing is going the way it should for us...*we're having a bad day.*

We call it *"Good Friday"*, this day when Jesus was crucified. But for Him, *it wasn't a good day.* Just the evening before He had washed the dirty, smelly feet of disciples to demonstrate love and servanthood. He spent hours in the garden praying that He would be able to drink the bitter cup of death, and surrendered His will to the inevitable purpose set before Him. His followers fell asleep on Him in the hour He needed their strength the most. *He was betrayed with a kiss by a friend.* His friends all forsook Him, leaving Him to face His trials alone. He felt a soldier's fist in His face lifted against Him in anger. He endured a trial that was unjust, unlawful, and unfair. False witnesses maliciously twisted His truth. His face felt the cruel fists of the soldiers' hands as they relentless beat Him. Then, they took Jesus to Pilate, who washed his hands of the matter and turned Him over to the cold, hatred filled mob. They freed a murderer and condemned Jesus to death. He was brutally beaten as they plowed into His back with cat'o'nine whips. They spit on Him, mocked Him, and crowned Him with thorns. They nailed Him to a cross and placed the Holy Son of God between two thieves. They gave Him vinegar to drink when He thirsted. The heavens turned dark and the earth shook...and the Father turned His face from Him. Then...He died. *No, Good Friday wasn't a good day for Jesus, but it was very, very necessary.*

It was necessary so that we could love and be loved. It was necessary for His blood to flow so that we could be cleansed from sin. *No, it wasn't a good day for Jesus, but it was necessary for mankind.*

April 11

It's Not What it Appears to Be

Matthew 27:54 "...Truly this was the Son of God."

> *Some things are not what they appear to be.*

The meek appear to be weak. The wealthy appear to have it all. Hollywood offers a facade of happiness. Serving Jesus may appear to be a joyless life of no fun. The wealthy can buy the best medical attention - *but not divine health.* Money can buy lots of expensive toys - *but not fulfillment.* Hollywood can only offer what it really is - *an imitation or hyped up version of real life.* Serving Jesus brings more fulfillment, greater happiness, true joy and more adventure than you'll ever find anywhere else! *But we all know better. It's not always how it appears!*

To the religious leaders Jesus was someone who trampled upon their cold hearts with His fiery truth - *not their Messiah.* To the Jewish people Jesus was someone to take Barabbas' place as a common thief - *not their Deliverer.* To the Roman soldiers who tore open His back He was a criminal receiving punishment - *not the Great Physician.* To Pilate He was an extraordinary, faultless man - *not the King of Kings.*

But, to the Centurion on guard at the crucifixion, He was the Son of God! Out of all these people who had an encounter with Jesus, one got it! Jesus was no criminal, nor a common thief...**He was the Son of God...Emanuel...God with us!**

Others also were able to recognize the truth about Him. To the thief on the cross *He was the entrance into Paradise.* To Lazarus *He was the Resurrection!* To Blind Bartimaeus *He was the Sight Giver.* To the woman caught in adultery *He was Life Changing Hope.* And...*He is so much more!*

The truth will always come out! Someone today needs to hear this...if you've been misunderstood or lied on...the truth will come out! To the one who has been misrepresented or deceived - Jesus will give light to the situation. Some of you appear to be insignificant, but the truth is this...You are a Child of God, and His Purpose, Plans and Destiny will take you to the palaces of the great and mighty. To those thought to be of no consequence, God will position you to influence governments and rulers.

The truth will always come out! The entrance of light will always bring out the truth.

April 12

Trust Him In the Silence

Luke 23:52, 53 "This man went unto Pilate, and begged the body of Jesus. And he took it down, and wrapped it in linen, and laid in a sepulcher that was hewn in stone..."
Matthew 27:66 "So they went, and made the sepulcher sure, sealing the stone, and setting a watch."

It's silent. Little is heard except for the sound of weeping. It's a quiet, somber group that has gathered...these few men and women who had walked with Jesus. Occasionally you might hear one of them recounting an event during the past few years spent with Him. Perhaps they spoke quietly of the day Jesus fed the thousands with two fish and five loaves. Each conversation might well begin with, *"Remember when Jesus..."* You can hear the sob in their breath as they speak. The eyes that brightly saw the miracles of Jesus were now dim with tears. *The voice they loved so dearly was now silent in the tomb.*

Perhaps they heard echoes of voices from the crowd of yesterday...voices that mocked Him saying, *"He saved others; let Him save Himself...if He be Christ, the chosen of God." "If..."* They heard Him declare that He was the Son of God, that He was building a Kingdom. ***But now, all those dreams were silent, as silent as the voice that spoke them.*** Did they remember or even understand what their Lord said about the third day? I don't know if they comprehended the words of hope and promise on this second, silent day. What would they do? Maybe go back to fishing, or whatever it was they did before they met Jesus. The religious leaders believed something would happen tomorrow, what could it be? Could Jesus, the One who raised dead folks, raise Himself? It's very silent on this day after Jesus died, as thoughts and sorrow filled their hearts and minds.

How do we handle the silence? Can we hold on to the promises even when they are dead and silent? Can we believe that He is resurrection life? It may seem like hope is gone and the promise has been sealed up, lying dead in a tomb with enemy

124

soldiers guarding it to make sure is stays dead! What do we do when we pray, and pray, yet He remains silent? My friend, we keep believing! We keep trusting Him in the silence. *Today is just a testing day, but tomorrow...is the day of miracles!*

April 13

Both Hands Tied

Revelation 1:18 "I am he that liveth, and was dead; and, behold, I am alive for evermore, Amen; and have the keys of Hell and of Death."
Matthew 27:2 "...They bound Him..."

I have those days when it seems my hands are tied and I can do little about certain situations. How many of us would do more *if* our hands were not tied! We'd give more of our time. We'd pay our tithes and give bigger offerings. We'd do more for others. We'd bless the Church. We'd give to missions. We'd pray more. We'd be more faithful. We'd worship more passionately. But, it seems that *something* always ties our hands, keeping us from doing what we ought to do or want to do.

Jesus defeated the devil with both hands tied! They tied his hands to the whipping post as they laid open His back. They tied His hands to the cross as they drove the spikes into His flesh. He was tougher than the nails that pinned His body to the cross. Just when Satan thought he had finally won, Jesus stepped into hell and stripped him of his victory, his power and his power over death, hell and the grave! He ripped from Satan's grip the control over man's souls. When He burst forth from the tomb He came forth with great might, all power and supernatural authority. He went in beaten up and tied down, *but came out as King of Kings and Lord of Lords!*

The next time you feel beaten down and tied up, *remember that Jesus beat the devil with both hands tied*! He overcame all so that we, too, can overcome! Our Big Brother took on Satan with both hands tied behind His back, and defeated him once and for all...*and He did it for us*! You are not powerless, nor defenseless! We have power over the "something" and "someone" who loves to keep us tied up, bound up, and held up. We have been given great authority in the Spirit, for it's not by might, nor by power, but by His Spirit that we are victorious!

April 14

The Lion Revealed

Revelation 5:5, 6 "And one of the elders saith unto me, Weep not: behold, the Lion of the tribe of Judah, the Root of David, hath prevailed to open the book, and to loose the seven seals thereof. And I beheld, and, lo, in the midst of the throne and of the four beasts, and in the midst of the elders, stood a Lamb as it had been slain, having seven horns and seven eyes, which are the seven Spirits of God sent forth into all the earth."

So many precious people are going through fiery trials that test their faith in Him. We wonder, *"Did we come this far just to face a stone wall that seems unmovable?"* Feelings of despair seem to grip our hearts as defeat seems closer than victory. But, hold on, dear one, because God is about to unveil His strength and power *in us* through these tests and trials!

There He hung, this Lamb of God who was slain from the foundation of the world. He had just been betrayed by a close friend, abandoned by one who had just promised that he would never betray Him, and suffered unspeakable agony in a garden of prayer. And now... He hung on a cross with His flesh torn to ribbons from a scourging that was so harsh that He could no longer stand under His own power. He, like a lamb offered up for slaughter, offered no resistance as they tore into His flesh with their hatred and malice. But...there's more! *His last cry of "It is Finished" was not the sound of a lamb, but was uttered with the roar of a Lion*! His last breath was taken in victory, not defeat, *as the stricken Lamb of God revealed the Lion of Judah!* In His final moment we see not just a slain Lamb, but a strong Lion! His momentary defeat was the lead-in for His ultimate victory! *The day they killed the Lamb they unveiled the Lion!* He did not go out defeated, but victoriously!

Beloved, it may seem like it's over and finished, but the Lion has the final Word! What looks like the end is only the beginning! *The Lamb may be silent, but the roar of the Lion shouts victory!* The Lamb shed His blood for remission of our sins, but the Lion's roar declares our triumph! Our tests and trials will reveal the Lion in us!

Sometimes we feel like we are lambs on display as the wolves test our faith, but the Lion inside us will roar, bringing our enemies to their knees! *Feeble attempts to kill our destiny and dreams will serve only to unveil the awesome power of the Lion inside of us!*

April 15

He Nailed It!

Matthew 28:6 "He is not here: for He is risen, as He said..."

    Jesus nailed it! Through His suffering and death, He won victory. He won the victory over every sin, iniquity, sorrow, grief and sickness. When they nailed Him to the cross, they also nailed our sins, our sorrows, and our sickness. Each time the hammer drove the nails deeper into the flesh of Jesus, *He was winning one more battle... one more victory...*just for us so that we, too, might have victory over these things. But...that's not the end of the story...

    Some thought death conquered Him, however, on the third morning Christ arose from the cold clutch of death with great power and victory. Let's take Him off the cross and out of the tomb! He's not there...but sits at the right hand of the Father to make intercession for us! What a reason to celebrate! As we focus on the message of Easter and look at the price Christ paid for us, let's also remember *that He broke every stronghold, including death, and reigns forever!* He's not dead, but He nailed death, sickness, sin, and defeat to the cross!

April 16

Full Access

Matthew 27:51 "Then, behold, the veil of the temple was rent in two from top to bottom..."

Have you ever been denied access to some place that you really wanted to be? Perhaps you struggle with feelings that you don't belong or maybe you're just not good enough to be in elite company. Do you feel that there is always something blocking you or preventing you from obtaining the position or place that you desire to be?

Before Christ came ordinary people were not allowed access into the Holy of Holies. There was something that blocked ordinary people from entering in this sacred place. A thick, four inch veil separated this most holy place from mankind, and only the High Priest was allowed inside. A rope was tied around him in the event that he would have iniquity or unrighteousness in him and would die upon entering this holy place. *This was the place where the mercy seat and God's Holy Presence abided.*

When Christ shed His blood and died, His blood was placed upon the mercy seat for us. *The veil that was in the temple was rent from top to bottom, thereby forevermore allowing all who receive Christ entrance into the very presence of the Living God!* He took our filthy garments and gave us robes of righteousness. He removed the shame and gave us acceptance. We no longer need a High Priest to go before God on our behalf - Jesus Himself is our High Priest, interceding to the Father for you and I. We, who were called sinners are now called Priests and Priestesses! He is not just our God - He is our Father! We have full access to Him anytime we need Him. The next time Satan tells you that you're not good enough, not righteous enough or that you just don't belong, *tell him that you belong to the family of God, and you have been accepted by Christ.* You have full access into the promises, the power and the presence of the Most High!

April 17

The Cross - Our Standard

John 19:17 "And He bearing His cross went forth to a place called the place of a skull, which is called in the Hebrew Golgotha."
I Corinthians 1:18 "For the preaching of the cross is to them that perish foolishness; but unto us which are saved it is the power of God."

"The cross alone is our theology." Martin Luther

On a hill called Golgotha God raised His standard--the cross--to declare to Satan that the war for the souls of mankind was won! The cross was lifted high, bearing the Slain Lamb of God who, with a mighty roar, declared, *"It is finished"*! The battle between God and Satan had been waging since Lucifer was cast out of heaven, but on that day Jesus raised the standard, and with one final breath, won the war.

He broke the back of poverty! He broke the strongholds of iniquity and sin! He broke the chains of oppression and disease! He broke the spirit of heaviness and grief, removing the sting from death! Once and for all time, He defeated Satan and put him under His feet!

Yes, the Cross - the *standard of God's power to transform our lives.* The Cross - *the emblem of all that we count dear and precious.* The Cross - *the bridge between God and us!* The Cross will I treasure and cherish until the day I exchange it for my crown!

April 18

The Bondage Breaker

John 8:36 "If the Son therefore shall make you free, ye shall be free indeed."

Are you one of the many who are carrying burdens that are too heavy to bear? Are there chains that hold you back from walking in the fullness of Liberty and Freedom? Has sorrow and grief beset you, robbing you of the joy that strengthens and sustains you? Is there a stronghold that has snatched victory from your hands, leaving you empty, helpless and, defeated? *If so, I have a Word from the Lord for you today!*

The Bondage Breaker has come to set you free! There is nothing to heavy, too hard, too impossible, or too besetting that He can't take care of for you. Are you struggling with an illness that you can't shake? He is the Healer of all your diseases! Have sorrow and depression taken hold of your spirit? He is the healer of broken hearts and the giver of joy! Is there a besetting sin, an unresolved issue, or a stronghold that has a hold on you? He came to free you, and those whom He frees are forever freed! Are you struggling with finances and can't see a way out? He is your Provider, so why should you worry or fret! Jesus came to destroy the works of Satan! He came to liberate those who are held prisoner by sin, sickness and hopelessness. There is no authority or power that is greater than His!

Why be bound when you can be free! *He is your Bondage Breaker*! He has come to set you free!

April 19

A Fallen Foe

Isaiah 54:17 "No weapon that is formed against thee shall prosper; and every tongue that shall rise against thee in judgment thou shalt condemn. This is the heritage of the servants of the LORD, and their righteousness is of me, saith the LORD."

Defeat is inevitable for your enemy. *Your foe has fallen and has been placed under your feet by the Blood of Jesus Christ.* The tongue that has risen against you in judgment is condemned by the Word of the Lord. God will avenge His children and send restoration and healing to those who are wounded in battle. Lift up your heads, for our redemption is near!

You may have taken some hits...but you are not defeated! Your knees may have buckled under the onslaughts, but you are not down! You have His favor...His crowns you with His loving-kindness! You are a Child of Promise...and Heir and Joint-Heir *with Christ Jesus!* Lift Up Your Head! He causes you to triumph in ALL things! *It might not look so good right now, but hold on because God has the final Word...and it is a Word of Victory!* Your armor might have a few dents and dings, but it is strong and able to prevail against every attack. Hold on to the Word....it will not fail you. Your enemy is a fallen foe, so rejoice and lift up your head!

April 20

The Power Belongs to God

Psalm 62:11 "God has spoken once, twice I have heard this: That power belongs to God."

Last Tuesday evening I sat in my back yard contemplating the changes that we as a Nation are facing. As I sat there feeling great uncertainty about our future, I turned my eyes upward...and gazed upon a sliver of the moon that was shining and glowing in the still, dark night. I realized this same moon that was lending her light to me was the same moon that shinned upon Adam and Eve, Abraham, Daniel, and Jesus! It was the same moon that bathed our forefathers in her light as they sought Divine Direction from God for the birth of our Nation. She saw change after change through generation after generation. *She was there at the conception of this world and she will continue to shine until her creator says..."No More!"* **She does what she was created to do...shine and glorify Almighty God.** As I gazed at the moon, I was reminded that God was there in the beginning, He will be there when time ceases to exist, and *He is still in control of this world.*

Power belongs to our God. He controls this universe, commands the moon to shine, and tells the stars to dance. He is a Refuge and Defense for His people. He reminds us that, regardless of who sits upon earthly thrones, the power still belongs to Him. That will never change.

If we are facing uncertain tomorrows, let us go with full assurance of the knowledge that ultimate power and authority is His. If you need reminding of God, look at the moon and there you will see God's faithfulness and His power shining in the darkness to dispel fears that sometimes invade our hearts and minds. He still has power over the moon...and He retains power over the kingdoms of this world.

April 21

God Has The Final Say

II Timothy 2:13 "If we believe not, yet He abides faithful; He cannot deny Himself."

God is faithful to us!

Many of us have had great testings of our faith recently, but God has remained faithful to each of us, reminding us that *He is in control* and our lives are in *His more than capable hands*! **He has the final say!**

Be reminded today that the enemy is a liar and a deceiver, so don't believe *anything* he says to you. He is quite good at taking circumstantial evidence to make his case, but there is no truth nor real evidence to support his lies. He is a master of deception and loves to take a small pebble and make a mountain out of it, *but God's Word* will remove the mountains. He will come at you like a roaring lion, *but God's Word* will put him on the run! He'll try to get you to believe that it's just not going to work out...*but God's Word says* He orders your steps and has ordained victory for you! He will tell you that you are sick unto death, *but God's Word decrees* that we are healed by the stripes of Jesus! He will whisper his lies in your ears telling you that everything is out of control, *but God's Word says* that He (God) reigns forever and ever! He will try to convince you that you are going under, *but God's word says* we are going over! He will try to make you believe that you will never be blessed or prosper, *but God's word says* we are blessed going in and blessed going out!

He is in control. Nothing alarms Him, or takes Him by surprise. Nothing is too big for Him to handle, or so small it escapes His attention. When the winds of adversity begin to blow, He remains seated. When raging waves billow over us, He governs their temper...I need not be moved ... Because God has the final say!

April 22

He Knows All About You

Hebrews 4:15 "For we do not have a high priest who is unable to sympathize with our weaknesses, but we have one who has been tempted in every way, just as we are - yet was without sin."

Jesus knows! He knows everything you are going through, every hurt, every pain, every disappointment, and even your hopes, dreams and joys.

Why would the Son of God choose to suffer so much shame, pain and sin known to the human race? He knew unspeakable loneliness, felt the crushing guilt from sin and endured the shame of the cross. Why did He feel the weight of every sickness and disease upon His back? He knew that these are all things that we would feel. He did it for us, so that He could understand what we feel. Jesus knows...

I find it difficult to talk to someone who has no clue about what I am feeling or going through, or to discuss my dreams and visions with someone who simply doesn't care. But when someone has walked in the shoes that I am walking in, I can express my thoughts and feelings clearly and openly, knowing that they can understand. Sometimes it's hard to find someone who really knows and understands us. But, we have a Savior who felt everything that we feel...and He is available to us anytime we need Him. We can tell Him everything, holding nothing back, and *He understands because He felt it too*. When we feel misunderstood by others, Jesus understands. When we feel shut out and have no one to talk to, we can talk to Jesus. When we are inconsolable with grief, Jesus shares our pain. When others have turned on us and forsaken us, Jesus will stand with us because He, too, knew what it was like to be forsaken. When all hell has come against us, we can go to Jesus, because He faced the full force of hell's fury and defeated it. When we have a dream we want to share, we can tell it to Jesus, because He dreams with us. Jesus knows...

April 23

Lord, I Need You

Matthew 8:24-26 "And, behold, there arose a great tempest in the sea, insomuch that the ship was covered with the waves: but he was asleep. And his disciples came to him, and awoke him, saying, Lord, save us: we perish. And he saith unto them, Why are ye fearful, O ye of little faith? Then he arose, and rebuked the winds and the sea; and there was a great calm."

"Mom, I need you!" My grandson is a busy little boy and very independent, often to the dismay of his mother. He tries to do everything himself, but sometimes...he will realize he cannot do this by himself and needs help. When she hears that little cry, *"Mom, I need you,"* immediately she runs to him, knowing her child needs her help.

"Lord, save us! We perish," cried out the disciples. The storms were blowing, *but Jesus was asleep in the boat.* The disciples did all they could to keep the boat steady, but even the most skilled boatmen could not conquer the raging waters that threatened to sink them. Panic set in and they just knew that all was lost - they would perish in the storm. They were helpless against the storm...*and Jesus was asleep*!

Do you ever feel that He is asleep and unaware of the storm that is blowing against you? All of your knowledge and skill cannot abate the storm, for this storm is greater than you. You pray every prayer you can think of, you call every prayer warrior you can reach... but the storm has not ceased. There is one prayer you can pray that will get His Divine attention..."*Lord, this child needs you. Jesus, I need you now!"* This simple, but profound prayer will reach the heart of the Master as few other prayers can do. When we come to the point where we realize we cannot take one more step without His assistance, it is then we become fully dependent upon Him. *Our desperation and need can be heard in our cries, and quickly He will come to our rescue, calm the storm, and quiet our fears.*

April 24

Run After God

Psalm 42:1 "As the hart panteth after the water brooks, so panteth my soul after thee, O God."

The longer I am in this world, the greater my hunger for Him grows. *I am intensely, keenly aware that I am made for another world.* There is another kingdom that I belong to that outshines any mortal kingdom on earth. I long for Him, and passionately pursue His presence.

I look around and see many who are so unsatisfied... hungry for something they can't explain. I see Christians who are unhappy and unfulfilled...and I want to say to them, *"Run after God."* If we would only pursue Him the way we pursue our goals, our jobs, or that special someone, we would find what we are seeking. As we get closer to the return of our King, all the offers and enticements of this world are but mere shadows and poor substitutes of what He offers. They cannot satisfy the deep longings and intense desires that burn in our hearts for Him. His voice beckons us to Him, and resonates deep in our souls, bidding us to come closer to Him. He whispers, *"Come closer, pursue Me, seek Me...and you will find Me."*

Today, take a drink from the Artesian Wells that flow from His Presence. He will quench our thirst and satisfy our hunger for Him as we pursue His Presence and run to Him.

April 25

I Am With You

Matthew 28:20 "...I am with you always, even unto the end of the world."
Job 28:3 "He setteth an end to darkness..."

There are times we will go through where we feel completely alone and as though there is no one who can truly understand this place we find ourselves in. We can be completely surrounded by family or be in a crowd of friends...*and still feel that we are all alone*. Even our Savior seems out of reach as our prayers appear to fall upon deaf ears. The trial we are going through seems to have no end in sight! But, as real as this feels...there is a truth that supersedes this moment of empty solitude...*He is with you and will walk you through this dark place*.

Job realized that *every trial has a beginning and an end*. He was as low as anyone could be as clouds of darkness obscured the light of day, yet *He trusted in the One he could not see*. He put his trust in Jehovah, even when everything he had was taken from him. He had walked as a prince among men. His wisdom was sought after by everyone. Young men listened when he talked. He had riches, wealth, and children who walked in the ways of the Lord. Suddenly, everything that mattered to him was taken away...except his faith in His God. Although Job didn't understand what was going on or why he had to go through such a fiery trial, he knew that as sure as the trial had a beginning, it also had an end!

Your trial will not last! Your storm will cease and the waters that threaten to overtake you *will* subside. Let God impart His peace that passes all of your understanding...*and know this*...there is an end to your dark days and the Savior will walk through every step of this trial with you. *He is with you, even unto the end of this trial*!

April 26

Some Greater Thing

1 Peter 4:12, 13 "Friends, when life gets really difficult, don't jump to the conclusion that God isn't on the job. Instead, be glad that you are in the very thick of what Christ experienced. This is a spiritual refining process, with glory just around the corner."

The trials you are going through are just stepping stones into some greater thing - something far more precious than silver or gold!

There will be tests that we must take so we can advance to the next level. God will never put us in positions that we are unprepared for, but faithfully takes us through the stepping stones of fiery trials to prepare and equip us *for some greater thing.* Your faith will be put to the test. Your stand for Christ will be tested. You will go through tests of trustworthiness, loyalty, commitment, submission, obedience, and endurance. Your love walk will be tested. *Each test is but a stepping stone into something far greater*! Glory awaits you just around the corner! You can be sure that ***God is very near*** and is walking you through your trials one step at a time. He provides grace for the moment and strength to make it through, so don't become faint in your faith, but rejoice knowing that greater things await you.

You can make it! You will get through each test by standing on the Word, holding up your shield of faith, and by your testimony! We are made overcomers by the Blood of the Lamb and the word of our testimony. (Revelations 12:11) Embrace these tests knowing they are leading you into something greater, something far more glorious than the place you are in now!

April 27

God Remembered

Genesis 8:1 "And God remembered Noah..."
Genesis 19:29 "...And...God remembered Abraham..."
Genesis 30:22 "...And God remembered Rachel..."

None of us like to be overlooked or forgotten, but sometimes it happens. To be acknowledged and remembered is a need we all have, and brings us much satisfaction and joy.

I think about Noah floating above the earth for many days and nights, wondering if his feet would ever touch the ground again. It was a lonely, solitary time in his life, *but God remembered Noah!* Then, there was Abraham, God's friend. Perhaps he also felt forgotten about, especially when years went by without seeing the promise. *But God remembered Abraham*! Then, there was Rachel! How her heart ached to have children, yet she was barren and could not produce. There is probably no greater ache or pain to a woman than to be childless. *But God remembered Rachel*!

Do you feel forgotten about or perhaps unnoticed by others? Do your acts of love and kindness to others seem unreciprocated and unappreciated? Does your labor of love go unrewarded? *Are you in the boat with Noah, wondering if the sun will shine again?* Or, maybe you identify with Abraham as you wait upon God to fulfill His promises. Perhaps, like Rachel, you feel barren and ache to hold new life in your arms. My dear friend, just as God remembered them, *He also remembers you.* He has not forgotten about you, nor has He abandoned you. He is with you and will reward your labor of love. He remembers His Word to you and will bring it to fruition. Don't be downhearted, but know that God has the final say...and He remembers you.

April 28

Does God Get Mad?

I John 3:1 "Behold, what manner of love the Father has bestowed upon us..."

Last night my youngest granddaughter, Ashtin, asked this question, *"Did you ever get mad at God?"* She then went on to say that she did once when He didn't heal her as quickly as she wanted Him to when she had hurt herself (she's nine years old). She then made this statement that really got my attention, *"He never gets mad at us, and always forgives us."*

I thought of the many times I have heard people rant at God, angry with Him because of things that had happened to them, or upset because, like my granddaughter, He didn't answer their prayers quickly enough or in the way they wanted Him to. It hit me pretty hard that *this Wonderful, Amazing and Loving Father who gave us His very best takes a lot of abuse from us humans.* Sometimes we remind me of really young children - we talk too soon, move too fast, and don't listen. We throw tantrum fits when we don't get our way, always wanting candy instead of a good healthy meal. (Doesn't this sound like a lot of us!) Yet, as Ashtin pointed out, He never gets mad at us, but is very patient, kind and loving with us. Oh yes, He does chasten us when we need it, but always with love and with our best interest in mind. He loves us that much! But, *He isn't to blame* when things don't go our way. He is there - loving on us, forgiving us, and restoring us. He never holds grudges, gets grumpy or loses His cool! Wow! What an amazing God!

If you think God might be mad at you for something you did, let me assure you today, He is not mad at you! You are loved unconditionally!

April 29

Quick to Help

Ps 46:1 "God is our refuge and strength, a very present help in trouble."

Thunderstorms swept across our part of the country yesterday, announcing themselves with loud thunder and pouring rain. As my daughter and I worked in the office, she commented on the storms, mentioning that her son (who was 4) was afraid of thunder. It was his day to ride to daycare with another parent immediately after his morning preschool class. For a few minutes it looked as though the storms were going to clear up and she sighed with relief. It was almost time for him to get out of school when the thunderstorms rolled back in with a vengeance. She scooped up her purse, headed out the door while calling to me that she was going to get Blaise'. *She couldn't stand the thought that her little boy might be afraid of the storms and there would be no one who understood his fears*, so she quickly ran to get her son.

Beloved, we have a caring Father who is even more concerned about us. *He will quickly come to our rescue when storms* roll in that overwhelming us with their darkness and noise. He is quick to run to us when we stand small against the forces of storms that threaten our security. He is there when the billowing waves of adversity come against us. Our Father is there to speak peace to us when the sounds of the thunder shake us to the core. Not only does He quickly run to our sides, but He is also our place of refuge, and gently pulls us into safety, security and peace. His very presence strengthens us, for we know we are in safe hands. Storms will blow in and out of our lives, but we have an anchor, a refuge and a very present help in our times of trouble. Lean on Him today and trust Him through the storms.

April 30

They Have No Wine

John 2:3 "And when they wanted wine, the mother of Jesus saith unto him, They have no wine."

We'll never truly impact the world until the emptiness in our lives and in our Churches is filled. How can we offer them anything when we, ourselves, are empty, void, and filled with hopelessness. We put on our Sunday faces while around others, but the mask falls away when we are alone and no one can see how empty we are. We look the part of a Believer, but inside we are void and empty. This cry can be heard in many of our Churches and Homes..."*They have no wine!*"

People are crying out for fulfillment and for Someone to fill the emptiness. Many Churches that were once ablaze with fresh fire from Heaven and filled with passion and love are but a shadow of what they used to be. They go through the same motions, say the same prayers, and leave the same way they came in. Passionless sermons have replaced passionate preaching. Love once flowed freely for God and men, only to be replaced with a form of godliness and cold hearts. *They have no wine!*

The Spirit of the Lord spoke to my heart this morning and said He was going to fill His vessels with New Wine! Joy will return and love will flow freely between believers. Don't be surprised when you hear Him calling your name - just do what He says do! He is preparing and positioning those who hunger and thirst for Him to receive the outpouring of His Spirit as spoken of in Joel. He spoke this... *"I am breaking through denominational walls, geographical walls, and religious walls by my Spirit!"* No more will this cry be heard, *"They have no wine"*, for the Lord will fill His vessels.

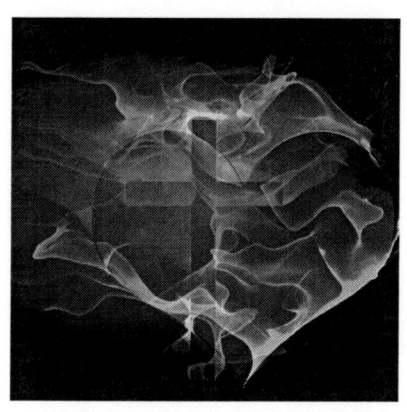

May

How precious is a Virtuous Woman...
Her price is greater than Rubies
(Proverbs 31)

May 1

Women of Virtue

Proverbs 31:10 "Who can find a virtuous woman? For her price is far above rubies."

Women...we are one of those mysteries that sometimes only God can understand ... and another woman! We laugh when we want to cry, and cry when we should laugh. *We wait by the phone for a call to let us know they arrived safely.* We volunteer for good causes, and fight for what we believe in. We are the pink ladies in hospitals, and delivery persons to bring food to shut-ins. We are the Mother Teresa's and Princess Diana's reaching out to those who are unwanted and unloved. We are fragilely made, yet can bear burdens that would sink a 6 foot, 4 inch man. *We are feminine and dainty, and brave and strong.* We cry with our friends and rejoice when something wonderful happens to them. We will hang in there when everyone else has quit. The heart of a woman is unmeasured in value, yet given freely to those needing love.

Proverbs described a virtuous woman as having more value than rubies - a precious and rare stone. A man finds a good thing when he finds a Godly woman, and is blessed to have her heart. She is the fragrance that will beautify his home, and the essence of all he can desire. You will find a woman behind every great man, whether it be his mother, wife, sister, or friend. *Today, we celebrate all women everywhere who love, laugh, weep and dance, who carry burdens too big, and receive too little in return!* We celebrate our Mothers, Grandmothers, Wives, Sisters, Daughters, and Friends.

May 2

Carriers of Rain

John 7:37, 38 "...If any man thirst, let him come unto me, and drink. He that believeth on me, as the scripture hath said, out of his belly shall flow rivers of living water."
1 Kings 18:41, 42 "And Elijah said unto Ahab, get thee up, and drink, for there is a sound of abundance of rain. And Elijah went up to the top of Carmel: and he cast himself down upon the earth, and put his face between his knees."

Did you know that you are *a carrier of the rain* and you have what someone is thirsting for? Jesus said that out of your bellies shall flow rivers of living waters - waters that minister healing, hope, and salvation to those who are thirsty.

There was a great drought in the land and it had not rained for three and a half years! Elijah had spoken the Word that draught would come...and come it did! Can you imagine the devastation, despair and desperation of the people? What they wouldn't give for a drop of water to quench their hot thirst. Thank God for a man who knew what to do! *Elijah went to the top of the mountain, put his face between his knees and prayed!* This position is called the birthing position. **He had to birth the rain!** Giving birth is not an easy process, but *what is inside has to be pushed out!* Sometimes it is very laborious and requires every effort of strength you can muster. But what is on the inside has to come out!

Child of God, we have within us everything we, and others need. If our walk with God has become dry and formal, or if our church is not flowing and moving as it should, **then it's time for us to get in the birthing position and call for the rain** - the rivers of living water that lie within us to come forth, bringing life, healing and refreshing! Let it be your prayers birth the latter day rains!

May 3

Diamonds in the Rough

Isaiah 45:3 "...I will give thee the treasures of darkness, and hidden riches of secret places, that thou mayest know that I, the Lord, which call thee by thy name, am the God of Israel."

Many of us have beautiful and secret treasures inside of us, just waiting to be exposed and discovered! God has placed in us amazing talents and glorious gifts that He wants to showcase!

No one looking at this young shepherd boy would have expected him to be the next king! *Yet, within the heart of this young shepherd beat the heart of a giant slayer and a mighty warrior.* Hidden in the depths of his soul was one of God's greatest worshippers! David would one day trade his smelly shepherd's cloak for the royal garments of a king!

Perhaps you think that no one recognizes the unique abilities and God-given gifts that are hidden deep within you! Maybe you have been overlooked as others were presented for promotions and titles. But, the time will come when *the need will call out for the gift that is within you!* If you are in a holding place right now, just know that God may have you on the back side of the dessert to learn faithfulness! He is teaching you how to hear His voice! He has you in a place of training, sending lions and bears to test your strength so that one day you can face your giant and defeat him! The world may see us as chunks of coal, but beloved, God sees us for the diamonds we are! When the giants come to fight, it will be the shepherd boys who have been in training that will take out the giants! It will be the diamonds in the rough who will show the majestic glory of God! He is preparing us - *so get ready to be showcased!*

May 4

God Uses Clay Pots

2 Corinthians 4:7 "But we have this treasure in earthen vessels, that the excellency of the power may be of God, and not of us."

You have been selected and chosen by God and for God as a vessel He can use! See, God uses clay pots! Pots that are earthen vessels and are yielded, pliable and trainable!

Clay pots break easily, but God says in Psalm 51:17 *that His sacrifices are a broken spirit and contrite heart!* He doesn't despise us because of our brokenness, but instead uses our broken places to glorify Him! Clay pots are not indestructible and sometimes crack! God turns away from the proud and arrogant, but loves the humble and meek! We are full of imperfections and filled with flaws, yet He chooses to use us in spite of these things! Why? *So that the excellency of His power is of Him...and not of us!* He uses ordinary people like us to show His glory to and through! What a God that He is so mindful of us and can use our imperfections, mistakes, flaws and weaknesses! What a God that He chooses to use clay pots instead of perfect marble vessels! He loves to use clay pots - pots that have been molded on a potter's wheel and fashioned by the Master's own hands! He has poured great treasure into us so that God can be God! As a precious Minster said to me, *"If His glory is what is leaking out, then I will rejoice in the broken places."*

May 5

Daughter of Abraham

Luke 13:16 "And ought not this woman, being a daughter of Abraham, whom Satan hath bound, lo, these eighteen years, be loosed from this bond on the Sabbath day?"

You are a Child of Promise!

To the Pharisees this little woman was a nobody...a nothing and certainly not worthy of the attention she was receiving, nor of the healing that took place. Why her? Why bother? *However, Jesus saw her for whom she was...a Daughter of Abraham.* He stopped the Pharisees criticism by calling her a Daughter of Abraham! Abraham...the father of Israel, the one who answered God's call, the one to whom the promise was given - a promise to make of Abraham a great nation, a nation through which all the nations of the world would be blessed. This woman is heir to all the blessings of God. *And as a daughter of Abraham, she is called to be a blessing to the whole world.* She is not just a sad victim - only a nameless woman with a bent back - *she is a daughter of Abraham, an inheritor of the promises, a part of God's great salvation of the world.* She was entitled to the benefits and the blessings of Abraham. Perhaps she had long ago forgotten who she was and just accepted her condition and circumstances that life had thrown at her. *But then Jesus came and proclaimed her as a Daughter of Abraham...a Child of Promise!* He reminded her that God had much better things for her. He loosed her from her affliction and set her free!

You, as an Heir and Joint-Heir with Christ Jesus, are entitled to the great benefits of Calvary! Christ redeemed us and loosed the bondage of affliction, addiction, poverty and disease from us. You may have been "bent over" by cares to heavy to bear, but you are still somebody! Never forget that you are a Child of Promise, a Seed of Abraham, and an Heir of God, and you are entitled to benefits that He paid for at Calvary. It doesn't matter how the world sees you or what they think. *You may have been bent over and thought of as*

151

nothing, but Christ Jesus came to lift you up and declare to all that you are His and you are Precious! Let go of all the stuff that keeps you bent down, discouraged and defeated, and rise up in victory, power, and His righteousness! Walk as an Heir and Joint-Heir of Christ...as the Seed of Abraham...as a Child of God!

May 6

From Barrenness to Joy

1 Samuel 1:17 "Then Eli answered and said, Go in peace: and the God of Israel grant thee thy petition that thou hast asked of him."
Isaiah 54:1 "Sing O barren, thou that didst not bear; break forth into singing..."

Shamed. Rejected. Grieved. Forgotten. Taunted. Forsaken. Desolate. Robbed. She felt all of these things, even though she was deeply loved by her husband. *She could not have children.* Her heart felt ripped from her when she looked upon the children of others. She grieved deeply, not understanding any of this...*until she went to the House of God and found the answer she needed.* There...things changed...she changed...and her life was never the same.

Some of us can identify with Hannah, for we, too, don't understand why we are not being blessed as others are. *We feel the intense pain that being barren brings and know all too well the shame of rejection and the loss of our dreams.* Our longings are so deep that words fail us and no one seems to understand the depths of our desires. We are faithful, we are loved, *yet something is greatly lacking in us...we must bring forth children or we will die.* We feel Hannah's pain of being barren. The dreams we hold deep inside have produced lonely, aching hearts that long to have fulfillment and *to be given a future.* There is probably no greater pain than that of being barren and infertile. The pain is indescribable and can only be understood by someone who has felt that sorrow. Added to the pain and grief are the pointing fingers who shame and criticize us for being barren. *Yet there is hope...*I believe we will find our answers when we go to the House of the Lord and seek Him, as Hannah did, with all of our hearts.

The same God who closed Hannah's womb opened it and she produced a child that few others can begin to compare with. It is said of Samuel that not a word of his fell to the ground. There was a seed of greatness that was planted in Hannah's heart and spirit before it ever reached her womb. *Sometimes it is out of our nothings that we produce some of the greatest accomplishments this world will ever see.* Before the seed of destiny can fill the barren womb, it must first be seeded into your heart and spirit. It must be so deeply imbedded that no foe, no antagonist, no hater of your dream can discourage you from hoping and believing that God will open up your womb and you will bring forth life...a future...and a destiny. Time cannot erase the hope and desire when God seeds your destiny into your spirit. In due season, you will reap your harvest. In due season God will open your barren womb and fill it with the desire of your heart. In due season God will give you what you desire and the seed of destiny will produce something great and tangible. Be like Hannah...dare to plead with God for your dream, or, like Abraham, lose your doubt when you gaze upon the stars that reflect the greatness of your God.

May 7

A Kept Promise

1 Samuel 1:11, 24 "And she vowed a vow, and said, O LORD of hosts, if thou wilt indeed look on the affliction of thine handmaid, and remember me, and not forget thine handmaid, but wilt give unto thine handmaid a man child, then I will give him unto the LORD all the days of his life, and there shall no rasor come upon his head....And when she had weaned him, she took him up with her, with three bullocks, and one ephah of flour, and a bottle of wine, and brought him unto the house of the LORD in Shiloh: and the child was young."

Keeping my word is important to me. My father taught us that a man's word is his bond and every effort should be made to keep our word.

I admire this woman, Hannah, for she was very real with the Lord. Hannah took nothing for granted, nor did she make a vow lightly in the heat of the moment. Hannah knew what it was like to agonize in her soul and to deeply desire something so strongly that she would do anything to get it. A Baby! Hannah wanted a baby and knew that it would take a miracle from God for her to have one. She made this vow to God..."*Give me a son and I will give him back to you!*" Hannah kept her vow to God and brought her little baby boy - the one she covenanted with God for, the one she longed for with all her heart - and gave him to the man of God to raise in the House of God. She willingly surrendered the one that brought her honor and defined her as somebody...the one that took her to a place that, without him, she could only dream about. Hannah could have revoked her vow. She could have justified keeping this little baby by saying, "*Lord, I know you don't really mean for me to give up something that You gave me.*" Or, "*Lord, that promise was made when I was under emotional duress. I didn't know what I was saying. You won't hold me to that, will You?*" Hannah entrusted her most precious and valuable treasure back to God. **She realized that everything belonged to God and she was just the keeper of those things He sent to her.**

Sometimes we hold back those things that are most dear and precious to us, afraid to relinquish them into the hands of God.

How important is it that we keep our vows? *Samuel would have never become the great Man of God that He was had he remained in Hannah's hands!* The vow his mother made and kept was the key to his future as a Prophet that anointed Kings. Those lips that made a vow to God also fulfilled that vow and whispered, *"Here he is, Lord. He is yours!"* Those hands that held her newborn son tightly to her also lifted him up and released him to the Lord. Is it important that we keep our vows? Oh, yes! **God honors those who keep covenant with Him!**

May 8

The Plea for the Impossible

Matthew 15:28 "Then Jesus answered and said unto her, O Woman, great is thy faith, be it unto thee even as thou wilt…"

We give up too easily. We forget that we are in a battle. We are sometimes too complacent, adopting the motto, *"Whatever will be, will be."* We accept our circumstances as something we cannot control or change. But that is wrong thinking and victim mentality! Beloved, as heirs and joint-heirs with Christ, there is so much more that God has for us than for us to just settle with what we now have. We must learn how start exercising this great gift of faith. Dare to believe God for the impossible!

Faith will petition God for the impossible! In Matthew 15, we read about the woman of Canaan whose daughter was vexed with a devil. She had heard about Jesus, the miracle worker and how He could rebuke devils and they would obey. She cried out to Him for mercy, but He answered her not. Did she give up and go home crying? NO!!! Did she get mad at Jesus because He didn't respond to her first plea? NO!!! *She bowed down and* WORSHIPED *Him, anyway*! She was persistent in her faith and *believed in the provision of faith!* She refused to waiver and was able to leave with her plea for the impossible granted!

How many of us can say that Jesus marvels at our faith? How many times have we heard Him say to us, *"Be it unto you as you will?"* Too many times we settle for wimpy faith that rarely gets exercised that soothes our carnal minds by believing for things that are already possible. I want to challenge us today to have faith for the impossible things! Dare to believe that God will give you what you ask Him for. Search the scriptures for His promise and Word to stand on when you take your request to Him...*and let your faith plea for the impossible! Great things happen to those who have great faith!*

May 9

Wings to Soar

2 Corinthians 3:17 "Now the Lord is the Spirit; and where the Spirit of the Lord is, there is liberty."

Several years ago I assisted my daughter in her work in adoptions by taking some of the pregnant girls to their doctors appointments. These young women were making plans for their unborn babies to have better opportunities in life than what they could give them. They would carefully choose the parents for their babies, making sure these adoptive parents would be able to provide for their babies what they were unable to. I remember one of the girls writing a letter to her unborn child to tell in her own words why she had made this choice to place him for adoption. She wrote, *"These parents I have chosen for you will give you roots. I will give you wings."* She could not provide the roots for her child, but by releasing him into a future that was better than she could give him, she was giving him wings to soar...wings to reach potentials and opportunities that would be hindered had she kept him.

We can find our roots in Christ, yet He also gives us wings to soar. *The potential and plans He has for us are unlimited and boundless.* He has a plan of hope for our future. He has set before each of us an individualized destiny that only we can walk in. He gives us new hope, new directions and new promises that will fulfill us. He keeps us grounded and balanced with His Word, and give us freedom and liberty in His Spirit. Where the Spirit of the Lord is, there is liberty. We find freedom only in Him! He frees us from the past and releases us into a future of bright promise. He loves us so much and wants only for us to be free to walk in our destiny. He doesn't get angry when we "miss" it, but is patient and gentle with us.

The love of the Father is indescribable and almost unfathomable. He has great places that He wants to take us to, and doesn't want us held back by past failures, rigid formalities and mundane mindsets. *Soar with Him today...and take a trip upwards. Spread your wings...and release yourself into His hands!*

May 10

Take Him To His Mother

II Kings 4:19 "...And he said to a lad, carry him to his mother."

It was a beautiful sight in our Sunday Evening Worship Service last week...*mothers and sons praying together.* Some were younger mothers and sons, and some were older whose sons also had sons. It wasn't planned...it just happened when an invitation to pray was given. Mothers were weeping as they prayed over their sons... you could see the tears streaming down their faces as they earnestly brought their sons to the heart of the Father. It was a scene that will forever be fixed in my mind.

There is something tender, yet fierce about a mother's heart for her children. ***That same love can be found in the heart of the Church.*** God refers to His Church as a woman, His bride. He entrusts all of His precious children into her care. He, like this father whose son was ailing, knows where the cure can be found for His hurting children...*take them to their mother..take them to the Church.* The original plan for the Church was designed in such a way that there should be no one lacking anything, but all needs could be met through the Church. I believe the Father's heart still cries out when one of His little one's is hurting..."***Take them to the Church.***" There is a holy and sacred bond between the Church and her children, just as there is between a mother and her sons and daughters.

David also knew this truth when he said in Psalms 27:4, *"One thing have I desired of the Lord, and that will I seek after; that I may dwell in the house of the Lord all the days of my life, to behold the beauty of the Lord, and to inquire in His temple."* The Church provides a covering for us, offering us protection, strength, comfort, healing, encouragement, and vision for our future. *She is there, like a spiritual Mother, pleading for her children.* She is there to provide guidance for them and discernment. As we celebrate our Mothers, let us also consider and value the role of the Church in our lives. She was set up by God for us and is a gift to those who treasure her wisdom.

May 11

The Love of a Mother

John 19:25 "Now there stood by the cross of Jesus his mother..."

I've heard that a Mother's love is the closest thing to the love of God. As I reflect upon some of the awesome women of faith, I see love in its purest form. Until a woman becomes a Mother she will never know the ecstasy of love and the deep pain of love that only motherhood brings.

Mary's womb carried the Great I Am. She was there when He took His first breath, His first step until He took His last step and His dying breath. She was there when He performed His first miracle...indeed it was at her quiet urging that He turned the water into wine. *She saw Him take lame men by the hands as He healed them...and recalled how His tiny little fingers once curled around hers as she taught Him to take His first steps.* She took great pride in Him when He fed the 5,000...and remembered how He once nursed at her breast. *The last tribute and great act of love Jesus gave was to His mother while He hung on the cross dying. His final thoughts were of His Mother.*

A Mother's love is a reflection of His love for us in its most tender form. Athletes praise their Mothers! Presidents honor their Mothers! And, we give thanks for every Mother who taught her children to pray and instilled in them a faith that will prevail through good times and tough times! Thank God for Godly Mothers!

May 12

Night Praisers

Psalm 134:1 "Behold, bless the Lord, all you servants of the Lord, who by night stand in the house of the Lord."

It is said that on a clear day you can see forever. I'd like to add this... *on a clear night you can see the evidence of our Awesome God! His handiwork is displayed as Heaven rolls out a blanket of midnight blue velvet alit with bright, glittering lights of shining stars and the soft glow of a radiant moon.* I love standing under this canvas of majestic praise, and feel amazingly close to my Creator as I behold the faithfulness and beauty of His love. The sounds of night praises fill the atmosphere as Nature unfailing sings her songs to her Creator. I am privileged to enjoy the sweetness and the beauty of these night praisers...and am gently reminded to offer my own night praises to my Creator!

Night Praisers! David filled his temple with praisers twenty four hours a day, seven days a week. *No wonder he loved to go to the House of the Lord! Psalm 134 was written especially for the night praisers!* In the desperate, long hours of the night...God has night praisers...people who know how to praise Him in the darkest hours. Their praise is not contingent upon blessings, but comes from hearts in love with Him! Night praisers know that weeping endures for a moment, but joy comes in the morning! Night praisers understand solitude, loneliness, and separation...and still lift up their voices in songs and praises!

Are you one of those night praisers? Perhaps you are in a night season in your life, and you feel isolated and alone. Can you still open your heart of love and pour out worship upon Him, even in the darkest hours? Are you associated with the ones who not only praise Him when things are going well, but praise Him when you are in the fiery trials, the dark nights, and the deep valleys? ***God is looking for Night Praisers - so go ahead - lift up your voice in the night and let your song be heard!***

May 13

Worship Through the Blindness

Luke 18:37, 38 "And they told him, that Jesus of Nazareth passeth by. And he cried, saying, Jesus, thou Son of David, have mercy on me."

Faith is hearing the voice of the Spirit when you cannot see your way clearly. *Faith worships through the blindness!*

Bartimaeus could not see Jesus coming, but he did hear the clamor of the crowds. He heard many voices that day, some that ridiculed him, some told him to shut up, and perhaps some of the voices came from his past telling him he would never be anything but a beggar. But, Bartimaeus heard the one name that took him from his seat of hopelessness into the arena of worship. He heard the name of Jesus! That name caused Bartimaeus to worship the Savior, even though he couldn't see him. When told to shut up, he responded by worshipping even louder! His worship and cries got the attention of Jesus and opened the door for him to have an audience with the Great Healer. *He was forevermore changed that day.*

Sometimes all we hear is the noise of the crowd - confusing, constraining and negative. We sense by faith that the Lord is near, yet we can't see Him. Voices from the past fill our ears with hopelessness and voices of the present loudly demand that we keep quiet. But above all the noise...above all the voices we can hear the whisper of the One Name that will take us from our seat of desperation and into the atmosphere of worship - an atmosphere that is charged with faith! Our worship and faith will connect us with Jesus, gaining us entry into His presence where we will be restored and revived. We can learn from this blind man to worship through our blindness and trust the One who has the power to change our circumstances! Faith lets us hear His voice even when we can't see Him! Our faith will cause us to worship Him through our blindness!

May 14

Touch Them In Love

Galatians 6:1, 2 "Brethren, if a man is overtaken in any trespass, you who are spiritual restore such a one in a spirit of gentleness, considering yourself lest you also be tempted. Bear one another's burdens, and so fulfill the law of Christ."

So, so many people are in pain. Their wounds go far beneath the surface, but they cover them up with small talk and smiles that don't quite reach the eyes. People are suffering silently, and many feel they have no where or no one to turn to. Instead of reaching out to their Family of Faith, they pull away and isolate themselves to lick their wounds in their own private hell. *This should not be so...but, oh, how they need to be touched and healed.*

We all need a safe, soft place to fall...a place where our hurts and wounds can be tended to without fear of rejection, criticism, and judgement. *Instead of running from the Church, we should be running to her...for support, for love, for forgiveness, for strength, and for restoration. The Church is God's gift and blessing to every Believer.* She is His arms extended, His Wisdom spoken, His heart for the lost, and is a carrier of hope. She is not a program, nor an institution, but is the Living, Breathing, Channel of God's Love, Power, and Chosen Method to share Jesus Christ with the world. *She is the best hope for this world*, and is the signpost pointing souls to Christ. She should be our safe place to run to and our soft place to fall. Oh, that our Churches would be the Beacons of Light that directs lost souls home. She is called to be the Refuge of Safety for the weary, the tired, and the hurting. This is what Her purpose is...this is what we are called to live, to do, to support...and be. We need to stop condemning the Church with our words, and begin pointing those lost, weary, hurting people to Her open doors and open arms.

People are hurting and their wounds are raw and bleeding. They are looking for a haven, a shelter from the storm, and a safe place to run to. The world is very unkind and cruel, but we are of a different Spirit. We are full of mercy and grace. We are kind and gentle, even to the unlovely and unlovable. We are carriers of hope and messengers of His love. We are burden-bearers and ministers of healing. We are His and are a part of His dear Church. He is calling His Beloved Church to touch them...the wounded, hurting hearts... to touch them in love.

May 15

Break Through In Worship

John 4:23 "For the hour comes, and now is, when the true worshippers shall worship the Father in spirit, and in truth; for the Father seeks such to worship Him."
Isaiah 58:8 "Then shall thy light break forth as the morning, and thine health shall spring forth speedily, and thy righteousness shall go before thee; the glory of the Lord shall be thy rearward."

Each morning the sun breaks forth from the darkness and displays its lovely rays of light and hope to the world. The skies reflect the glories of the sun's light. You can see beautiful hues of pink, purple and a glimmer of gold coloring the skies as the morning breaks. Those rays assure me that the sun will soon appear.

Isaiah 58:8 tells us that *our morning will break forth*! There is a promise given to each of us that we will see light breaking forth over our horizons, illuminating everything that has been hidden away! We will behold the glories of the Lord with our eyes! As the Son begins to shine, glimmers of hope are resurrected and we can see more clearly than we've ever seen! Health springs forth! Righteousness reigns!

*The Presence of the Almighty is manifested through His creation...*and He bids us to join Him in the celebration of the new dawn breaking forth. It's easy to get "caught away" for hours as I lay before Him, basking in His love. Cares and sorrows grow strangely dim as I gaze into His loveliness. Hope is restored, vision is renewed and joy returns when I am caught up in Him. The more I see Him, the more I realize that worship is all about Him, for He is the only One who is worthy of our worship.

Let today be a day of break through worship. Worship Him... and see the beauty of His glory reflected in His creation.

May 16

Beauty in the Sanctuary

Zechariah 9:17 "For how great is His goodness, and how great is His beauty..."
Psalms 96:6 "Honor and majesty are before Him: strength and beauty are in His sanctuary."

Yesterday was one of those busier days for me that was filled with meetings and things to do, most of them unplanned! In the early afternoon in the heart of Old Tulsa in between meetings, I found a place of beauty and serenity. Tucked away in one of the older, more gracious neighborhoods was a beautiful little lake that was a habitant for swans, ducks, turtles and fish. I stood there, absorbing this beautiful and picturesque scene. Time slipped away as cool breezes brushed across my cheeks, bringing serenity and grace. I thought about the Garden of Eden and how beautiful it must have been - the original sanctuary of the Lord! I thought about our little sanctuary called Passageway and how the Lord so graciously beautifies it with His presence. I thought about people who gave their lives to Christ - people who once had a hard and bitter countenance but now shine with an inner beauty that expensive cosmetics and surgery cannot begin to compete with. They, too, are sanctuaries for the Spirit of the Lord!

Our Father loves beauty and created it for us to enjoy. Today, if possible, find a place of beauty that will soothe and calm your soul. Listen for it in the laughter of children or the songs of the birds! Let it wash over you like a gentle breeze that will blow away the cobwebs of cares and sorrows. There is beauty to be found in the sanctuary of the Lord!

May 17

Free to Dance

Psalms 30:11 "You have turned for me my mourning into dancing..."

Can you hear it? The sound of dancing and rejoicing? It's a sound that has been silent in many of our churches and even in our personal lives. But...*it is a sound that is returning to the Bride of Christ!* Our weeping may endure for a night, but our joy is coming! And *when joy comes,* there will be a lot of dancing going on.

I remember when my niece, Amanda, was two years old how much she loved to dance. She would dance for no reason, without any music, and for the sheer enjoyment of it! Her little feet would start tapping and moving, and she would dance with all of her heart, strength and body! It was quite something to behold! She would lift our spirits and bring great smiles to our faces as we watched her enjoying herself in dance*! Reminds me of someone else who danced before the Lord with all his might and strength*! He didn't care about the mockery of his wife or the stares of those looking on - he found great pleasure and *strength* in his dance unto the Lord!

Christ has made us free to dance! He has turned our sorrows into joy and our mourning into dancing! When was the last time we cast off the bands of heaviness and released the spirit of praise that caused us to leap for joy in the presence of the Lord? We have a reason to rejoice and a purpose for dancing! One of the most precious things about being filled with the Holy Ghost is *He gives us power to praise*, sing, dance, and leap for joy, whether we are in a valley or on a mountaintop...or in a prison cell or in the marketplace! Let the laughter return to the Church! Our freedom to rejoice and dance does not come from the external but from within us! Let's let go of our inhibitions and "*get our dance on*"! Let the dancing and rejoicing return to the Church

May 18

I Have A Song

Ephesians 5:19 "Speaking to one another in psalms and hymns and spiritual songs, singing and making melody in your heart to the Lord."

Several years ago my daughter, Crystal, had a little yellow canary named "Tweety." This little guy would sing...*all the time!* His songs were sweet and pure, and brought her great joy. My daughter took a job in Texas and eventually brought Tweety with her, but...*he sang less and less.* When she moved back to her home in Tulsa, Tweety was joyfully delighted. *His songs began filling the atmosphere...He sang with great joy and gusto!* (He was a lot like God's people who couldn't sing in a strange land and hung their harps on the willow trees.) *He was so glad to be home!*

We must not let our songs go. *We must not cease our singing and making melody in our hearts.* Many things will try to steal our songs, but we can be determined to keep singing - regardless of circumstances. Paul sang while in a deep dungeon, even though he was beaten with many stripes and had heavy chains placed on his hands and feet. He refused to let his song be silenced! Our greatest and most meaningful songs and worship are sometimes birthed in our greatest trials.

Maybe you are like me, and not the best singer, *but sing anyway!* I thank God for the songs He gave me during my times of trials and discouragement. We've got great worship and praise songs that inspire and bring great joy when we sing them. We've got the old hymns that tell of God's faithfulness and the promises of better things to come. There are so many varieties of Christian music today...find what you like and get involved with the song! Make melody with your heart! Sing! Sing joyfully! Let your heartsongs come forth!

May 19

Held Back No More

Philippians 3:13 "...This one thing I do, forgetting those things that are behind me, and reaching forth unto those things which are before."

Often we are our greatest hindrance to doing what we are called to do. We sometimes use our weakness, failures and pain as an excuse to hold us back from fulfilling our destiny. *But God doesn't buy the excuses!* He created us to overtake and overcome - to be more than conquerors! He fashioned and designed us in His very own image - we are made into His image and likeness, and in Him there is liberty and freedom!

Moses tried to use his speech as an excuse, *"I stutter, God"*, but God would not buy it. Moses led his nation out of slavery. He was destined to lead! Gideon excused himself by saying, *"I'm just a farmer"*, but God saw in him an amazing warrior who would win one of the most amazing battles ever by using 300 men to defeat a great army of thousands. Rahab could have said, *"I have a bad past"*, but she chose God over her past. Ruth could have said, *"I don't know anyone, they are all strangers to me"*, but she left everything familiar behind and stepped into her future. Esther tried to excuse herself by saying she would die if she went before the King without him calling her, *but God sent her anyway!*

Our excuses can hold us back, *or we can let them go and move forward with God.* We cannot let our failures, mistakes, or the unfamiliar hold us hostage any longer, but let's step into our destiny and fulfill it!

May 20

Let Your Song Be Heard

Philippians 4:4 "Rejoice in the Lord always, and again I say rejoice."
Acts 16:25, 26 "And at midnight Paul and Silas prayed and sang praises, and the prisoners heard them, and suddenly there came a great earthquake, so that the foundations of the prison house were shaken; and immediately all the doors were opened and everyone's chains were unfastened."

And again I say rejoice! One of the younger boys that attend our church just loves this little song, *"Rejoice in the Lord Always."* You can count on Zack to sing this song during children's church. He sings it with much gusto and fervor; and with a great smile upon his face! Oh that we, too, would rejoice with songs of praise and worship like this little guy does!

We have songs within us that are waiting to be released - songs that are locked up in the deep recesses of our hearts and spirits. The world is waiting for those songs to come forth! The world needs to hear our songs! Songs that tell of the mighty works of God! Songs of deliverance and victory! Songs of unity and harmony!

Don't allow your songs to remain or be silenced! Sing with gusto and fervor! As we release the songs inside of us, we will experience chains being broken off of us. Our songs of deliverance will release the captives and set them free! Our songs of Praise will usher in the mighty rushing winds of the Holy Ghost! Our songs of worship will bring us into the throne room of God! Let your song be heard and sing out with gusto, fervor, and great joy!

May 21

The Joyful Sound

I Kings 18:41 "...For there is a sound of abundance of rain."
"For faith has caught the joyful sound, the song of saints on higher
ground." - Higher Ground

There is something deep inside of me that keeps me pressing
on! *There is a sound* that I can hear in my spirit that urges me
forward! *There is a hungry ache* inside of my belly that tells me that
there is so much more that God has for us than what we have now.
There is a vision set before me that I must see fulfilled! *My faith tells*
me that there is joy ahead on higher ground!

It's time for the latter rain! It's time for the sound of joy to
resonate deep within the hearts of God's children! It's time for the
church to stand tall upon the mountains and declare that Jesus Christ
is Lord and will soon return for His bride! I can hear the sound of the
abundance of rain that is fast approaching...and I am excited! Saints,
this world needs a mighty move of God! This generation hasn't seen
the power and the glory of the Lord...yet!

I believe that soon the Spirit of the Lord will be poured out
upon all flesh, giving mighty revelations of who He is and exposing
the glory of His power! My heart aches when I think about this
younger generation who have yet to see the power, might, glory and
wisdom of God. But my spirit rejoices to know that very, very soon
they will see for themselves what we have been talking about for the
last twenty years! The abundant rain is falling...and we are ready!
Listen closely and you, too, will hear the joyful sound of singing that
is coming to the believers!

May 22

Joy That Remains

Habakkuk 3:18 "Yet I will rejoice in the LORD, I will joy in the God of my salvation."

Regardless of the circumstances, we can rejoice! An attitude of gratitude will give us strength for our journey! We need the strength that joy brings, for it will cause us to run through troops and leap over walls! Joy is contagious! *I'd rather be spreading joy around than anything else!*

Many people in the body of Christ are weary because joy has been depleted, leaving them weak and struggling. Friend, everyone has their share of troubles, but *it is how we face them that will determine our outcome*! We can be victims or victors! I choose to be a victor, for it is God who girds us with strength and makes our way perfect! I refuse to allow circumstances to steal my joy! I refuse to allow how others treat me to rob me of my strength!

I love the scripture that says, *"Weeping may endure for a night, but joy comes in the morning!"* Beloved, our night is ending as morning light is peeping across the horizon. Our time of weeping is just about over...and joy is coming to the Body of Christ! Strength is returning to the Church! Jesus gives us joy that the world cannot take away. Trials can't remove our joy! Circumstances cannot change our joy! We refuse to let Satan steal our joy! Rise up and sing unto the Lord, be joyful in our Savior, for the joy of the Lord is our strength today!

May 23

Love Is Spoken Here

Ephesians 4:15 "But speaking the truth in love, may grow up into him in all things, which is the head, even Christ."

Yesterday I saw a sign in the Christian bookstore that read, *"Love is Spoken Here."* I thought, *"That should be the motto of every Church and every family."* How different the Church would be if everyone spoke love!

Speaking in love doesn't mean that we avoid the truth, but that we use the truth wisely with the objective to win souls! Sometimes love demands that we still our tongue when we are dealing with argumentative people. Sometimes love urges us to speak up, for the circumstances will demand that we be quiet no longer to win a soul or correct an untruth. We speak the truth to uplift and exhort. We speak the truth in love to restore those who have wandered from God and into sin. We speak the truth to instruct and guide. We speak the truth to encourage and admonish. We speak the truth to correct and persuade. Always, we speak the truth in love!

Love speaks volumes!

May 24

Heart Treasures

Ten'der-heart'ed a. 1. Having great sensibility; susceptible of impressions or influence; affectionate; pitying; sensitive.
Ephesians 4:32 "Be ye kind one to another, tenderhearted...".

    She was only following her heart...a heart that is so much like her Heavenly Father's. He was another stray that had found his way to her home...and stayed. There they were, the two of them on the side of the road in the old convertible with the top down, She had stopped by the vet's office to get an allergy shot for the stray dog who was smelly, losing his hair and walked a little lopsided. The car had stalled and she needed a jump, so she called me for help. That's when I saw who she had with her...*it was him! "I can't believe you have taken another dog in,"* I later told her. *"But, Mom,"* she replied, *"this one is a really good one...one of the best dogs I've seen. He is so smart."* She went on to list all of his wonderful abilities, his feats and everything that made him really special, *blatantly overlooking his smell* and the fact that he had lost almost all of his hair because of allergies. Marcy was simply being who she was designed to be... *tenderhearted and kind.* Her heart treasures saw only great worth and treasure in this stinky, hairless dog.

    Oh, that we could also be so tenderhearted and kind to each other and deliberately overlook the faults in others. If only we would stop focusing on the mistakes and failures that are so obvious and see the treasure inside of people. If only we could be the kind of people that uplift and encourage instead of demean and criticize. I guess I don't like being around nit-pickers and faultfinders, know-it-alls and holier-than-thou attitudes. I'd rather be around people like my daughter who can go to anyone (animal and human) and give them a hug, a kiss, and a great big smile, and make them feel loved and special. That's what Christ does for us...*He sees the King that is waiting to shine...the Princess that longs to be recognized.* He very graciously offers us His unconditional love...you know...the kind that makes us feel very special and very favored, even when we're stinking and less than beautiful. Shouldn't we do the same for others?! We'd sure win a lot more hearts for Him!

May 25

Step Into Grace

Psalm 84:11 "For the Lord God is a Sun and Shield; the Lord bestows [present] grace and favor and [future] glory (honor, splendor, and heavenly bliss)! No good thing will He withhold from those who walk uprightly."
James 4:6 "But He gives us more and more grace (power of the Holy Spirit, to meet this evil tendency and all others fully). That is why He says, God sets Himself against the proud and haughty, but gives grace [continually] to the lowly (those who are humble enough to receive it)."

Few words are as beautiful to me as "**Grace**". It conveys everything that is lovely and beautiful and God-like about our wonderful Savior. Mercy forgives us of sin, but it *is grace that enables us to abstain sin.* Mercy is what grace offers and grace is what love offers.

I find we sometimes expend ourselves by doing things the hard way, leaving us tired, weary, and discouraged. It is during challenges and trials *we can step into grace and receive God's enabling favor to do what He wants us to do.* Grace is poured upon us like rains in dry seasons, like healing oil upon tender wounds, and offers us His help...His hand...His favor. Grace wipes the tears from our eyes and gives us courage to try again. Grace heals the broken places in our hearts, giving us strength to rise from our ashes of mourning and step into joy. Grace empowers us to overcome sin and resist temptations. He is our Sun and Shield, withholding no good thing from those who humbly receive His grace.

Today may be a day of difficult challenges, if so, step into grace. Perhaps you will encounter someone who will try the limits of your love, but step into grace. His grace will not only see you through, but will give enable you to do what He calls you to do. *Whatever comes your way, by the grace of God you can make it!*

May 26

The Art of Being Still

Psalm 46:10 "Be still, and know that I am GOD…"

There is a lost art of being still before the Lord and waiting upon Him. Waiting upon the Lord is so hard because *we are by nature impatient and have a need to hurry things along.* Most of us have full plates that leave us with little time to ourselves, and even less time to give to the Lord. So, even in our quiet times with Him or in our worship services, we will find ourselves *"hurrying Him up."* Many times the presence of the Lord will linger as He waits for us to acknowledge and worship Him so He can in turn refresh our spirits. The great men and women of faith have learned the art of being still in the presence of the Most High. Wisdom has taught them that the only way out, over, through or around is by Him and through Him, and to wait for Him. They have found that the best spent time is time spent in His presence.

This is something that most Christians lack…being still before the Throne of God. Isaiah 40:31 *"But they that wait upon the Lord shall renew their strength; they shall mount up with wings as eagles; they shall run, and not be weary; and they shall walk, and not faint."* Once you come into his beautiful presence you won't leave the same. Jesus had a talk with Martha about the most important things. She was so caught up in *doing* that she found no time to sit in His presence and hear what He had to say. Many of us are like Martha, busy doing and serving, but have very little time to actually be in the presence of the Savior. *We wear ourselves out and don't understand why we are always tired and why the joy has left us.* We have forgotten to be still and let Him be God. We try to force things to happen because we are too impatient to wait for God. If we can learn the art of being still, God will do so much more for us than we ever dreamed…and we'll be able to enjoy all the blessings He has prepared for us. The most important thing we can do is to be still, and wait upon Him.

There is a haven for us found in waiting before Him. It is a place of stillness and quiet, and a place where we can really know this great One that we serve*! It is here we are built up, strengthened, restored and refreshed.* He just LOVES for us to come into his presence.

May 27

The Pearls in Tears

Psalm 56:8 "You number my wanderings; Put my tears into Your bottle; Are they not in Your book."
Psalm 126:5 "They that sow in tears shall reap in joy."

There is something precious about the tears of the Saints. They are so valuable to the Lord that He has a special place for them. For several days now I have seen pearls, heard pearls and felt pearls in my spirit. Beautiful, luminous, transparent, huge pearls. I wondered why I keep seeing these pearls and the Lord let me know *that these pearls are the tears of the Saints.* More precious to Him and of unspeakable value, they are costly, priceless and very, very dear to His heart.

What may seem painful to us for a moment is only a transitional place where we are being shaped and formed into beautiful pearls. And when the pain has ceased, joy will overflow and we will see the beauty of His love in our lives. When the moment of grief has passed we will dance with joy and shout with gladness of the marvelous works of the Lord! The tears we have shed for lost souls will produce a great harvest of joy! Our tears we have shed upon the altars of sacrifice and obedience will render a great victory! *The tears that have soaked the steps to the throne will open the doors of heaven as Our God hears our cries!*

There will be a time of tears, but we will also burst into song and dance as the joy of the Lord fills our hearts! There will be a time of pain, but out of the ashes of hurt there will arise pearls that will adorn and grace the palace of the King!

May 28

Beauty in the Brokenness

Luke 7:37, 38 "And, behold, a woman in the city, which was a sinner, when she knew that Jesus sat at meat in the Pharisee's house, brought an alabaster box of ointment, And stood at his feet behind him weeping, and began to wash his feet with tears, and did wipe them with the hairs of her head, and kissed his feet, and anointed them with the ointment."

The beauty of the Lord can be found in broken people. The sweet savor of His Presence is released through our tears and our heartaches. *We find Him to be the sweetest when life is often the bitterest.*

Mary took her costly and beautiful alabaster box...and brake it open to release the expensive fragrance that was inside. She poured it upon Jesus...and *the scent of her worship filled the house.* Had her box remained unopened and unbroken, it's costly beauty would have never been released. As she released the ointment from her beautiful box, she also released her soul to worship Jesus. *Her tears fell like rain upon His dear feet, soaking into His skin and becoming a part of Him.* Bending low to the ground she kissed those feet now wet with tears, and then dried them with her hair. *She was in her most surrendered and humble position* as she worshipped Him with her tears and her brokenness.

As you go through your time of brokenness, release your soul and pour out your worship to Him. *Keep nothing back from Him,* for it is in the sweet release of your broken worship that He finds the beauty that was locked away in your heart. Broken worship is costly and comes with a high price. Be willing to release the beauty of brokenness in your worship!

May 29

The Heart Test

Jeremiah 11:20 "But, O LORD of hosts, that judgest righteously, that triest the reins and the heart..."
Daniel 1:8 "But Daniel purposed in his heart that he would not defile himself with the portion of the king's meat, nor with the wine which he drank..."

You have something of such importance and value that the very forces of light and darkness contend for it. Your children want it. Your spouse or lover wants it. Your friends want it. Your Church wants it. Your boss wants it. The world wants it. Satan wants it. *God wants it!* What is this amazing, precious, priceless thing of value that so many are competing for? *It's your heart! There will be many "heart tests" in life that will reveal Who and What has your heart!*

The paths we take in life are driven by the purposes in our hearts. Our successes, failures and responses to them result from heart issues. Motives and agendas are hidden in the heart. Destinies are first revealed in the heart. Choices are made and characters are shaped in the heart. The issues of life and death are found...in the heart!

"Create in me a clean heart," was the passionate prayer of One who had a heart after God! Rubies and diamonds and gold cannot compare to the beauty and rare cost of a pure heart! There is nothing more sacred, more precious, and more desired by God than a heart set ablaze with His love! No wonder we are told to guard our hearts with all diligence. The world looks upon the outward and makes its judgments, but God sees the inner heart of man...and judges the contents of the heart! What we hold in our heart is too priceless to lose and too rare to find.

May 30

Conditioned By Conflict

Psalms 119:71 "It is good for me that I have been afflicted..."

Sometimes we wish life would be just a little bit gentler with us, or a little bit more kind. It would be an ideal world if men ruled justly and fairly, and we were without want or need. How difficult it must be for our missionaries to look upon the faces of children who breathe their last breath because there was no food or medicine available to sustain their lives. How cruel life can be to take a dear one from us who brought us such joy and happiness. We must trust that God has reasons to allow us to go through these heated fires of testing. ***God uses conflict as a fire drill to reveal what our true values and allegiances are.*** Our reactions betray what is most important to us. Conflict strips away the pretense and self-delusion and shows us what we treasure the most and where our heart truly is.

God receives glory each time we triumph over trials! He allows us to be conditioned by conflict so we can partake in His glory! He will allow Satan to come against one of His children as He did with Job so that some greater thing can be accomplished! It's for our good and His glory!

Our stand in the conflict shows the world what faith in God can accomplish! We are trained for service through trials and tests, but we are seated with Christ in heavenly places each time we endure the hardness as a good soldier of Jesus Christ! Think it not strange concerning this fiery trial...***God is just polishing us to show us off!***

May 31

Remembering Who I Am

1 Peter 2:9 "But ye are a chosen generation, a royal priesthood, an holy nation, a peculiar people; that ye should shew forth the praises of him who hath called you out of darkness into his marvelous light."

Yesterday I took a trip down memory lane and was reminded of who I really am in Christ Jesus. I went back to a place of happier times when my future looked promising and bright, a time when God amazingly opened doors for me in high places with some awesome people. *Life moves on swiftly, and sometimes the residuals of continual warfare can leave us numb and dull to the promises of our destiny in Christ Jesus.* As I reflected upon that time in my life, I realized that *God has much better for me than my current circumstances have dictated,* and I just needed reminding of who I am.

★ *I am an heir of God and a joint heir with Christ Jesus! All the promises of Abraham are mine through Christ Jesus (Gal. 3).*

★ *I am a Priestess of the Lord, hand picked and chosen by Him. It is He who anointed me, called me, choose me, and I owe no one any apologies.*

★ *I am Redeemed and Forgiven - and that's enough for me to reach my destiny.*

★ *I am loved, and called to love. No one can pluck me from His hand, no matter how hard they try.*

★ *I have a future in Christ that is bright and filled with hope, for He knew who I was while I was in my mother's womb, and has carefully and intrinsically designed the plans He has for my life.*

★ *I am rich in love and mercy, and have all that I need provided by His benevolent hand.*

★ *I am not ashamed of the Gospel, for it is life to me and to my children, therefore I boldly preach the cross of Jesus Christ to whosoever will receive Him.*

★ *I am somebody, not because of my own good deeds, but because I belong to Him.*

Today, I will do my very best to live up to whom I am - His! I will walk with my head held high, regardless of the circumstances life has thrown at me. I will boldly face my giants and, as my grandson would say, smack them between the eyes with the Word of God. I will give thanks to God for the provision I have today, and trust Him that tomorrow is in His hands. I will remind myself often that I am not just "anybody" but I am His...and that's the best me that I can be.

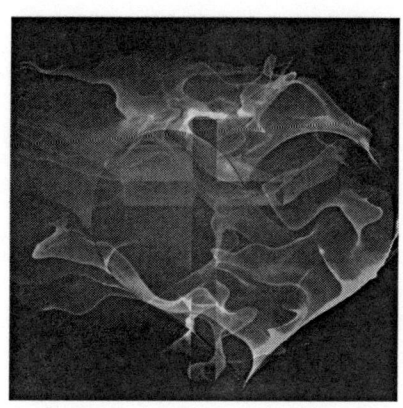

June

In the heart of every man
Beats the desire to be someone's hero!

June 1

The Great Promise Keeper

Numbers 23:19, 20 "God is not a man, that He should lie, nor a son of man, that He should repent. Has He said, and will He not do? Or has He spoken and will He not make it good. Behold, I have received a command to bless; He has blessed and I cannot reverse it!"

The year was 1988. My daughter had been praying and believing all year for divine healing for a dear and precious man who so deeply wanted to be a testimony of God's goodness, but on November 4 of that year, the Lord called him to glory. She was heartbroken and couldn't understand why God did not heal him. God, in great compassion and wisdom, spoke to her in the early morning hours that followed and said that this dear man was now a part of that great cloud of witnesses and his testimony would live on. Peace came to her, even though she didn't understand how this could be. *Six years later a home was built for troubled women and named after the man. His name was a testimony to all who entered the home.* Although she had forgotten what God spoke to her in those early morning hours, *God never forgot!* He remembered His word to her and brought it to pass! He is the great Promise Keeper!

It is not possible for God to lie, nor can He forget His promises! We may forget some of the wonderful blessings He has promised to us, but He Never Forgets! The Word tells us that God honors His Word, even above His Name, and we know that there is no name higher than His! See, in His name is full provision for every thing we will ever need! In the beginning was the Word and the Word was God! His Names mean provision, but His Word IS the provision! He ALWAYS makes good His Word! It will never fail us...ever! It's not a hard thing to Step Out On His Word when we understand that HE IS THE WORD! Praise God! When we step out on His word, we are stepping out on HIM! I encourage you today to bring to His remembrance all of the promises He gave to you. Bind Him to His Word! Have faith, that in due time, He will make good His Word! He is the great Promise Keeper!

June 2

Heroes of Faith

Hebrews 11: 33, 34 "Who through faith subdued kingdoms, wrought righteousness, obtained promises, stopped the mouths of lions, quenched the violence of fire, escaped the edge of the sword, out of weakness were made strong, waxed valiant in fight, turned to flight the armies of the aliens."

We need some heroes!

Our pulpits are filled with powerless men who pray powerless prayers over powerless people! Aren't you tired of going to dead churches that sing dead songs and preach dead sermons? *Isn't it time for some changes in our churches?* **Isn't it time for faith to step up and voice her victory?** *Isn't it time we pray prayers that avail much? Isn't it time for leaders to manifest the anointed power of the Living God to their congregations?* We need some spiritual leaders who aren't afraid of the battles, who proudly wear their battle scars with honor, and who are determined to preserve through the pressure. I expect miracles and answers when I pray. I expect the enemy to back down when I face him with the Blood and the Word! We need people who expect! We need heroes who have:

Dominion Over Distress
Praise under Pressure
Power over Problems
Faith that Fights Fearlessly
Strength in the Struggles
Authority over Adversity
Triumph over Trials
Testimonies from Tests
Been Conditioned by Conflict!

Heroes are born out of hardships! **Heroes aren't appointed - they are anointed!** Heroes aren't ordained - they are divinely ordered! Heroes aren't people pleasers - they are purpose driven! Heroes aren't just called - they are chosen! Heroes aren't discriminative -

they are people who are available, willing and teachable! Heroes aren't proud or arrogant, but are humble and willing to do whatever is necessary! God is looking for heroes who won't back down, compromise or settle! He has qualified you to do all things in His name!

June 3

Giant Slayers

2 Samuel 23:8 "These be the names of the mighty men whom David had…"

    Do you know that you are a giant slayer? We are called to slay giants!

    First, there was Joshua and Caleb! When the others said *"We can't,"* they said, *"We can."* Then there was David, a shepherd boy who took on the giant of intimidation. Next, there were the mighty men who followed a giant slayer…Let's take a look at who they are and what they did:

    Adino (He lifted up his sword and slew 800 men at one time)

    Eleazar (Smote the Philistines until his weary hand clave to his sword) means *God has helped*

    Shammah (Wrought a great victory by defending the ground and destroying an entire troop) means *Fugitive*

    Abashi (Lifted his spear against 300 men and slew them all) means *Desirous of a gift*

    Benaiah (Slew a lion, a mighty Egyptian, and two lion-like men) means *Built up by Jehovah*

    Elhanan (Slew Goliath's giant brother) means *Whom God has graciously bestowed*

    These men all had a choice to make…*keep running or take a stand.* They came to David looking to find hope and a future with an outcast who was on the run for his life! They found a leader who would not quit, but chose to reload! They found a man with the reputation of a giant slayer…and became men with like reputations. They slew giants!

    We have been given the power and authority to slay giants! We are called to slay the giants of addictions and slavery, disease and poverty, sin and iniquity! We do not warfare in the natural, but our battleground is in the spirit realm, and it's full of giants! We are called to overcome and overpower them. ***We are…giant slayers!***

June 4

Men Who Won't Quit

2 Samuel 23:9, 10 "After him was Eleazar...one of the three mighty men...he arose and smote the Philistines until his hand was weary and clave to the sword..."

Thank God for men who won't quit and who refuse to give up!

For several days I have been thinking about this warrior who was one of David's mighty men of valor. ***He fought so hard and so long that his hand could not release his sword.*** His sword actually cleaved to his hand and his hand could not release it! What a man! What a warrior! I can visualize his hand wrapped around his sword as he fought against the enemy. He was no coward nor was he a quitter. His courage and determination are pretty hard to beat. His loyalty was second to none. *He was a man's man, fighting valiantly for a leader whom he loved.* His obedience to his Captain is inspirational. David had could not lose a war with such a man fighting at his side. *He had only one goal, and that was to give his all to his calling.* He was not sidetracked from his mission. Not much is said about him today, but he was a true hero and warrior to be respected. His name was Eleazar which means, *"God has helped."*

May God give us such men as this who will not quit nor be distracted from their purpose. May God give us such men whose loyalty and valor testifies to this generation that mighty men can still be found. Thank God for men who have the heart of a warrior beating strongly in their breasts and whose eyes are not turned from the mark! Thank God for the men who take a stand for their faith and family. Thank God that He is raising up men who will get involved and won't quit until we taste victory. Thank God for men who won't quit!

June 5

God's Mighty Men

Zechariah 10:5 "And they shall be as mighty men, which tread down their enemies in the mire of the streets in the battle: and they shall fight, because the LORD is with them..."

King David was extremely blessed! He had a few good men in his group of vagabonds and misfits! These men recognized that he was God's man, and saw his vision, and felt his heartbeat, and got behind him! ***They knit their hearts with his and refocused their vision to see what he saw.*** They became one with him in his purpose and in his destiny!

Every leader needs a few of these mighty men to help propel the vision into being! Every successful ministry has the backing of a few good men! Thank God there are still a few good men to be found - men who will commit to a God-given cause that is not their own, men who will help build the dreams of others who have received a commission and vision from God.

My son-in-law, Wayne, has become invaluable to me. His integrity, devotion to his family and faithfulness to the service of God is one of the greatest blessings in my life. Just knowing that he loves my baby girl and my granddaughters is a blessing, but having him work side by side with me in the church is an added benefit! My other son-in-law, Ronnie, is one of those fishermen like Peter - *he can cast a line into the water and always pull in a fish!* He has that "fisher of men" calling and anointing that amazes me! There are other "good men" that God has brought to help in the church - men who pray and sow their talents into this ministry! Men who help support this ministry financially! *Men who have greatness of spirit know how to humble themselves before God.* They may be few in number - *but they are great in spirit!* I thank God for the few good men who see my vision and have lent themselves to help fulfill it! It only takes a few good men who know the heartbeat of their leader and of God to get the job done!

June 6

Wake Up, Mighty Warriors!

Joel 3:9 "...Wake up the mighty men, let all the men of war draw near..."

Men of God, get ready! The Spirit of the Living God is calling your name and giving new orders to faithful men of valor! He is searching for men who will do exploits for Him. Men who are trustworthy and true! Men whose eyes are upon the Savior and will not be turned aside!

As I was reading about some of the Biblical heroes of faith, I thought, *"We need such men as these!"* Were they a special breed? No, but these were ordinary, normal people - just like us! They were not "super" men, but were courageous and strong, and possessed great determination and zest. They were visionaries, with purpose and destiny. They were faithful and obedient to their callings and duties. They were men who simply believed God was bigger than their foes.

Men and women who dare to step up and assume their responsibilities and submit to the Mighty Hand of God are men and women who will achieve great status and honor. Men and women who are not ashamed to stand up for the right and defend the innocent are people that God can trust with His greatness! Men, wake up to your destiny, for the Lord is drawing you into your purpose! *You are a mighty man of valor!*

June 7

The Heart of a Champion

Hebrews 11 "...By Faith..."

Attitude says a lot! You can have a "can do" attitude of faith that will take you to some pretty great places! Mountain moving faith was deposited into your spiritual bank account...you only have to access it!

David, Joshua, Moses, Abraham, Elijah, Paul, Peter...these all had one thing in common - *they had the hearts of Champions.* They faced insurmountable obstacles, but were equipped with the right spirit and mindset. When the odds were against them, they saw an opportunity for God to do something spectacular. Their focus was upon the Lord and the prize that was set before them. *They were men of commitment - they gave all of themselves wholly over to the Lord, not holding anything back.* They were all men of prayer and knew how to get answers from the Lord. They were humble enough to serve others and great enough to lead the people to mighty victories. They refused to quit because they were convinced that victory was eminent!

We, too, can be Champions for God! When we commit to His service, we can become mighty in the Lord and dare to believe God for impossibilities! See setbacks as opportunities for God to step in. See giants as grasshoppers, and obstacles as faith-builders. Focus on Him and the prize that is ours to pursue! It's time for the Champions of the Lord to arise, overtake and possess!

June 8

Champions of Faith

1 Samuel 18:17 "Saul said to David, There is my older daughter, Merob, whom I will give you in marriage if you become my champion and fight the battles of the Lord..."

The world is looking for a Champion - someone who will fight the battle and win! The Church is looking for men who have hearts of Champions and who will fight this good fight of faith! Do you hear Him...*perhaps He is calling your name to stand and be counted as a Champion of Faith!*

We are called to fight a good fight of faith (1 Timothy). A champion is described as a person who fights for or defends any person or cause; or to act as a champion of; defend; support. Christ empowered us to become champions for Him just as He did David. *The secret to defeating giants lies in our faith. If we believe we can, then we will!*

The world always recognizes true champions. Saul recognized David's potential as a warrior and tried to entice him with false promises! The world will try to seduce God's mighty warriors today with promises of fame and fortune, but *true champions don't need worldly promises to be successful.* We are committed to the call and to the cause, and have engaged in spiritual warfare, refusing to compromise our faith, and are willing to pay the price. Champions of faith are determined and persistent, and are willing to step out in faith, going where others fear to step! Champions realize that there is a prize to be gained and are passionate about obtaining it.

June 9

Fallen Champions Arise

Judges 16:21, 22, 28 "But the Philistines took him, and put out his eyes, and brought him down to Gaza, and bound him with fetters of brass; and he did grind in the prison house. Howbeit the hair of his head began to grow again...And Samson called unto the Lord, and said, O Lord God, remember me, I pray thee, and strengthen me..."

We see it a lot these days - *fallen champions*. Once great men of God, they have succumbed to a temptation or weakness, destroying the effectiveness of their testimony. Hearts are broken, lives are affected and faith is damaged. The body of Christ takes the blow from these hits, and feels the pain and humiliation of a downed Champion.

The story of Samson is one of the saddest in the Bible. Samson was a mighty man of power and might. His greatest weakness was *he thought he was invincible* - nothing could touch him. He became involved with someone whose assignment was to find his weakness and destroy him. (Be careful who you hang out with.) His eyes were put out and he was harnessed to a grinding wheel in prison. *The goal of our enemy is to steal our vision and render us useless and to aimlessly go nowhere.* But, God is a God of second chances! Samson's hair (strength) began to grow again. Hear the anguish plea as he cried out to the Lord, *"Remember me, O Lord."*

God hears the cries of fallen Champions who are crying out to Him today. He hears the plea of their hearts that say, *"Let me finish my course."* His mercy and grace reaches out to them to restore and forgive. A true Champion will not stay down - He will arise from the ashes of shame, humiliation and disgrace to complete the mission he was assigned. There is a second chance for us today because of His mercy and loving-kindness. We may be crippled from our fall, but we can get up and still fulfill our purpose. We may have been going in circles, blind-sided, but God can restore us. Get up, shake the dust off, and keep going! We can still fight, we can still win, we are still overcomers - as long as we get up again.

June 10

Our Heavenly Father

Malachi 4:6 "He shall turn the hearts of the fathers to the children, and the heart of the children to their fathers..."
Ephesians 3:14 "For this cause I bow my knees unto the Father of our Lord Jesus Christ."

Many of us are making plans to show our Fathers just how much we love and appreciate having them in our lives. *Fathers are deeply imbedded in the heart of God, designed by Him to impact the next generations to come!* Godly Fathers are gifts to each generation, designed to guide the future in wisdom. God loves Fatherhood! Fathers were so important that He appointed one for His Son, Jesus! When teaching us how to pray, Jesus instructed us to call Him, Our Father!

He is Our Father! The One who turns planets and gives the stars their twinkle is always near to His Children, ever ready to respond to their cries and prayers. We have a Heavenly Father that loves us with an everlasting love! He has assumed His role and responsibility of being our Father with great wisdom and delight! He, the Father of our Savior, gave His best Gift to us - His Own Dear Son, so that we would have eternal life with Him. He gently speaks hope to us with each sunrise, and whispers peace in the moonlight. His breath is in the winds that blow across our cheeks, restoring and reviving our spirits. His voice calls out to us when we have lost our way, urgently calling us back to safety. His greatest desire is to have a deep and intimate relationship with each and every one of His children. He knows us by name, and like a good Father, knows our desires and dreams!

To all the Fathers...be greatly blessed and reminded that you are the instrument God chose to impact the next generation! *The day is coming when the Spirit of the Lord will draw the hearts of the Fathers to the sons...and the hearts of the sons to their Fathers.*

June 11

The Message of The Test

1 Peter 4:12 "Beloved, think it not strange concerning the fiery trial which is to try you, as though some strange thing happened unto you..."

I know that you, like many of God's precious children, have had your share of tests and trials. Perhaps you, like so many of us, even wondered what the purposes of these tests were. Maybe you have even questioned, *"Why this test?"* Beloved, there is great purpose and value in every test we go through!

Embrace the message of the trials, for they hold the keys to your future victories! There is something the test has to say that will profoundly impact your faith. *The purpose of the test is not to defeat you, but to make you strong.* The trial is come, not to harm you, but to make you wiser and more confident in the God you serve. The message of the test speaks loudly of His trust in you to weather the storms of life. He knows what lies ahead, and in His infinite wisdom, chooses each test with care, concern, and loving thought. Provision for your future can be found in your current test. Listen to the message of the test and you will find that God is preparing you for some greater thing.

None of us like the tests, but oh, what character is worked in us through these trials! What wisdom is deposited in us because of the tests! What strength is developed in us! What glory awaits us on the other side of the test! Oh, how brightly and clearly we shine once we have been polished by the trial! Listen and learn, for the keys to your destiny are found in each test and trial you go through!

June 12

Called and Committed

1 Samuel 22:1, 2 "David departed and escaped to the cave Adullam: and when his brethren and all his father's house heard it, they went down with him. And every one that was in distress, and everyone that was in debt, and everyone that was discontented, gathered themselves to him; and he became a captain over them..."

Commitment. Loyalty. Trustworthy. Not common traits to be found these days. But...for those of us who are Set Apart and Hidden Away, we will pass through the Cave of Commitment before we ever walk in the *Fullness of Sonship.*

David, on the run from Saul, came to the cave called Adullam, *which means refuge.* With David came a group of people who were in *distress, discontented and in debt*! What a group to be a leader of - certainly not the popular crowd! But it was in this cave of refuge that these rejects and losers *taught us what it means to be committed to a leader, loyal to a cause, and the value of trustworthiness.* In this group of four hundred or so were some mighty men of valor - amazing warriors and valiant men who took out giants! They knew how to fight and the importance of commitment to their captain. These men came to David for protection, training and a cause. By learning how to lead this group, David was also learning how to lead a nation. He committed himself to this rough group of outcasts, winning their loyalty and trust. David made up his mind in the cave to not give up, give in or give out! People were attracted to him, not because of his charisma or intellect, but because of his devotion to his people.

May God give us those who know something about commitment, loyalty and trustworthiness! Give us leaders who are committed to their people and people who are committed to their leaders! We are coming out of our caves of commitment in a blaze of glory, and will confuse those who knew us as nothings and nobodies! The willing and obedient, committed and faithful are rising up as the true Sons of the Living God! Get Ready - Get Committed!

June 13

Burst Forth In A Blaze

1 Samuel 22:5 "Now the prophet Gad said to David, Do not stay in the stronghold; depart, and go to the land of Judah. So David departed and went into the forest of Hereth."

We are coming out with a blaze of glory!

We have been hidden away in a cave of refuge, learning how to be committed and faithful. We are surrounded with the dejected, despised and in debt! But we are coming out! We are not content with what we see going on in churches. We know there is more and we won't settle for less. We won't accept what the world has offered to us and have refused the watered down, compromised version of the gospel that is prevalent today. We have tasted the sweetness of victory when we faced our Goliath, and we know *there is nothing that tastes as good as God's glory!* We are hungry for more and are pressing on and pressing in to see the salvation of the Lord. We are unified and strengthened through our cave of commitment experience, and we are ready to face the giants!

There is a prophetic utterance coming forth that is commanding us to leave our caves or refuge and go to Judah! Judah - the voice of praise! Judah - the place of victory! Judah - the path to glory! Listen to Gad...he's giving instructions! Listen to the prophetic voice speaking - He's giving us directions! Listen to the Spirit - He's telling us victory is near and it's time to go forth in a blaze of glory! The hands that have grown weary are rising up in praise! The steps that have stumbled are dancing in victory! The voice that has been silent is ringing out in song! We are coming out of our caves in a blaze of glory!

June 14

Consumed by the Call

Revelation 12:11 "And they overcame him by the blood of the Lamb, and the word of their testimony, and they did not love their lives so much as to shrink from death."

Every Believer has been entrusted with a God-given dream...a vision...a calling. *The success of our dream or calling is largely dependent upon us...and our commitment to it.* Until it consumes us like a burning fire, until it fills our every waking moment, until we are willing to walk alone with the dream, until we are willing to risk all for the sake of the call...it will mostly lie dormant in us. The difference between success and failure is the difference of being sold out or being partially involved.

Sold out people will always respond to the God-called cause! Something inside of you will *always* rise up to fight if you see that dream threatened in any way. The cost of the dream is the laying down of our lives and surrendering our will to His. *When nothing will satisfy and you just can't settle for less than the dream...you are on the path to selling out. When your hunger for the call consumes you and you lay aside all to answer the call, then you are answering the call. When you are willing to risk everything, and spend and be spent to live out the dream, then you are found worthy of the call.*

Jesus gave up everything to answer His call...we should be willing to do the same. There is a seed of greatness that God has planted in you, but it can only come to fruition when your will has died and His has become yours. Once you believe in your dream, others will as well. No one wants to follow someone who isn't completely consumed by their vision or dream, but give us someone who believes in something so strongly they are willing to give up everything! They are sold out and cannot be bought, compromised, or defeated!

June 15

An Excellent Spirit

Daniel 1:3, 4 "...He should bring certain of the children of Israel, and of the King's seed, and of the princes. Children in whom was no blemish, but well favored, and skilful in all wisdom, and cunning in knowledge, and understanding science, and such as had ability in them to stand in the king's palace..."

Once you meet someone who has an excellent spirit you will never forget them. *They have that "something special" in them that defines them as "the King's Seed."* There is a purity in them that is rare and precious. Their convictions and faith in a Holy God will never allow them to bow a knee to an idol or defile themselves with the pleasures of this world. *They have special ability to stand in the King's palace!*

We find in the Bible several young men who had "an excellent spirit." Joshua, Caleb, Joseph, and then Judah's sons...Daniel, Hananiah, Mishael, and Azariah. *These men did not compromise, even when the best of the world's temptations were placed at their feet.* They stood for God unapologetic, and purposed to serve God, even to the death. ***They were God pleasers, not world seekers***! They gave Him their allegiance, their loyalty, *and their lives.* They were men of excellence, virtue, and purity. They found His favor, His blessings, and His Divine Presence that would take them from ordinary men to men who are remembered for their excellence.

God is looking for such men and women today...those whom He can trust to bring into His high courts. He is looking for those who are excellent in spirit...those who, like Daniel, are determined to not defile themselves, but to live holy, acceptable lives that please Him. *You have the Seed of the King that is implanted in your spirit by the Holy Ghost. Develop it! Nurture it!* Let the old man die and let the Spirit of Excellence, the Spirit of the Divine Nature of Christ come alive in your heart! These are the people He is coming back for...those who are found without blemish and without spot or wrinkle! Choose excellence over mediocrity and integrity over compromise! You will never ever regret who you are!

June 16

A Heart of Integrity

Daniel 1:8 "But Daniel purposed in his heart that he would not defile himself..."
Daniel 6:4 "...But they could find none occasion nor fault; forasmuch as he was faithful, neither was there any error or fault found in him."

Three things that God love dearly and Satan despises are *faithfulness, purity and integrity.* It is these traits in the Church or in the life of a believer that are most frequently under attack. If we compromise them, our testimonies are but empty words that impact no one. We are known by all men by not so much as what we say, *but by how we live.*

The more I look at the life of Daniel, the more I am impressed by his integrity, his purity, and his commitment to His God! Daniel purposed in his heart that he would not defile himself. One of the reasons we see so much shame, disgrace, and departing from the faith is because *many fail to purpose in their hearts that they will live the Holy, acceptable life that Romans 12 talks about.* Over and over we read where Daniel exalted and blessed God, refusing to accept any credit or glory that was His. His heart of integrity would not allow him to own something that was God-given. Daniel not only had an excellent spirit, but was also a man of prayer. Finding no fault in Daniel, his enemies attacked him through his prayer life, but still he refused to compromise, even though it meant going into a lions den. We know the story...he came through triumphantly.

When we refuse to compromise our integrity and purity, *our lives will speak for themselves, causing some to hate what we stand for and others to trust in what we possess.* Like Daniel, integrity and standing for what we believe will put our testimony to the test, but God will always show up for those who stand for Him. Like Daniel, we might face persecution from those who oppose what we stand for, *but God will deliver us also!*

June 17

The Fellowship of Friends

Daniel 2:17, 18 "Then Daniel went to his house, and made the thing known to Hananiah, Mishael, and Azariah, his companions: That they would desire mercies of the God of heaven concerning this secret; that Daniel and his fellows should not perish with the rest of the wise men of Babylon."

It pays to have good friends, especially the kind who know how to touch heaven for you! If you are like me, you cherish a good friend, because you know just how rare they are! Good friends are not perfect, but they are God sent and know how to cover your back when you are under attack.

Daniel had three friends who had his back...*friends who knew how to pray and get results*! These friends had walked through captivity with Daniel, had joined him in refusing to defile themselves with the King's meat, and *were bonded together in unity that comes from pure, selfless love.* David had a few such friends...the story of Jonathan and David's friendship was a type and shadow of the blood covenant Jesus made with us. There is the story of the brave, loyal soldiers who loved David so much that they went through enemy lines and back just to get a drink of water from a well that David reminisced about. *Great men recognize and understand the need to have trusted friends who will put their loyalty to the test and walk through the fires of hell with and for them.*

Rare? You better believe it! *If you have such friends, Celebrate them! Cherish them! Value them*! Overlook their faults and see the integrity, the loyalty, and the selfless love that defines them as "friend." Are you this kind of friend? *Do you know how to get on your knees and bombard heaven until God answers for your friend?* If so...you are in excellent company with great men and women of excellent spirits! You, too, will share in the blessings when your friends are blessed! I am thankful for every friend who will seek Heaven on my behalf, cover my back when I am attacked...and be there through thick and thin!

June 18

"But If Not" Faith

Daniel 3:15-18 "...Who is that God that shall deliver you out of my hands? Shadrach, Meshach, and Abednego, answered and said to the king, O Nebuchadnezzar, we are not careful to answer thee in this matter. If it be so, our God whom we serve is able to deliver us from the burning fiery furnace, and he will deliver us out of thine hand, O king. But if not, be it known unto thee, O king, that we will not serve thy gods, nor worship the golden image which thou hast set up."

God loves bold faith! In spite of circumstances and situations, *God has people who will not bow to worldly idols nor compromise their faith! They serve Him out of love and not for selfish gain.* Some serve Him for what He can give, but when the money runs out or times get tough, God is the first One they blame. Some serve Him out of fear of going to hell, but when the fears abate they go back to their old ways. Some are pleasure seekers and when the "newness" or the "thrill" is gone...so are they! *But not some!*

The more I read about Daniel and his companions, the more I am impressed with their devotion, their faith, and their courage. An enraged king asked them, *"Who is that God that shall deliver you out of my hands?"* He underestimated their faith...and their God! He gave them one more opportunity to compromise, to bow to him...but they would not. Boldly proclaiming that their God was indeed able to deliver them not only from the fire, but from the hand of the King... their faith took them to a higher dimension... *but if not.* They had the "Job" faith...though He slay me, yet will I trust Him! Their faith took them through their fiery test. Not only did He save them, *but He personally showed up and walked them through their fire!*

Do you have *"if not"* faith? Are you so committed to Jesus that you can say like Paul, *"Nothing shall be able to separate me from the love of Christ?"* When others mock your faith and your

God, can you boldly proclaim that your God is indeed able to deliver you from the trials you are going through? *God thrills at bold faith, faith that isn't alone for a ride, but faith that perseveres through storms and tests!* I challenge us today to get bold with our faith... and watch God walk us through the fires that cannot touch us!

June 19

Is Your God Able?

Daniel 6:20 "And when he came to the den, he cried with a lamentable voice unto Daniel: and the king spake and said to Daniel, O Daniel, servant of the living God, is thy God, whom thou servest continually, able to deliver thee from the lions?"

It's easier to make a stand for Jesus when you believe in Him. Unless you truly believe He is Who He says He is, you will never make the full commitment to Him that He is worthy of. *You will never convince anyone to believe in something or someone that you have little faith in.*

Years before he faced the lions, Daniel had purposed in heart that he would not defile himself. He had boldly taken a stand for the God he believed in, causing many to hate what he stood for, but inspiring others to believe in Who he stood for. Daniel could have nursed his injustices with a less than excellent spirit, and defile himself with a bad attitude, self pity, thoughts of revenge, and unforgiveness. He could have allowed the spirit of offense to take over and rot his soul...but instead he maintained an excellent spirit that brought him favor, promotion...*and bitter enemies.* His enemies could find nothing about Daniel to fault or criticize....*so they attacked his faith in his God,* hoping to destroy him through his faith. The king, having observed Daniel's faith and stand, assured Daniel upon being placed into the den..."*The God you love and serve will deliver you.*"

Your faith will also be tested and questioned. *"Is your God able to deliver you?"* Can you, like Daniel, go fearlessly into the den of lions? Can your faith sustain you when it is all that you have? Is your faith strong enough to inspire others to believe in the greatness of our Awesome God? Yes and absolutely...if you, like Daniel, love and know the God you serve! *When you stand for Him...He will stand up boldly, gloriously, and splendidly for you!*

June 20

Go To The Faith Place

Judges 6:12 "And the angel of the LORD appeared unto him, and said unto him, The LORD is with thee, thou mighty man of valor."

There is a place we can go that will elevate us to the status of a Champion! *It's called the "faith place".* It is the place where mountain movers are birthed and champions are created!

While it is human nature to cling to the comfort zones and safe places, *it is Divine nature to embrace the Faith places* - the place that will take us to new dimensions where champions walk. It is the place where peace abides and our spirits dare to believe for impossibilities! Faith people who walk in faith places are God pleasers! God loves risk takers who leave the comfort of complacency to take on the giants of mediocrity and impossibility. He is looking for men and women of valor who are willing to risk everything to gain what He offers.

He may be calling you to go somewhere you've never been before - *Go, for He is with you!* You may feel compelled to do something you've never done before - *do it!* You may have a dream that God wants to make a reality, but fear grips your heart when you think about the impossibility of that dream - *trust Him!* We want to know the whys and hows, but *all we really need to know is that He is calling us to do this and He is with us!* God doesn't always give us the full plan, but wants to know if we are willing and obedient to do what He says do. He wants us to get out of the safe place and go to the faith place - the place where ordinary men and women become Champions of Faith!

June 21

Sacrifices of the Heart

Genesis 42:36, 37 "And Jacob their father said to them, You have bereaved me: Joseph is no more, Simeon is no more, and you want to take Benjamin. All these things are against me. Then Reuben spoke to his father, saying, Kill my two sons if I do not bring him back to you; put him in my hands, and I will bring him back to you."

I wept as I read the story of Joseph and the reunion with his brothers, and I felt the sorrow that must have been overwhelming to them all. Although Joseph knew who they were, they were unaware of who he was...and *only knew him as a great ruler of Egypt and **not a brother**.* Condemnation weighed like heavy chains upon their guilty souls, and a heavy-hearted father who lost so much now faced losing even more. Sins of the past now demanded a sacrifice and *someone would have to pay.* The famine that was starving their bodies brought to surface the lies, deceit, and anguish that was hidden for many years. A family that was once intact and was the hope of all nations was now broken and torn apart. Their sins had caught up with them demanding that the debt be paid. A sacrifice would have to be made. A vow was made by one of the guilty brothers who broke under the weight of guilt and shame..."*Kill my own two sons if I fail to bring my brothers back.*" Sacrifices of the hearts were demanded....and offered.

There is nothing heavier to bear than the weight of guilt and condemnation. *Our Churches who were once filled with the glory and power of the Lord are now broken and stained with sin.* Once we offered hope and the saving power of Jesus to the world, but now offer empty entertainment and powerless programs. We cry out as Jacob, *"Joseph is no more, Simeon is no more, and now you're asking me to give up the last of my sons? Our hopes are gone, our future looks bleak, and now you want me to give up that which matters the most?"* Grievous sorrow has replaced the joy of the Lord, and we have lost our way. We make vows that are born out of desperation and anguish, but have little ability to carry them out. We know we must go back to the Source, but guilt and condemnation strike fear in our hearts to stand in the Presence of a Pure, Holy God. Our sins have found us out.

But there is a Joseph - *a Jesus* - whose heart is weeping over our condition. Guilt prevents us from seeing Him as our brother and Savior, and too often we see Him only as a Judge. No, it doesn't seem like we really know Him, but *He certainly knows us and weeps at the words of guilt and shame that come from our lips.* He has much to offer us and, just as Joseph forgave his brothers, Jesus also offers us complete forgiveness and reconciliation. He is closer than we think, and ready to receive us with open arms! He, and He only, will remove the heavy burdens of shame, guilt and sin that we have carried far too long. He only asks for our hearts...hearts that are willing to sacrifice everything to find the joy, forgiveness, and acceptance that He gives.

June 22

Take Your Brother

Genesis 43:13, 14 "Take also your brother, and arise, go again unto the man: And God Almighty give you mercy before the man, that he may send away your other brother, and Benjamin. If I be bereaved of my children, I am bereaved."

There are moments in our life when the *demands of a test will cause our faith to shine more brightly than ever before.* We find shining faith of this magnitude in the tests of sacrifice when we are willing to let go of what matters the most to us. It is found in the heart-wrenching prayers and cries of the Priests of the Lord *who weep for what once was and is gone,* and in the anguished plea of a Pastor or Parent crying out on behalf of the children. It is the same anguish that is heard as Esther cries out, *"If I perish, I perish!"* It is the same desperation heard in Rachel as she pleads, *"Give me children, lest I die."* That same painful cry can be heard in the voice of the Father as He pleads with us to intercede for each other, *"**Take your brother with you. Don't leave anyone behind**!"*

I hear the anguish of this father's cry..."*Joseph is no more! Simeon is no more! **Take also your brother!**"* And I see the trust, the faith that was a part of who Jacob was shining more brightly at this moment than at any other time in his life. The only thing he placed on the wagons of any real value was his youngest son. *He had to let go of that which he loved the most if he and his children were going to live,* and he had to put Benjamin in the trust and care of God. I can picture this old man as he tenderly places his boy on the wagon that would take him away. I can hear the plea, the desperation, and the anguish in his voice as he repeatedly tells his sons, *"Take him with you. Don't let him out of your sight. He is of utmost value to me. Take him to the place of life, of provision, of bread so he can live and not die. Guard him with your lives."* And finally, he passed his test of submission to God's will, *"If I am bereaved of my children, I am bereaved."*

The magnificent response of Reuben and Judah came out of hearts that knew pain, guilt, and sin, and from shoulders that were beaten down from burdens too painful to bear. They accepted full responsibility for their brother and were willing to make sacrifices to atone for their mistakes. They did not mind being inconvenienced to protect their brother. Once they would have been jealous that another received so much attention from their father, but now they protected that love, and vowed to do everything in their power to keep him safe. The commission was given...*and received with great humbleness and gravity.* Should we not do the same? We have been given that same commission. *We are our brothers' keepers.* Our hearts should ache at the thought of a brother or sister in danger, peril, or distress. We need each other! Not only do we need to rid ourselves of the excess things that have no real value, but we must rid ourselves of the petty jealousy, the strife, and the division, and care for one another as befitting heirs of God. We, like Reuben and Judah, need to grow up and assume responsibility for our brothers and sisters. *I hear the anguished plea of our Heavenly Father crying out to us, "Take your brother, watch over him, don't let him out of your sight...Take him to the place where there is life, provision, and bread. Don't leave anyone behind!"*

June 23

Be Strong In The Lord

Ephesians 6:10, 11 "Finally, my brethren, be strong in the Lord, and in the power of His might. Put on the whole armour of God, that ye may be able to stand against the wiles of the devil."

You are stronger than you think!

These tests that come your way are sent with God's permission. He knows what is inside of you and what you are made of, even better than you do. He has allowed certain things to test you that will refine and redefine who you are. *You will make it because He believes in you.* Your armor is God sent and specially anointed for this season in your life. You are fully equipped to handle whatever tests come your way, for your weapons of warfare are mighty and strong. Your strength seems insufficient, but He sends His power to you. Your enemy is tricky, sly, and conniving...but greater is He that is in you than he that is in the world!

You will pass this test. You are stronger, wiser, and braver than you were before. The test has revealed something powerful and potent that was perhaps lying dormant in you...a greater measure of faith and a greater measure of power! You are endued with His power, His strength, and His great faith in you to succeed! Be strong in the Lord...for greater things await you!

June 24

Don't Settle

Genesis 45:27 "...And when he saw the wagons which Joseph had sent to carry him, the spirit of Jacob their father revived."

Sometimes we cheat ourselves out of the best blessings because we settle for the first things we see. Remember the story of the blind man whom Jesus touched? Jesus asked, *"How do you see?"* He replied, *"I see men walking as trees."* And although that was a great improvement from seeing nothing to something, he needed a second touch...a second sign...to receive the fulfillment of the blessing.

The enemy would love for us to stop at the first sign. The first signs can throw us off course, causing us to settle for second best, and will deny us of our future. The first sign Jacob saw from Joseph was a bloody coat that fooled him. The second sign from Joseph was the wagons of provision. *The first sign nearly destroyed Jacob, but the second sign restored him.* The first sign of trouble can paralyze us, but the second sign of blessing can redeem us. The first sign of doubt can cripple us, but the second sign of faith can anoint us. The first sign of disaster can defeat us, but the second sign of victory can exalt us. The first sign of difficulty can ruin us, but the second sign of provision can prosper us.

We must not stop at the first sign! Look for the second sign. Persistent faith will not be defeated by how things appear to be, but believes the sure promises of God. We must not settle for the crumbs from the table, nor dwell in the land of mediocrity, hopelessness and second best. There is a second sign appearing on the horizon bringing hope, prosperity and destiny.

June 25

Listen...Someone is Cheering for You

Hebrews 12:1 "Therefore we also, since we are surrounded by so great a cloud of witnesses, let us lay aside every weight, and the sin which so easily ensnares us, and let us run with endurance the race that is set before us."

You have far more who are for you than against you! All of heaven is cheering you on! The great cloud of witnesses are standing up for you, and trusting you to win this battle you are fighting. Cheers and cries from these champions fill heaven's airways, saying, *"Get back on your feet! Victory is eminent! Stand! Fight! Recover All! You were made to win!"*

"Do you see what this means - all these pioneers who blazed the way, all these veterans cheering us on? It means we'd better get on with it. Strip down, start running - and never quit! No extra spiritual fat, no parasitic sins. Keep your eyes on Jesus, who both began and finished this race we're in. Study how he did it. Because he never lost sight of where he was headed - that exhilarating finish in and with God - he could put up with anything along the way: Cross, shame, whatever. And now he's there, in the place of honor, right alongside God. When you find yourselves flagging in your faith, go over that story again, item by item, that long litany of hostility he plowed through. That will shoot adrenaline into your souls!" (Hebrews 12:1-3 Message Bible)

This place you are in is not final, but greater victories lie ahead of you! This momentary setback is just temporary! He is right there with you, urging you forward, compelling you onward, and has placed your enemy under your feet! There is a place reserved for you in His Hall of Champions, so don't waver, don't quit, and don't settle! You *can* make it because *He* is with you!

June 26

I Will Not Let Go

Genesis 32: 26 "And he said, Let me go, for the day breaketh. And he said, I will not let thee go, except thou bless me."

Don't let go of your faith. Hold on to your dream that God seeded into your heart, for it is through dreams and visions that God shows us our purposes.

Before the Angel, he first had a dream...a dream in which God spoke amazing promises to him, promises that he had heard his father and grandfather speak of. Years later, still living in fear and tentative hope, Jacob has this second encounter with the Lord, *but he had to wrestle with the Lord to receive his blessings.* His faith and determination overrode the fears, the guilt, and the condemnation he might have felt. He became a changed man while wrestling with the Angel of the Lord...he was left with a limp, but his faith was stronger and more assured. He left the encounter broken and humble, but in his brokenness he was more of a man than he had ever been. He left with a name change...no longer was he called Jacob the deceiver, but Israel...the Prince of God!

There was something about this man that got Jacob's attention. Deep down in his soul Jacob knew that this man, this Angel of the Lord, would forever change his life. Beloved, we, too, will have an encounter with the Lord that will leave us changed, full of purpose and full of hope. *We may have to wrestle for it, we may have to overcome our failures of the past, and we might leave broken...but we will leave blessed of the Lord.* Determine to say as Jacob said, "I will not let go until You bless me." Some things are worth wrestling for! Some blessings must be wrestled for! Don't let go!

June 27

Anoint Your Words

Proverbs 18:21 "Death and life are in the power of the tongue: and they that love it shall eat the fruit thereof."
Psalm 141:3 "Set a guard upon my mouth, O Lord; keep watch over the door of my lips."
Job 4:4 "Your words have stood men on their feet."

The words we speak are a powerful force, setting things into motion that can build us up or tear us down. One word spoken in anger can destroy a life or break a heart. One unkind word spoken can inject a soul with bitterness and rejection. One harsh word can kill the seed of the greatest dream. *We can nurture our dreams and build bridges into our destiny by the power of our words.* What's inside of us will come out through the words we speak. Angry people say angry things. Critical people criticize. Sad people speak sadness. Hopeless people say despairing words. Pessimistic folks prophesy doom and gloom! Wise men speak wisdom! *Children of Light speak words of life, hope, purpose, and destiny!*

Our words should be anointed with grace and mercy. Every word spoken should be anointed in love and peace. Our words should bring life, hope, peace, reconciliation, and encouragement to those who hear them. We are not of this world, but are called to sit in heavenly places with Christ Jesus, speaking those things He spoke and sharing the Good News to those around us! Our mouths should not be filled with words that condemn, hurt, or bring pain to our listeners, for those are they ways of the world. We have the power to speak into lives...what are we speaking?

What do your words say about you? Is your tongue used to bless or curse? Are your dreams built up or torn down by what comes out of your mouth? Say what God says and speak what He speaks! *Agree with His Word!* Allow His Word entrance into the deep recess our your heart and spirit...and your mouth will line up with what He says!

June 28

The Power of Unity

Ephesians 4:3 "Be eager and strive earnestly to guard and keep the harmony and oneness of [and produced by] the Spirit in the binding power of peace."
Ephesians 4:13 "Till we all come in the unity of the faith, and of the knowledge of the Son of God, unto a perfect man, unto the measure of the stature of the fullness of Christ."

Oh, the great things we can do when we come together in unity! It's about coming together for Something and Someone who is so much bigger than us...*It's about Jesus, His Ministry and His Body! It's about unity and coming together in peace!* Why, even the animals are smart enough to realize unity works! Look at the geese who fly in formation and how they create a power source for those following. Watch and be amazed at the unspoken unity in the flock. When the one leading becomes weary and tired, he falls to the tail end of the formation *to rest on the wind power of the others*, as another leader steps up to the plate!

We are called to be One in the Spirit and One in the Faith, knit together in the binding power of peace! We are called to be perfect in unity and faith so we can grow into the fullness of Christ. It's about us rising to the occasion to do what He saved us to do - be One Body and One Spirit! If Christians would ever get their acts together we could turn this world upside down for Jesus! When we tear each other down, we are tearing down the Body of Christ. When we speak against the Church, we are condemning Him! When we rebel against the purposes of our Pastors, Teachers, Apostles, Prophets, and Evangelists (who are His Gifts to us), we are rebelling against God.

Too many times we don't get on board with the Church because the ideas didn't come from us. *We think we know so much more than the God-appointed leaders He has set over us, so we close a deaf ear to the message and refuse the message bearer!* This should not be so! Think of everything we can accomplish when we come together in unity! If one can put a thousand to flight, two can put ten thousand to flight! Our prayers are so much powerful when we pray in agreement! Our labor is far more productive when the Body gets involved! Our impact is felt all over the world when we speak as One, act as One, and walk as One! Churches are built, Souls are won, Burdens are lighter, Lives are changed and this Gospel is preached to the World when we work together! We are tied together in love, knit together in peace, and joined together in the Spirit! *Oh, the great things we can do for Christ when we walk in unity!*

June 29

Ties that Bind

John 17:20-21 "Neither pray I for these alone, but for them also which shall believe on me through their word; that they all may be one; as thou, Father, art in me, and I in thee, that they also may be one in us..."
Ephesians 4:3 "Be eager and strive earnestly to guard and keep the harmony and oneness of [and produced by] the Spirit in the binding power of peace."

The more I connect with Him, the more I find myself connecting with His Body of Believers. I will often feel someone tugging at my heart and *something in my spirit tells me to pray for them.* Sometimes the Lord will arouse me from sleep to pray for someone; other times I feel so connected with a person that I just *"can't get them out of my mind."* I later found out that this person was in need of prayer at the very moment I felt the urge to pray for them. It is the Supernatural Bond of the Spirit that connected me with these other members who needed the under-girding of prayer or encouragement.

This is what Jesus prayed for...that *we would be One in the Spirit with Him and with each other!* It is a rare thing these days to find people who are willing to knit themselves together. Oh, how precious and how pleasing it is to the Lord when we bind together and become as One! We are Divinely connected in Him! Our souls are knit together in such love that even distance and time cannot destroy the ties that bind! A soul tie is like a bridge between two people, a connection that can't be explained. I think of the soul tie between David and Jonathan: *"And it came to pass, when he had made an end of speaking unto Saul, that the soul of Jonathan was knit with the soul of David, and Jonathan loved him as his own soul."*

He loved him as his own soul! Oh, that we could be so connected! Oh, that we would be willing to take the plunge and invest ourselves into our brothers and sisters in Christ! *"**Make us One**,"* was the pleading prayer of Jesus! My prayer also is, *"Lord, give us ties that bind! Let us feel so connected with each other and the rest of Your Body that we know exactly what's going on in the Spirit! Teach us to love each other as You love us!"* Blest be the ties that bind!

June 30

There is Always Hope

Romans 5:5 "And hope maketh not ashamed; because the love of God is shed abroad in our hearts by the Holy Ghost which is given unto us."

Look around and you will see the faces of hopelessness. Look into the blank eyes of those who have lost all hope...and *you will see empty nothingness*. So many people are without hope and are just going through the motions, numb to feelings, numb to faith, and numb to life. They live just getting by and making it through one more day. This spirit of hopelessness and despair has even penetrated the Churches. We can barely hold our heads up and our worship is flat, lifeless, and dull. Trials are endured instead of embraced as challenges that make us stronger and victorious. We fight on in the battle, but we fight as those we are going to lose. *We fight as those who have no hope...*

May I say to you...*there is always hope*! Our hope lies in Jesus Christ. *He is our Door of Hope and will not allow us to be shamed or disappointed as long as we trust in Him!* We have hope because we have His love. Why should we be cast down when Jesus is our Lord! *There is always hope...until the last breath is taken...there is hope; until the war is over and the battle is finished...there is always hope; and until God says enough...there will remain hope for us!*

We are not victims in life, but we are Called, Chosen, Set Apart, Declared Overcomers, More than Conquerors, and Champions of Faith! We are not as the world that has no hope, but we have the blessed hope of better things to come. Talk to yourself in your moments of hopelessness. *Tell yourself that you are no victim, but you are mighty and strong in Christ Jesus, who causes you to always triumph*! Get up from your bed of despair. Let the wings of hope began beating in your breast, and as hope begins to beat again, the strength of God will conquer and defeat the spirit of hopelessness. We win! In the end...we win! As long as there is life, as long as there is faith, and as long as there is God...there will always, always be hope!

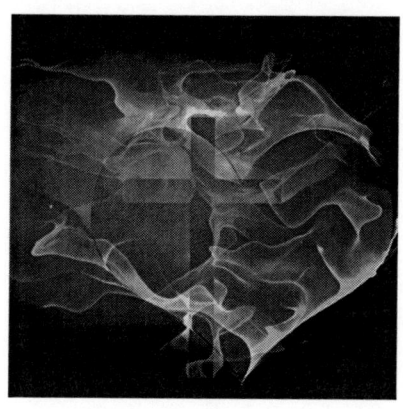

July

The clear summer nights are lit
up with a thousand lights
Reminding us to Shine brightly for Jesus...

July 1

You Are A Person of Interest

Deuteronomy 14:2 "For thou art an holy people unto the Lord thy God, and the Lord has chosen thee to be a peculiar people unto himself, above all the nations that are upon the earth."

You are of great importance to someone who cares deeply about you. You are a person of interest to the Lord.

Almighty God has taken a deep and personal interest in us, and has chosen us to be His. He created us with unique abilities and talents, and longs to be involved in our plans. He did not copy and paste us when He formed us, but designed us to be different from everyone else. *He has a personal interest in us and wants to be very involved in the fulfilling of our destiny.* Sometimes we think we have everything figured out...we are using our talents and skills, have made our plans for our future, but yet we are on the wrong path headed for a future that can bring disillusionment and disappointment. Our own plans, without God's direction and guidance, will never bring the complete fulfillment that we are so desperate to achieve. Sometimes we think that if we get God more involved in our lives, He will deny us the things we think we want the most. But when we understand that He created us to live a life of purpose, fulfillment, achievement and satisfaction, it is easier for us to turn the reigns over to Him. *He takes great personal interest in us, and will not deny us any good thing.* He has reserved the very best for us...if we have the faith to trust Him. He will not lead us down the wrong paths...if we give Him control of our lives.

He loves us and dreams great things for us...dreams that can only be fulfilled if we cooperate with His plans for us. *Everything else is second best!* He thoughts are towards us and His plans are amazing. We are people of interest, set apart and chosen for His purpose...and He wants us to involve Him in our plans.

July 2

You Have Been Chosen

2 Corinthians 4:7 "But we have this treasure in earthen vessels, that the excellency of the power may be of God, and not of us."
1 Samuel 13:14 "But now thy kingdom shall not continue: the LORD hath sought him a man after his own heart..."

Some folks often despise the little things, thinking these tiny, small things are beneath them. They want big things and the positions of influence and power that often result in pride setting up a throne in the hearts. They think insignificant, little things and nobodies are beneath them and not worthy of care, of giving proper attention to, or of heartfelt involvement. *Such thinking arises from a certain ignorance of the value of little things.* Our thoughts and measurements of what is important are so different from God's, for *we focus on the quantity, but God is looking for quality.*

God chooses His vessels with a different point of view than man does. He looks at the little ways a person conducts themselves. He chooses a faithful David from a sheep field when men choose a handsome Saul for his strength. He chooses Joshua the servant to be the next Leader. He chooses a small army of 300 with lamps and trumpets instead a great massive army. *Your greatest moments in life are the moments of obedience. Every small act of obedience is a stepping stone into God's greatness!* It is the hidden things that God looks for in His chosen vessels: integrity, honesty, commitment, faithfulness...*and always obedience.* **Chosen vessels are always vessels of quality.**

You have been chosen by the Hand of God...hand-picked to be His vessel of honor and to bear His name! The magnitude of our calling should awe us. When we stand in the presence of God, responding to His calling, we should stand reverently and honestly before Him. *Not only have we been found, we have been chosen.* As Philippians 2:3, 4 says, "*Don't push your way to the front; don't sweet talk your way to the top. Put yourself aside, and help others get ahead. Don't be obsessed with getting your own advantage. Forget yourselves long enough to lend a helping hand.*" (The Message) And then...God will send the promotions and the honor, and He will receive the glory!

July 3

Dare To Be Unconventional

Mark 11:22 "...Have faith in God."

God is looking for people who are willing to risk everything for their faith...*people who will go to the extreme in their faith to get what they need.* I confess that for the most part, I do my best to comply and conform to protocol and policies and to obey the laws of our land. I believe in order and doing things right. It is what God expects from us. *However, there is a place in my faith-walk that takes me far beyond the ordinary, mundane thinking and into the supernatural realm where my faith can move mountains!*

God has precious believers who will not allow traditions, formalities and convention stand in their way of getting to Him. *Sometimes we need to ignore the protocol to get to the miracles!* Jesus healed seven times on the Sabbath...something very unconventional in His day. *Sometimes we have to separate ourselves from our needs to get to the miracles!* The Centurion Captain told the Lord, *"Just send Your Word and my servant will be healed. Your Word is enough!"* Sometimes *we have to be willing to be buffeted and bumped to get to the miracles.* The woman with the issue of blood had to press through the crowds and risk being poked, and pushed, yet she pressed through until she touched the hem of His garment. *Sometimes we have to risk being insulted to get to the miracles.* The Syrophonecian woman only wanted a crumb of healing for her daughter, and refused to be denied by Jesus, even though He told her she was not a part of the "right" group of people. *Sometimes we have to worship through our blindness to get to the miracles.* Bartimaeus would not let the crowds hinder his worship, but only cried out louder until he got the attention of Jesus! *Sometimes we have to be willing to go the unconventional way to get to the miracles.* Four young men refused to give up on their friend's miracle, and literally went through the roof to get to Jesus! *Sometimes we have to be willing to give our most precious gifts to get the blessings.* Mary gave her most valued gift to the Lord...precious anointment that cost about a years wages, and poured it upon His feet in extravagant worship.

Where there is a will, there is a way! Where there is faith, the way has been made! Our faith is creative when it comes to getting our needs met! When we are desperate enough, hungry enough, thirsty enough, and willing to do whatever it takes, we will touch the miracles! Dare to be unconventional with faith - it will take you on exciting journeys and into the land of miracles!

July 4

The Cost of Freedom

John 8:36 "He whom the Son sets free is free indeed!"

I attended a Salute to Veterans concert with my daughter and five year old grandson, Blaise. The room was full of older veterans and their families. My dear friend was also singing and remarked, *"This is a great country!"* I thought, *"Yes, this is the best country in the world...and these brave men and women sitting here tonight fought hard for the freedoms and liberties we so enjoy today."* Freedom and liberty demanded a terrible price, but it was a price they willingly and proudly paid. ***Many say they love our country, but these brave soldiers proved it.*** One of the most touching moments was the clips showing the bombing of our ships at Pearl Harbor as it told the story of one soldiers' survival. This living, in person, hero shared how when he surfaced from the sinking ship he noticed our flag was not flying. *He bravely went back into the ship to where the flag was kept, took it out, and amidst the bombings, climbed the ships mast to hang the flag.* Many of the survivors later shared how the sight of our country's flag flying high gave them courage and strength to press on. My grandson learned something of great value last night, as did I. *Freedom and liberty comes with great cost.*

Jesus Christ also paid a terrible price for our freedom and liberty from sin and eternal death. He, too, willingly paid the price for my salvation. There was no flag hanging as an emblem of my salvation...only the spotless Lamb of God hanging on a rugged tree with blood streaming down from His dear head, face, back, hands and feet - the precious blood of Jesus that atoned for the sins of the world. Yes, there was a war going on that day...the greatest war in history...but victory was wrought and freedom and liberty offered to whosoever will come. *Freedom comes with a price.* I am proud of my country and of the men and women who bravely have fought for her and continue to fight for her. I am prouder still of the One who calls Himself King of Kings and Lord of Lords...

July 5

Not Might, Nor Power

Zechariah 4:6 "...Not by might, nor by power, but by My Spirit, saith the Lord of hosts."

We serve a God of wonders who spoke our world and universe into existence and breathed eternity into the soul of Adam! *He breathed and everything that was in His mind was released into existence!* The heavenlies were formed by His Spirit! No wonder He tells us that it is not by might nor by power, but by His Spirit!

In the midst of the power and wisdom of this world, there is a Redeemer who with just a word calmed a tempest! With just a word He resurrected a dead Lazarus and widow's son! With just a word He opened blind eyes and deaf ears! *If we must be impressed, let us be impressed with the greatness of our God!* If we want to be awed, read about the power of His word! He has not changed and is the same now as He has always been! *Just as the Spirit of the Lord moved upon the waters in Genesis 1:2, so He is once again moving upon the earth!* The Spirit of the Lord is moving upon us bringing great revelations! It is not power and might that we need, but the Spirit of the Lord falling on us and filling us! When His Spirit is welcomed, wanted, and sought after, He will come, raining upon us all that we thirst for!

July 6

Our Good - His Glory

Romans 8:28 "And we know that all things work together for good to them that love God, to them who are the called according to His purpose."

If Job, Daniel or Joseph could speak to us today, I believe they would tell us that the trials they went through were for their good and God's glory! They had to walk it out, not knowing how it would all end, but nevertheless trusting God with a faith that was remarkable! This should inspire us to know that in our own times of testing and trials, something good will come out of them that will bring great glory to God!

I have often shared how God uses pain to birth a pearl. A small grain of sand will become lodged in the oyster that causes irritation and pain. The oyster will begin coating that irritant with layer after layer of mother of pearl until a beautiful pearl has been formed. The greater the irritant and pain, the more glorious the pearl! God puts us in the center of a stage, turns on the spot light and says, "Let me demonstrate and prove what I am in the life of this child of mine." So even though it's a time of testing for us, it's a time of glorifying Him in a way that the smooth places in our lives could never do. He uses our pain and irritants to form beautiful pearls in us!

We will sing great songs of deliverance only when we have been greatly delivered! We can sing songs of great victory only when we have achieved great victories! God can showcase the beautiful pearls in us once we have gone through great trials and testings...and *He will* showcase His pearls!

July 7

Before and After

2 Corinthians 3:18 "But we all, with open face beholding as in a glass the glory of the Lord, are changed into the same image from glory to glory, even as by the Spirit of the Lord."

You've seen those ads that show the 98 pound weakling being bullied on the beach. Then...fast forward to the after that shows him buff and strong, taking out the bully! Or, what about those makeover shows that transform homelies into beauties. You've seen the before and after pictures - wow, what a difference!

Jacob was a deceiver, but a son of promise. Before his encounter with the angel, Jacob was a con-artist who stole his brothers' birthright, and relied upon his wit and strength. Before, Jacob was a coward who ran away to a place where the deceiver was deceived! Fast forward where Jacob came to the place of his makeover called Peniel, which meant, facing God. A great transformation occurred! After the struggle, Jacob's strength was diminished, but God's was increased. After the struggle he changed from a deceiver to a prince! Before he was a coward and 98 pound weakling, but after he was a prince that had favor with God and man!

Yes, we go through some trials and tests! But we come out stronger than we went in! We may go in as weaklings, but we come out as powerhouses! *We may go in looking timid and afraid, but we come out looking like champions and kings!* It is through each test that we are changed into His image, going from glory to glory! Now that is a transformation!

July 8

Give God Time

Isaiah 49:23 "...I am the Lord; for they shall not be ashamed that wait for me."

We serve a God of precise timing. The planet we live on is precisely calculated to spin on its axis once every 23 hr. 56 min. The earth moves around the sun, in an elliptical (but nearly circular) orbit, once a year. Because of this, and the tilt of the earth's axis, *we experience the seasons.* This orbit also causes a solar day to be 24 hours instead of 23 hr. 56 min. God has exact and precise timing to carefully plan the seasons. *If planet Earth can trust God for exact and precise timing, shouldn't we as living, breathing humans formed in His image also trust Him to perform the things He has appointed for us!*

We sometimes get so impatient with God and don't give Him the time He needs to perfect the things He has appointed for us. We rush into things without waiting for God to say, "Go." Many times we miss the mark, or get ahead of God, or don't wait for Him. We will often find ourselves "out of sync" with God, or with what's going on in the Church as we try to hurry Him up. He has exact and precise timing and has carefully planned each season for us. Our greatest blessings will come as we wait upon Him for His perfect plan. We must not get distracted or anxious by what we see or feel. He has great plans for us that will be delivered to us in His perfect timing! God is working things out for our good!

GIVE GOD TIME! Even when the knife is in the air, you will see the ram in the bushes. Give God time, even when Pharaoh's armies are on your heels, a path through the waters will be opened up. Give God time, even when the brook is dry, we will hear the guiding voice. Trust in His perfect timing!

July 9

Who Are You?

Acts 19:15 "And the evil spirit answered and said, Jesus I know, and Paul I know; but who are ye?"

We have two choices once we meet Jesus Christ - *we can have an experience or we can have a transformation!* I prefer the transformation, especially since I don't like the ways of the old man very much! We can be sincere, serious followers of Jesus or we can be Sunday Christians. We can know Him or we can know about Him. I prefer to know Him.

Hell knows those who know Him...and trembles when you speak His Name! Hell recognizes those who have the dunamis power of God blazing in their hearts and souls! Evil spirits flee from the presence of a blood-washed, born again, Spirit-filled Child of God! Your name is known, not only in the portals of Heaven, but in the gates of Hell. Not because of you - *but because of He who lives in you - Jesus in you is what makes the difference!*

We can get ourselves into some pretty serious trouble when we just go for the experience and not the transformation! Our feeble attempts to overcome the old sinful nature result in frustration and defeat. But once we allow Jesus to transform us, to renew our minds, and to cleanse us from the shame, guilt and sins of the old life, we take on His nature, His love, and His forgiveness. We have His power working in us...and even Hell knows who we are!

July 10

There Will Be A Day

1 Sam. 2:7 "God brings death and God brings life, brings down to the grave and raises up. God brings poverty and God brings wealth; He lowers, He also lifts up. He puts poor people on their feet again; He rekindles burned-out lives with fresh hope, Restoring dignity and respect to their lives— a place in the sun! For the very structures of earth are God's; He has laid out his operations on a firm foundation. He protectively cares for his faithful friends, step by step, but leaves the wicked to stumble in the dark. No one makes it in this life by sheer muscle! God's enemies will be blasted out of the sky, crashed in a heap and burned. God will set things right all over the earth, He'll give strength to his King, He'll set His anointed on top of the world!"

Things will not remain as they are now, but one day soon, our King will render our enemies helpless and bring us out of the shadows. This season will pass as a new day dawns, bringing restoration, gladness, and fresh hope!

We sometimes feel as though we have been battered by the winds of adversity that have blown fiercely against us. We have poured every ounce of strength into that which He has called us to, but the results have been disappointing. We have given everything we have had to give and now feel empty and desolate. Our strength has waned and we feel burned out with life. We wonder when we will ever be on top again. *But, there will be a day when the tides will change and the God who put you in this place where you are now will bring you out!*

He will raise us to our feet again! We will stand tall and with heads held high as our God restores His Church with His power and His Glory. *The flames that have died will burn again with fresh hope!* He will restore our dignity and bring respect to His beloved people. He will lift us out of these ashes of defeat and seat us in high places. There will be a day when God will set everything right. *Our King will come and restore us to places of honor, righteousness, and power.* There will be a day...and it won't be very long. If you can just hold on a little longer, He will not disappoint.

July 11

Every Injustice Will Be Made Right

2 Samuel 2:10 "God will set things right all over the earth..."

One day soon every injustice will be made right. Every wrong will be made right. It's enough for me right now...and gives me the strength and faith to keep fighting the good fight of faith!

Each unfair, unjust deed *is* remembered and logged into His Book of Life. Nothing escapes His sight, but He sees the unrighteous acts committed against the innocent. We can't understand why little children go hungry and are starving to death. We don't understand why life is so very good for some...and so incredibly difficult for others. We find it hard to comprehend why men love the darkness rather than light. It astounds us when evil is called good, and good is called evil. Why do the innocent pay for the crimes committed against them by the guilty. We wonder why these things are allowed to continue. *But there will be a day when God says, "It is enough!"* There will be a day when He will no longer tolerate the injustices against His children...and *He will send His King to put an end to the reign of sin, unrighteousness, and injustices.*

Our King has not forgotten about us! Our Messiah will come for us. On that day when we shall see Him, *every injustice will be made right.* One look into His eyes of love and all wrongs done to us will pass away, and we will remember them no more. On that day when we bow before Him, every injustice, every unkindness, and every hurtful thing done to us will also bow to Him as He rights every wrong. And for now, it is enough just to know He will rule justly and righteously.

July 12

Not Of This World

John 18:26 "Jesus answered, My kingdom is not of this world."

It grabbed my attention! The little blue Volkswagen in front of me captured my full attention as I read the following statement that was on the rear window... *"Not of this world."* I felt translated into another dimension and released from burdens as the full truth of that statement made its way into my spirit! The impact of this simple truth was profound and liberating, bringing my thoughts to the place where I have established my eternal citizenship! Yes, I am in this world, making my presence felt by bringing salt and light to it, but thankfully, *I belong to another Kingdom*! HEAVEN - it surpasses our vocabulary & imagination!

John describes heaven in Revelation. *"And I John saw the holy city...coming down from God out of heaven. And I heard a great voice out of heaven saying, Behold, the tabernacle of God is with men, and he will dwell with them, and they shall be his people, and God himself shall be with them, and be their God. And God shall wipe away all tears from their eyes; and there shall be no more death, neither sorrow, nor crying, neither shall there be any more pain: for the former things are passed away. And he that sat upon the throne said, Behold, I make all things new."*

Heaven is the dwelling place of God and the elect angels. The everlasting home of the redeemed. AN ACTUAL PLACE! In John 14:2, it's called *"Father's House"*, In Hebrews 11:16 , *"Heavenly Country"* Revelation 14:13 describes it as a place of *"Rest"* , 2 Corinthians 12:14 refers to it as *"Paradise"*, In Luke 13:29, Jesus calls it the *"Kingdom of God"*. We are temporary dwellers of this world and will one day be promoted....Released from the burdens of this world. One day we will receive furlough from the battle zone and relocate to a better climate. We will be instantly transported to the celestial city. Our citizenship and treasure should be in Heaven. There is something in man that earth cannot satisfy! No matter the case - earth cannot satisfy the longing! One glimpse of Heaven and earth loses it's value! The Eternal city is so wonderful that the best way for John to describe it is with contrast to earth! No more sun, night, seas, curse, death, tears, pain. *This world is not my home, I'm only passing through. My treasures are laid up somewhere beyond the blue. The angels beckon me from Heaven's open door and I can't feel at home in this world anymore!"*

July 13

Soul Winners Needed

James 5:20 "Let him know, that he which converts the sinner from the error of his way shall save a soul from death, and shall hide a multitude of sins."
Proverbs 11:30 "The fruit of the righteous is a tree of life, And he who wins souls is wise."

God loves sinners. In fact, He loves them so much He is sending YOU to give them the message that He loves them and desires to save them from their sins. Some will need convincing, some will reject His love, but some will receive the message and be transformed by the power of that love! *He has put out a "soul winners needed" sign* and is looking for applicants who can show His kindness, His love, His mercy, and forgiveness to. *Judgmental, condemning, self-centered, cold hearted, pleasure seekers need not apply.*

My heart was deeply moved when I met with the young parents who had just lost their baby. They expressed their belief and faith that their baby was sent to them for the purpose of turning hearts to Jesus and getting their souls right with God. They expressed hopes that perhaps some friend or family member would have such a desire to see their baby again that they would give their hearts to Christ. They were very *"soul minded"* and their simple, child-like trust that God would use their baby to win hearts to Him stirred my soul and moved me beyond words.

It's time we who are called by His Name become more *"soul minded"* and begin searching for someone we can share Jesus Christ with. We have the only truth that can transform lives. We serve the only Savior who has the power to forgive sins and cleanse unrighteousness. We don't hear many sermons today about soul winning, but it's what the churches need most - sermons preached with intensity, passion, and conviction that will light a fire in us and set our hearts ablaze with love for the sinners and concern for their eternal salvation. Our Churches need to be soul-saving stations that beckon all to Christ, leading men to salvation. Heaven has posted the "soul winners needed" sign...*I wonder who will apply!*

July 14

We Are Light

Matthew 5:14-16 "You are the light of the world. A city set on a hill cannot be hidden. Nor do people light a lamp and put it under a basket, but on a stand, and it gives light to all in the house. In the same way, let your light shine before others, so that they may see your good works and give glory to your Father who is in Heaven."

You possess the great ability to light the way for others to find Christ! Jesus describes Himself as *The Light of the World,* then tells us that we are the lights of the world! He exhorts us to let our lights shine before others, so they may see our good works and give the Father glory! *Our lights are our Christian Testimonies, just as salt is our Christian witness!*

Light is described as a form of energy and is always moving! When light energy ceases to move because it has been absorbed by matter, it is no longer light. Light is the symbol of the Divine Presence of a Holy God! Light exposes and dispels darkness. Light serves as a guide. Light is to be seen - there is no such thing as a secret Christian!

Does our Light shine brightly in the darkness of this world? Do we live lives that cause the world to see Christ in us? Do we take our Light with us when we leave the Church, and bring it to the lost and darkened world? How desperately this world needs for believers to shine brightly, dispelling the darkness around them. Shine brightly for Him, take Him with you everywhere you go, and let others see your good works!

July 15

Let Me Be Salty

Matthew 5:13 "You are the salt of the earth; but if the salt loses its flavor, how shall it be seasoned? It is then good for nothing but to be thrown out and trampled underfoot by men."

It's amazing to think that we have such a powerful impact on everyone we encounter - *sometimes good and sometimes leaving a bad taste!* Funny how long the bad taste lasts! But think about something you craved or desired and immediately wonderful memories will surface.

Have you ever been around a *"salty"* Christian? Just being in their presence was an uplifting experience, bringing encouragement and joy. Salt is a mineral with lasting effects. Jesus says, *"You are the salt of the earth."* He is saying that those who follow Him are like salt: ***They are called to make a difference in the world.*** The difference we make is *"the flavor"*, causing others to develop a thirst for Christ. It only takes a little salt to flavor a whole community, a whole neighborhood, or a whole workplace. As Christians we are called to season the lives of others and to influence the people we come in contact with. Salt is hardly seen. Yet too little of it leaves a bland taste and too much of it can ruin your food..

We have the wonderful opportunity today to flavor someone's life just by being in their presence. All of us should desire to be salty and be a good influence on someone as we create in them a thirst for Him!

July 16

Take The Name of Jesus

Philippians 2:9-11 "Wherefore God hath highly exalted him, and given him a name which is above every name that at the name of, Jesus every knee should bow of things in heaven, and things in earth, and things under earth; and that every tongue should confess that Jesus Christ is Lord, to the glory of God the Father."

There is a Name...*a Name that we should take with us everywhere we go.* We should take it with us to work, to the grocery store, and to our schools. *We should take it with us to our business meetings, and when we stand before kings and presidents, governors and leaders.* We should keep Him close with us at all times, ever mindful of His holy Presence. This Name is the key to abundant living and life everlasting. Demons tremble at that Name and Christians rejoice in that Name, for in this Name only lies the hope of all mankind and the power to redeem a soul from death. This Name has the power to heal the sick and to raise the dead, to give sight to blind eyes, and peace to a troubled mind. Don't leave this precious Name behind, but take it with you everywhere you go.

Mrs. Lydia Baxter wrote this song that still blesses us today:

"Take the name of Jesus with you,
Child of sorrow and woe;
It will joy and comfort give you;
Take it then where'er you go.
Precious name, 0 how sweet!
Hope of earth and joy of heaven."

The apostle Paul in Colossians 3:17 proclaimed, *"And whatsoever ye do in word or deed, do all in the name of the Lord Jesus, giving thanks to God and the Father by hi*m." I admonish my fellow Christians everywhere *to take the name of Jesus with you all the way.* Carry His Name as a banner, lifted high for all to see!

July 17

48 Hour Challenge

Acts 13:47, 48 "For so hath the Lord commanded us, saying, I have set thee to be a light of the Gentiles, that thou should be for salvation unto the ends of the earth. And when the Gentiles heard this, they were glad, and glorified the Word of the Lord: and as many as were ordained to eternal life believed."

Are you ready for a challenge? We are called to be lights to everyone that we encounter, ministering the truth in love. They are there by divine appointment, and we are to see their needs, their loneliness, their longings, and reach out to them in love.

God is wooing people all around us and it's up to us to show them His light. Take a second look the next time we see someone in the line ahead of us at the grocery store. Look again at our co-worker who appears to have it all together, but is crying out to God in quiet desperation. Listen for the cries of the hurting and lonely. The Spirit of God has been preparing their hearts to receive the words of life that we have to offer them. He has appointed salvation for them and they will receive it with gladness. Ask Him to open our eyes and ears. Be soul-minded by bringing hope and life to those who are ready for Him. Are you ready? Are you willing? Someone is waiting for you to show them the way!

July 18

The Influence of Kindness

Ephesians 4:32 "Be kind and compassionate to one another, forgiving each other, just as in Christ God forgave you."

Kindness will influence more than eloquent words.

Kindness seems to be a thing of the past. Our culture is swept into the mindset of an "eye for an eye" and every day there are more examples of just how cruel people can be to one another. How refreshing it is when we find a kind person - a person who allows the love of Christ to flow through them to touch a heart that is burdened, hurting or discouraged. Oh that we would be kinder and gentler people - showing this present generation that we are the children of a loving and kindhearted God! We seem to think that by showing kindness we are showing weakness, but in reality we are showing the heart of the Father. The Psalmist said, *"Thy loving-kindness is better to me than life."*

To show kindness is to be considerate and gracious in all situations *regardless of circumstances*. This is indeed a difficult calling to answer but it is an essential one that we must answer to grow more like Christ. Kindness means that we care for the feelings of others and show them compassion, mercy, understanding, love and tenderness. *It means to be aware of a person's hurts, sufferings and problems.* The next time someone gets on your nerves, treats you badly, or mistreats you in any other way, remember that Christ died for them. Take time to be kind.

July 19

IF

Matthew 4:3 "And when the tempter came to him, he said, If thou be the Son of God..."
Genesis 3:1 "...And he said unto the woman, Yea, hath God said..."

One little word, yet it can plant seeds of doubt that become stubborn weeds in our gardens of faith. One little word, yet it can offset, tear down, second guess and uproot the best laid plans.

The serpent came to Eve and planted this tiny seed of doubt..."*Did God say?*" The seed of doubt found fertile ground and the rest is history. Years later, this same subtle attack was used against Jesus in the wilderness. He came when Jesus was weary, hungry, and weak, posing this one question..."*If...?*" *If you are the Son of God... Satan challenged the credentials of Jesus and Who He was - Son of God, Savior of the World, Prince of Peace, King of Kings...* His attempts to get Jesus to second guess Himself were futile, for *there was no fertile ground for seeds of doubt to grow.* Jesus, who was the Word, filled Himself with the Word!

We don't understand why God sometimes brings us to a wilderness...a dry, barren land of nothing where the wild animals hide...a place that is hostile and empty. It is in this place we face some of our greatest challenges of faith...*did God really say?* Satan comes to us in our moments of weakness, weariness and loneliness with his seeds of doubt. He will do everything he can to cause us to doubt God, His Word...and who we are in Christ. "*Did God really say that? Where are the blessings now? Don't you think if God was in this dream it would have happened by now? What are you going to do now...this didn't work?*" Fill up on the Word of God, resist the devil and he will flee! Cast down the "*if's*" and fill your mind with God's "*will's*"!

July 20

Our Eyes Are Upon You

2 Chronicles 20:12, 15 "...We have no power to face this great army that is attacking us. We do not know what to do, but our eyes are on You....Fear not and be not dismayed at this great multitude; for the battle is not yours but the Lord's."

He keeps reminding me to stand still. Stay focused and keep my eyes upon Him! He will amaze us with His God-ness! He tells me, *"Stand still and see my salvation!"*

Sometimes God just wants us to let Him be God! He just wants us to believe Him in spite of how it looks. God is ready and eager to show up and be God for us! He stands ready to defend those who trust Him. He is anxious to get involved in our affairs if we will simply cast our eyes upon Jesus! ***Stop asking, "Can God?", but say, "God Can!"*** He stands at the tomb of a dead Lazarus and calls, *"Come forth!"* He strides upon the waves of a storm *and commands peace.* His voice is heard in the trumpets and His glory shines in the lamps of a 300. His glory cloud rests upon the singers who sing *"Praise the Lord for His mercy endures forever!"* They behold His saving power as God comes through for them and He sets ambushes against the great army attacking them.

He keeps telling me, *"When you trust Me and look to Me, there is no need to fear."* Life can be difficult, and in the battle there are all sorts of struggles. If we will keep our eyes upon Him He will show us His salvation! Open the gates and let the King of Glory come in!

July 21

Help In The Sanctuary

Psalm 20:1, 2 "May the LORD answer you in the day of trouble; May the name of the God of Jacob defend you...May he send you help from the sanctuary and grant you support from Zion."

The Lord doesn't always answer when and how we want Him to, but we can be assured that *He will answer us in the day of trouble.* He *will* defend us against our enemies. He has provided a place where we can find help in troubled times...*it is in the sanctuary*!

The Sanctuary! Webster defines it as *"a consecrated place: the most sacred part of a religious building: a place for worship: a place of refuge and protection <u>where predators are controlled and hunting is illegal.</u>"* No wonder David loved the sanctuary! We find rest from the weariness in the sanctuary! We find hope and comfort. We find relief from the predators when we go to the sanctuary. The sanctuary is a place of worship, a place where our spirits commune with His. It is a place where we receive help and strength. God sends us help from the sanctuary!

God sends his support from Zion, and Friend, when he does, *watch out*. He will deliver, and He will do so in a mighty way. While some trust in chariots and some trust in horses, we trust in the Name that is above every name, the only Name by which we can be saved - *Jesus!* If you need help, go to the Sanctuary! Find a place to commune with Him. He will defend you. He will answer you. He will send you help and support in the days of trouble.

July 22

When I Need Him The Most

John 11:11 "He said to them, Our friend Lazarus sleeps, but I go that I may wake him up."

God is so good, isn't He! He never fails to show up *when I need Him*, especially in the most desperate times of my life! I can find Him on every page of my life, sustaining me, keeping me, comforting me, and forgiving me!

Jesus came to Martha and Mary when they needed Him the most! From their viewpoint it seemed that the Lord was too late and even He could not help them now. *But He came at the right time...the time when all hope was gone and all their dreams had died!* He came when their sorrow was inconsolable and their pain was unbearable. He came when they needed Him the most to recover what they had lost, to heal their broken hearts and to restore a future that had been snatched away. He came bringing light to their darkened minds and joy to their grieving souls!

He has always been there for me, especially during the times when I needed Him the most. He is with me always, but somehow, it is in the hours that are most desolate and lonely that I can feel His tender love the strongest! It is when I feel lost that He reveals Himself as *"The Way!"* It is when I feel pain that I know Him as *"My Healer"*! It is when I feel anxious that I know Him as *"Prince of Peace"*! I know that He will be there in all of my tomorrows, helping me to continue writing the book of my life!

July 23

Pay Close Attention

Isaiah 30:21 "Whether you turn to the right or to the left, your ears will hear a voice, saying, This is the way; walk in it."

Are you in transition? Is everything around you changing and you don't know if it is good or not so good? Does it seem there are so many different directions you can take, but are unsure which direction is the right path for you? *Then, pay close attention, for God has the answer you seek.*

We have entered into a season of prayer...a season of bending our knees to seek God's face for direction and understanding of the times. For many of us, it will usher in seasons of change, the season of new beginnings, and the season of new dimensions. As we earnestly pray the fervent prayers that avail much, we will hear the Word of the Lord directing us as He orders our steps. As we embrace our season of prayer, the Lord will send understanding, knowledge and revelation, as well as completion, fulfillment, and empowerment. It's time to let go of our preconceived notions, what we know and what we think we know...*and pay close attention to His voice.* It is not by might, nor by our own power, intellect, wisdom, talent, skills, but by His Spirit...so pay attention! He will reveal His secrets to us. He will give us divine instruction. Through prayer, the Lord will speak, *"This is the way for you to go...walk into it."* It is through prayer that we will obtain the information needed to take us to our next level!

The next season we walk into will be an important season. It is a time of letting go of the old carnal ways to embrace the new heavenly places! Pay close attention...be open to what He has for you, and where He will take you...*for He will bring you through floods and fires to establish you in this next season of your life. Prayer is the transportation that will take us...into our best, new season!*

July 24

What Is God Thinking

Isaiah 55:8, 9 "For My thoughts are not your thoughts, Nor are your ways My ways, says the LORD. For as the heavens are higher than the earth, So are My ways higher than your ways, And My thoughts than your thoughts."

Lately I find myself seeking God's face with a passion *to know what He is thinking.* The opinions of others aren't important, but what matters most is that my thinking is in alignment with His.

"God thinks purpose, passion, and vision, while we think need." (A. David) While we are so consumed with ME, God is thinking ALL. While we think NEED, God is thinking DESTINY! We think NOW, but God is thinking FUTURE! We forfeit our destiny and our future for momentary comforts and short term solutions. Like Esau, we fail to see the greatness of God's future plans and see only our immediate hunger and pressing need. Joseph saw beyond the pit, beyond the prison...and thought like God thought about himself. He could have asked, *"God, what ARE you thinking?"*, but instead he trusted that God's ways were much higher than his. He aligned his thinking with God's! He thought beyond the momentary discomfort of the pit, past the heartbreaking rejection of his brothers, and saw his future in God's thinking.

Many of us wonder, *"What in the world is God thinking?"* He is thinking hope. He is thinking future. He is thinking, "I *knew you in your mother's womb and I know the plans I have for you."* He is thinking of you today, and His thoughts towards you are thoughts of trust, love, compassion, and victory.

July 25

I Have Prayed For You

Hebrews 7:25 "Wherefore he is able also to save them to the uttermost that come unto God by him, seeing he ever liveth to make intercession for them."
John 17:20 "Neither pray I for these alone, but for them also which shall believe on me through their word."

There are and will be times when we need someone to stand in the gap for us, offering us the support of prayer from someone who can touch God for us. Many times requests for prayer come in to my office from all parts of the world from people who need answers and need them immediately. *We have seen God answer many of these prayers because we have reached out to Him in faith, believing that He alone is able to do what we can't do.* There are also times when *it seems* that our prayers aren't being answered, and Heaven has closed herself to us. Those are the times when we must trust that God has heard and will answer...for after all, we have called upon our Great High Priest who is seated at the right hand of the Father, and is taking our requests and prayers to the Father for us. *When Jesus prays...something has to happen!*

John 17 is all about Jesus' prayers for those who follow Him and those who will believe in Him. Jesus' phrase, *"them which shall believe on me,"* includes you and me. Jesus was praying for us when He walked this earth in the flesh! He even recorded this prayer in His Word, knowing we would be reading it. He wants us to know He was interceding for us to the Father! God has accepted His Son's prayer for each of us! That is why we are in Him today - because God answered His prayer for us!

He prayed for us when He walked upon this earth in the flesh... but He continues to pray for us! *He lives to make intercession for us,* taking each prayer, every request and every petition that we pray to His Father. *If anyone can get the Father's attention, it is Jesus!* If ever a prayer is answered, it is surely the prayers that Jesus prays! His prayers are not delayed, not held up, not hindered and not put on the back burner, but they are powerful, timely, and productive! Today Jesus is praying for you! He is interceding to the Father on your behalf!

July 26

That Your Faith Fail Not

Luke 22:32 "I have prayed for thee, that thy faith fail not..."

We are in warfare, not only for the well-being of our churches, families and nation, but *we are engaged in battles against principalities and spiritual wickedness that are attacking the very faith that we believe in.* This onslaught of demonic forces is relentless and can be devastating if we are not rooted and grounded in the truth. We are in a fight for our survival and the survival of Christianity as we know it today. Forces are at work to destroy our faith and shake us to the core, causing us to second guess God and question everything we know as truth.

Jesus told Peter, "*Satan desires to sift you as wheat,* or *Satan has demanded to have you to sift you.*" The sifting here refers to a repeated, violent shaking from side to side, then a tossing up and down. But then Jesus told Peter, "*I have prayed for you that your faith will not fail you.*" Although Peter had a setback, he rebounded in great faith and power. It was Peter who had previously asked the Lord to increase his faith! It is clear that Satan has waged this same attack against the Body of Christ today. Great men and women who have given their lives to Christ are being attacked on this level. Thankfully, we have a great Intercessor who is seated at the right hand of the Father...*praying for us that our faith will not fail us*! You know that when Jesus prays for us He will be heard! He tells us to hold on tight! He tells us that things are not as they seem and behind the curtain of darkness there is hope in Him. He is the finisher of our faith, so we must not toss our hopes aside, but stand firm in the face of adversity and unbelief.

Kick doubt to the curb! Show unbelief the door. Tell fear to hit the road and don't come back! Jesus is standing up for us today and praying for us to have the kind of faith that will stand toe to toe with the devil...and triumph over him. Pray as Peter prayed..."*Lord, increase my faith.*"

July 27

Only Believe

Isaiah 53:1 "Who has believed our report..."
Mark 11:24 "Therefore I say unto you, what things soever ye desire, when ye pray, believe that ye receive them, and ye shall have them."

Having done all, *stand and believe*. We must never stop believing!

Satan tries to get us to doubt God and His Word, just as he did with Eve in the garden. He uses trickery and doubt to bring us into disobedience to God's Word. Sometimes our mistakes and failures will hinder our faith and keep us from going forward, *but we must keep going*. We are in a fierce battle and must constantly be aware of the Devil's intention to neutralize and demoralize us. We are told that "our struggle is not against flesh and blood, but against the rulers, against the authorities, against the powers of this dark world and against the spiritual forces of evil in the heavenly realms." (Eph. 6:10). *We are in a battle and we need the help of God.* The enemy has marshaled his armies against us, but we must retaliate by believing only in the Word of Truth. Isaiah asks us, *"Whose report shall you believe?"* We must believe the report of the Lord! His report declares that we are free, we are healed and we are victorious in all things! Stand on the Word! When everything else has failed, stand and believe the Word! *Keep Standing. Keep Believing!*

Simple words spoken by Jesus, *"Only believe"*. If we can *"only believe"*, then the impossibilities become possibilities! The war is already won when we believe the Word. His word is infallible! His Word is the ultimate Truth! Nothing else matters except that we believe Him! Be a carrier of faith! Choose to believe!

July 28

Trust the Word

John 1:1 "In the beginning was the Word, and the Word was with God, and the Word was God."

One of the greatest truths I have learned is this, *"I can trust the Word."* We have a Friend who is closer than any brother, who will never leave or forsake us, and is completely trustworthy and dependable. He cannot deny Himself, nor can He separate Himself from His Word...for *He is His Own Word.*

The Gospel of John describes Him as **the Word that was in the beginning** and is now manifest in the flesh. Paul sees *Him seated at the right hand of the Father, interceding for us.* Peter acknowledges Him as the *Shepherd and Bishop* of our souls, a *precious, spotless Lamb without spot or blemish.* In Hebrews He is the *Author and Finisher of our Faith and the Word* which is powerful and sharper than a two-edged sword. Revelation tells us *He is the faithful Witness...* the *Prince of the Kings of the earth* who washed us from our sins in His own blood...*Faithful and True* **whose Name is called the Word of God.**

In these perilous times we live in with many departing from the faith at an alarming rate, *we can still trust Jesus.* His Word, when hidden in our hearts, will sustain us and keep us from sin, and is a Lamp unto our feet and a Light unto our paths. He is not a promise breaker, does not make vows lightly, but is a performer of His Word. *If He said it, then He will do it!*

July 29

He Remembers His Covenant

Genesis 9:15 "And I will remember my covenant…"
Genesis 40:23 "Yet did not the chief butler remember Joseph, but forgat him."

We've all been there…*forgotten by someone who promised to remember us*. Promises were made that were never kept. It's not a pleasant feeling to be forgotten about, is it?

When my youngest granddaughter, Ashtin, was two years old she would often say to us, *"Remember me?"* I don't know that she quite understood what "Remember Me" meant, however, she sure got our attention when she said it. She was not about to let us forget her or leave her out in anything!

We serve a God who remembers His promises and keeps His covenants with us! In fact, He has engraved us upon the palms of His hands so that we are always before Him and in His thoughts. When we feel that we have been put on a shelf and set aside, remember that He knows we are there. Just because we haven't seen the manifested promise doesn't mean that He forgot! The butler may have forgotten his promise to Joseph, but God set it up for Joseph to be remembered at the most important and critical time in the kingdom. God knew where Joseph was all the time and had never taken His eye off of him. So it is with us! We are not forgotten, but remembered by the One who matters the most! And, like Hannah, David, Nehemiah and Samson who prayed "remember me," we, too get our Father's attention when we cry out, *"remember me."*

July 30

God Hasn't Changed His Mind

Numbers 23:19 "God is not a man that He should lie, neither the Son of man that He should repent: Hath He said, and shall He not do it? Or hath He spoken and shall He not make it good?"

The Lord is true to His promises! He never goes back on His Word, but carefully guards over it to perform what He has spoken.

Sometimes we act as though we believe that God has changed His mind about some of the things He spoke. When delays come and things are held up, we begin to wonder and to question that God was in it or that He even spoke it. *Satan is especially fond of lying to us by telling us that we missed the boat or that we missed our season.* Although there are times when our own actions and doubt will alter things, God never intends for us to miss out on what He has planned for us. We can only do that when we allow doubt to rob us of our faith. Look at how long Abraham and Sarah waited for Isaac to be born! They could said, *"That wasn't really God"*, or *"Well, we really missed it on this one!"* They could have played the blame game with each other (in fact Sarah tried to take matters into her own hands with Hagar, and Abraham allowed it) yet God still fulfilled His original plan and promise to Abraham! So, even if we sometimes might veer off a little, be encouraged to know that God can get us back on the right track! Wow, what a great God!

When the enemy lies to us and tells us it's not going to happen, know *that GOD hasn't changed His mind, and neither should you!* Even if it takes a lifetime, keep believing the Word of God! Some things take time, so we must be patient, and trust God in the waiting, knowing He cannot lie and He cannot fail!

July 31

Put It In God's Hands

Isaiah 41:10 "...I will uphold thee with the right hand of my righteousness."
Isaiah 64:7 "We are all the work of your hands."

Hands tell a lot about a person. My grandson, Marty, has hands that speak volumes. Seems like they are always cut or bruised, for you see, Marty is a hard worker and has been since he was only twelve. Marty is a diesel mechanic...*and his hands prove it.* Haylee', my middle grand-daughter, has small, tiny hands, but they are quick and sure. She plays piano and saxophone, but her hands are strong from years of flag twirling in school. I would trust either of these hands with my treasures, *for I have found them to be reliable and true.*

Our Savior's hands bare the marks of His love for us. I remember a scene from "The Passion of Christ" where Jesus was tied to the whipping post. As His body took the lashings from the cat-o-nine whips, the camera flashed to the scene of His hands as they shook from the pain and onslaught of the beating. The Hands that held history and hold eternity were now tied and bleeding. They are scarred from nails that penetrated His tender skin. His hands told the story of His passion for us, and the mark of love is indelibly printed upon those pure, sinless hands.

God wants us to put our most valued treasures in His hands. He warmly invites us to entrust our deepest secrets, our hidden dreams, and our hungriest hopes into His loving hands. His hands are proven, sure and true. How can we *not* trust His Hands?

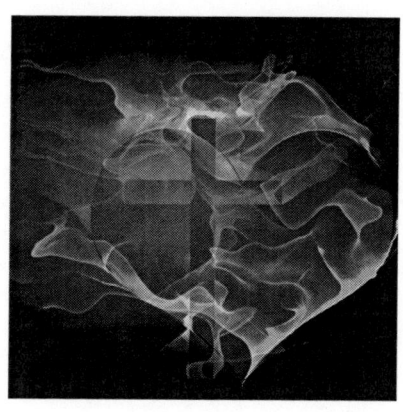

August

Be not weary in well doing…
For we shall reap if we faint not!

August 1

Expectant Waiting

Lamentations 3:24-26 "The Lord is my portion...therefore will I hope in Him. The Lord is good unto them that wait for Him, to the soul that seeks Him, It is good that a man should both hope and quietly wait for the salvation of the Lord."

Seems like almost everyone is in the *"waiting room"* right now. We know something has to happen, something needs to happen, and all we can do is wait! I don't know about you, but for me, waiting is the hardest part. I remember when my daughter, Myra, was waiting to deliver my first grandchild. The wait seemed to go on forever. We made a few trips to the hospital before it was time for Kristen to be born. We were tired of waiting and wanted her to come...now! I like to be actively involved, but when our hands are tied and all we can do is wait, it can leave me feeling a bit helpless. However, I have learned through the years to make the most of my waiting time. There is a productive way to wait upon the Lord...*it is to wait with expectation*!

There's a difference between waiting and expectant waiting. Expectant waiting is knowing that we are not forgotten, assuring us that God will come through for us. Expectant waiting tells us that in His timing everything will work out for our good. It eliminates the feelings of helplessness and hopelessness that we can find ourselves in while in the waiting room. It is while we are waiting and do not see anything happening that discouragement can often beset us. But take heart, dear one! *The Lord is good to those who wait for Him* and seek Him! He doesn't disappoint us when we put our hope in Him. He is completely trustworthy and faithful, and is very aware of our situations. Although we may at times feel powerless and helpless, He knows the situation we're in and will not leave us to face it alone. He has the answer and is the remedy. He alone is our portion and our hope, and He will not fail us. *Keep waiting expectantly*!

August 2

Get Jesus Involved

Zechariah 4:6 "...Not by might, nor by power, but by My Spirit, saith the Lord of Hosts."

We serve a great God who desires to be personally involved in everything that we do. *He doesn't want us to leave Him out of anything* - not the tears and sorrow, nor the joys and victories. He wants to be involved in our biggies and in our little, insignificant things. Oh, the difference He can make when we get Him involved! Things go better, the rough places are smoothed out, favor goes with us, and blessings overtake us.

Overwhelming circumstances will try to dictate our faith and tell us it's not going to happen. Martha told Jesus, *"Lord, he's been dead for four days and he is stinking by now."* Friends told Jarius, *"Don't trouble Jesus, your daughter is dead."* Peter said, *"But Lord we have fished all night and caught no fish."* The disciples told Jesus, *"We only have a little bit of bread and a few fish. We'll never feed this great multitude."* The widow told Elisha, *"The creditor is on the way and all I have is a little cruise of oil."* The disciples told Jesus, *"The taxes are due and we have no money."* Things changed when the Master got involved - the dead were resurrected, the fish practically jumped into the boat, a little food fed a multitude, and a cruise of oil never ran out. A fish personally delivered the tax money in his mouth to the disciple.

Jesus longs to be involved in our circumstances, in our dreams, in our families, in our churches, and in our careers. We make it a point at Passageway to not send anything out or do anything that is not covered in prayer and directed by Him. We involve Him in every decision we make, whether small or great. *If we don't hear from Him, we wait until He speaks.* He is the difference between not enough and more than enough, between death and life, and between poverty and prosperity. Our faith in Him will get Him involved in our lives. He wants to be the center stage, the director who calls the shots, the coach who calls the plays. Get Him involved - He will make the difference!

August 3

Are You A Dreamer?

Genesis 37:19 "And they said one to another, Behold this dreamer cometh."

They called him a daydreamer, one whose head was always in clouds. They made fun of his dreams and mocked him. His dreams aroused bitter hatred and tremendous opposition from others. His own brethren could not see who he really was. His dreams caused them to misunderstand him. Yet...he held on to his dreams and his integrity, even in the worse times of his life. I believe it was his dreams that kept him alive and gave him hope that there was a future for him. Though in prison, his dreams released him from captivity. *His dreams inspired him to never give up, no matter what terrible conditions he found himself in.* His dreams kept him from losing his sanity when he was betrayed by his own brothers and sold to strangers. One day...his dreams became his reality!

We grow great by dreams. All great men and women are big dreamers. They see things in the soft haze of a spring day, or in the red fire on a long winter's evening. Some of us let these great dreams die, but others nourish and protect them; nourish them through bad days till they bring them to the sunshine and light which comes always to those who sincerely hope that their dreams will come true. *Don't let anyone steal your dreams!* (Woodrow Wilson)

I believe we all have a God-given dream. *Hold on to it and don't let it slip away.* Refuse to let your current conditions dictate the death of your dream. *Nothing is impossible with God!* If He gives a dream, He is able to finance it. He is able to send Divine Connections to make the dream a reality. *Don't let Satan steal your dreams! Don't allow time to slowly strangle your dream!* God is bigger than we give Him credit for and has already mapped out a plan to fulfill our dreams! Entrust your dream into His care! Dare to dream God's dream for your life, then believe that it will happen.

August 4

Visionaries and Dreamers

Job 33:15, 16 "In a dream, in a vision of the night, when deep sleep falls upon men, in slumberings upon his bed, Then He opens the ears of men and speaks their instructions."
Proverbs 29:18 "Where there is no vision, the people perish..."

Jacob, Joseph, Solomon, Peter, Paul - *they were all dreamers.* Abraham, Daniel, Joel and many great prophets were visionaries! Some say that God is not in dreams anymore, but *those of us who have God-given dreams know the absurdity of that statement.* God has always used visions and dreams to guide and instruct men and women, and continues to do so today. If you are a dreamer, or a visionary, you are in the company of great people!

God gave kings and pharaohs dreams to get their attention. When the King had a dream and desired the interpretation, Daniel called upon God to reveal it to him...also in a dream. When God desired to reveal His heart, He gave His prophets and priests visions. When men are too busy to hear the voice of God, He speaks in the night when they are in slumber. He sends visions and dreams to seal His instructions. He uses visions and dreams to inspire, direct and guide His people.

Never, ever give up your dreams! Hold the vision firmly, and write it down! Dare to be a visionary! *Dare to dream big...for God has big dreams for us!*

August 5

Something Worth Believing In

Matthew 13:46 "And when he had found one pearl of great price, went and sold all that he had, and bought it."

What is it that makes the difference between success for some and not others? Why do some succeed with their dreams and goals, while many others spend their lifetime just dreaming about it? The difference is this...*is it worth believing in?*

A true believer knows there are two crucial decisions that must be addressed. The first is this: *Is this cause worth fighting and suffering for?* The second is this: *Is this cause worth laying down my life for?* Once having those issues settled, nothing will stop us from advancing, and nothing will separate us from our cause. We become consumed with the call...at all costs! It is the very thing that drove the Apostle Paul. He had a Divine encounter that changed his life and his perspective, he believed! Once he encountered Jesus, he knew this was Someone worth fighting for, spending for, and even dying for! The man who found the pearl of great price knew that it was something worth giving everything else up for! *Nothing could compare with it and he would never be satisfied without it.*

At some point we made a decision that this cause, this dream, this vision, this Christ was worth fighting, perhaps dying, for. He is worth believing in! The dreams He gives to us are worth believing in! He gives us something worth believing in!

August 6

Called, Committed & Consumed

Isaiah 6:8 "I heard the voice of the Lord, saying: Whom shall I send, and who will go for Us? Then I said, Here am I! Send me."

Some Christians don't like being labeled as radicals or fanatics anymore, yet when we are truly called and completely committed, *the call will consume us...and sometimes give us those unpopular labels*! It was "radicals" and "fanatics" who completely turned the world around with the Gospel...the Pauls' and Peters' who gave up all for the call! *No great accomplishment is ever achieved by mediocre attempts.* Churches are not built with non-committed members. No great revival ever broke forth out of passive, lethargic believers. No great deeds are ever accomplished by halfhearted attempts. To achieve any level of success, there must be complete belief and total commitment to the call!

We must defeat the killer of our dreams, the thief of our visions and the destroyer of our hopes. The cost of the call is the laying down of our lives. It means saying, *"Not my will, Lord, but Thine."* It means being willing to walk it alone when others don't see or share the vision. It means believing the Word of God even when everyone around us says it's impossible! When we, like Joseph, are forgotten or neglected, or purposely hurt, but we refuse to be offended or sting with the insult or the oversight, *then we are found worthy of the calling.* When our good is evil spoken of and when our wishes are cro: e¹ our advice disregarded, our opinion ridiculed but we refuse to let anger rise in our heart or even defend ourselves, *then we are truly worthy of the call.* When the only opinion that matters is God's and we refuse to allow negative opposition to kill the dream, then we are consumed with the call!

August 7

The Spirit of A Conqueror

Romans 8:37 "Nay, in all these things we are more than conquerors through him that loved us."

Jesus paid a great price, not only to purchase our salvation and redeem us, but also to make us overcomers and conquerors in our daily living. We all face giants, we all battle opposition and we all must deal with challenges that are a part of life, but thanks be unto Jesus Christ, we are overcomers in all of these things. *God has always had people who were champions and conquerors.* We are called to be conquerors!

If there were no challenges there would be no champions. *Challenges produce champions and battles produce conquerors.* Conquerors see beyond the challenges and into the victories. Conquerors know that they don't fight alone, *but the battle belongs to the Lord*...all we need to do is follow Him with all of our hearts! Conquerors understand that conquest is a life long commitment. Conquerors are determined people and are not swayed by opinions and opposition. Conquerors understand where their strengths lie. *Conquerors make Satan tremble*! Conquerors persevere!

Beloved, we are more than conquerors through Christ Jesus. *Within us is the power to conqueror fears, slay giants of intimidation and defeat the foes who oppose our God-given destinies.* The spirit of a Conqueror lies within each one of us because the same Spirit that raised Christ from the dead dwells in us!

August 8

Have Faith

Habakkuk 2:4 "...The just shall live by His faith."

Our walk with the Lord will always be a walk of faith. Faith is what takes us through the battles and the trials, and gives us the assurance that everything will work out for our good. It is believing without seeing. *Faith takes us beyond the unknown into God's reality...one step at a time.*

I really like what Patrick Overton says about faith..."*When you come to the edge of all the light you have, and are about to step off into the darkness of the unknown, faith is knowing one of two things will happen: There will be something solid to stand on, or you will be taught how to fly.*"

Faith in God produces the most solid foundation, even when all around us there is nothing but sinking sands. He is the Solid Rock upon whom we build all of our hopes and dreams. Faith empowers us to believe that when we step into the unknown that He is already there. Faith builds heroes who do exploits for God's kingdom. By faith...we understand that this world and all that is in it was formed by the Word of God. By faith we can subdue kingdoms, bring righteousness, obtain promises and stop the mouths of lions. Faith quenches the violence of the fiery trials and makes our weaknesses strong. *Faith teaches us how to fly!*

August 9

Rooftop Faith

Luke 5:20 "When Jesus saw their faith..."

Faith will move you from complacency into action.
These four friends mentioned in Luke 5 were determined to get their sick one to Jesus (don't we all needs friends like these). Unable to get through the great crowds, they looked for another way. One of them saw some steps leading up to the roof...and suddenly they *saw their opportunity and seized the moment!* I can imagine these boys ascending these narrow steps, cautiously yet quickly carrying their friend upwards until they reached the rooftop. They removed a portion of the roof, tied ropes around their sick friend's bed and slowly let it down...right in front of Jesus! *Faith finds the path to miracles!*

We just need to take our faith through the roof! Sometimes we must give our time and rearrange our schedules to make way for a miracle. Sometimes we need to give our talents and abilities to someone in need of a miracle. Extreme faith gives all of these and produces the spirit of a conqueror! God LOVES people of great faith...people who take believing to expectation! Faith cries out for the impossible. Faith is the precursor to miracles! Extreme faith allows God to work miracles in our lives. Are we willing to take our faith up a level? Let's take our faith through the roof!

August 10

Faith Expects Things

2 Corinthians 5:7 "For we walk by faith, not by sight."

We are having such a good time in our Wednesday Night Bible Class as we study on faith. Our small but happy class really gets into it as we laugh and share life changing truths of faith with one another. One thing we are getting is this...*faith is not all that complicated, but is simply believing and expecting God to do what He says He will do!*

If we look at what we see, we would quickly lose hope, but *when we see through faith, we see endless possibiliti*es for God to do great things! If we look at what we see, we would give up on everyone, but *when we see through eyes of faith, we see countless souls to win for Christ.* If we look at what we see, we would quickly give up on our God-given dreams and lay it all aside, but *when we see what God sees, we become clothed with courage, empowered with faith, and fueled with desir*e! We are called into a walk of faith that puts logic aside and simply believes God! Faith expects God! Faith expects God will hear our prayers! Faith expects God to answer our prayers! Faith expects impossibilities to become realities!

We need to look at our circumstances and situations through the magnifying glass of God's Word! It will completely change what you see and how you see yourself, your dream, and others around you! See everything through His Word...and then expect! *The level of your expectation determines the level of your faith.*

August 11

Optical Illusions

2 Kings 6:17 "And Elisha prayed, and said, Lord, I pray thee, open his eyes, that he may see. And the Lord opened the eyes of the young man, and he saw: and, behold, the mountain was full of horses and chariots of fire round about Elisha."

If we could sometimes see into the unseen realms it would amaze us, especially during times of uncertainty and threats from the enemy. We are ruled by our five senses and live according to the facts that are presented to our senses. However, for the Believer there is another realm that we are called to walk in...that of being seated with Christ in heavenly places!

Our greatest defeats come because of optical illusions and the belief that these illusions are truth. Satan will try to cloud our vision us by giving us half-truths and poor facts that will entice us into a false belief. He will tell us that we will never make it, that everyone is against us, and we will never achieve anything. His lies fill our ears telling us that we'll never be healed and will always be as we are now. Yet, God's infallible Word tells us that we are the head and not the tail, that we are overcomers and not defeated, that we are the healed of the Lord, for by His stripes we are healed! *The Word tells us that if God be for us, then who can be against us!*

If we could only see what God sees, then fear would never find a place to abide in our hearts. If we could look at the situation through the eyes of faith we would see that those who are for us are far more than those who are against us! Who shall believe the report of the Lord! His report declares that we are healed, redeemed, set free and more than conquerors! Let's not be fooled by the illusions of the flesh, but dare to look into the supernatural realm and see what God is seeing for us! See through the eyes of faith and dare to believe what the TRUTH says about you today!

August 12

Living By Faith

Isaiah 53:1 "Who hath believed our report, and to whom is the arm of the Lord revealed?"

The just shall live by faith and not by sight. Sometimes it is very difficult to not see the circumstances, for they are very real and very large in our view. The obstacles in our path can make us feel like grasshoppers in the path of giants, yet we know that *things are not always as they seem* and the truth is bigger than these mountains that are before us.

Isaiah asked, *"Who has believed our report and to whom is the arm of the Lord revealed?"* God reveals Himself to those who believe Him in the face of insurmountable circumstances. God is always on time, even when it would appear there is no time left for God to work. He is the creator of time itself and of all that happens in time. He has the power to speak life into those things which are dead. He can turn the tides of stormy trials with a wave of His mighty hand. He speaks and mountains tremble, He moves and the earth quakes. He has the power to override the reports of doctors who reach their limits and see no other course than to write death sentences. *Our faith activates God to move for us, reversing situations that seem impossible. Faith compels Him into action*!

Many people seek His hand of blessings instead of His face, but *those who know and love Him seek His face and His ways.* They know that in due season blessings will follow and overtake them. God loves it when we use our faith, for it is then He will make impossibilities possibilities! He tells us to call those things that are not as though they are! Faith makes it happen!

August 13

Called to Separation

Isaiah 49:2, 3 "And he hath made my mouth like a sharp sword; in the shadow of his hand hath he hid me, and made me a polished shaft; in his quiver hath he hid me; and said unto me, Thou art my servant, O Israel, in whom I will be glorified."

Have you ever felt that you were hidden away, that no one recognized who you were or what you had to offer? I, too, have sometimes felt hidden away and put on reserve.

God is going to raise up people that are not famed, great, or wealthy, but *humble servants with hearts on fire.* The world is waiting for the manifestation of the Sons of God. We may have been forgotten by man, but God is going to elevate us. We may have been despised by many, but God is going to glorify us! We may have been looked upon as nothings, but God is going to raise us up as mighty women and men. Like Joseph, we have been held in reserve, waiting for our destinies to unfold, staying true to the call. We have been set apart, sometimes not understanding what it's all about or why no one else understands us.

We are that Chosen Generation...part of the Royal Priesthood, and set apart by a Divine and Holy calling. There is a Holy Unction that has kept us going when others gave up. It has kept us separated and pure, and would not allow us to compromise when many others did. It has kept us on our knees, crying out to God to keep the vision and purpose alive in us as during the long nights of separation and sanctification. Yes, we have been set apart and hidden away...but for a purpose! *The Spirit of God will soon bring to light what and who we are all about*!

August 14

Compelled By The Call

Joshua 14:9, 12 "And Moses swore on that day, saying, Surely the land whereon thy feet have trodden shall be thine inheritance, and thy children's forever, because thou has wholly followed the Lord my God..Now therefore give me this mountain..."

    Can you hear it? Do you sense the deep echoing resonating in your spirit of a voice that will not be silenced, compelling you onward?

    If so, you are probably hearing the same compelling voice that Caleb heard for forty-five years, beckoning him like a neon sign lighting up the sky. A promise had been made years before, now the call of that promise was compelling him towards it and would not be silenced nor satisfied any longer. He was determined to possess his mountain, and nothing would prevent him from having it. Boldly he came before Joshua and said, *"Give me my mountain!"* Forty-five years earlier Caleb saw something that became fixed in his heart that did not diminish with the passing of time. For forty-five years Caleb held the picture of his promised mountain in his heart, and finally *the call of his promise compelled him* to go beyond his present and step forward into his future. He pushed aside the complacency and the voices of those who questioned his vision and who laughed at his dreams. It no longer mattered what others thought, but the only thing that mattered to Caleb was his mountain. *He dreamed it, he ate it, he talked it until his desire for the mountain could no longer be appeased by the life that was once satisfactory.* He could no longer live as others were content to do, but *the compelling call of the mountain bid him onward.*

    When God seeds a dream into our lives, *there will come a point in time when the call of our dream will urge us onward and upward until we possess the dream.* Obstacles will no longer hold us back, but our passion and commitment will overcome every hindrance in our paths. A life once satisfactory to us will become hollow and empty as the call of the promise becomes more urgent and passionate. Years may have rolled by us, but they cannot dim nor diminish the compelling call of our destiny. The hunger for it will grow, and we, like Caleb, will be armed with determination and courage to *"get our mountain."*

August 15

Hold On To The Promise

I Thessalonians 5:24 "Faithful is he that calleth you, who also will do it."

We define everything by time, but it is not so with our Lord! Time is a measuring stick used by man, but God is the beginning and ending of time. What may seem like a long time to us is actually perfect timing for God. *He is never too late, never too early and is always on time.*

God will often move quickly, answer prayers immediately and perform the miraculous suddenly. Yet, there are also times in our lives when we must wait upon God...*wait for the promise to manifest and wait for the fulfillment of our goals.* Abraham and Sarah waited a lifetime for Isaac. Caleb waited forty-five years to claim his mountain. Four hundred and thirty years passed between Malachi and the Birth of Christ. Anna, the priestess waited all of her life to see the Messiah. So, it is evident that we, too, must learn to wait upon the Lord for promises as of yet unfulfilled. But...wait...for it will happen in God's due time.

We can glean from Caleb's experience as we wait for our promise. Caleb was strong in his faith and stood against doubt. *He was strong in his faith even as the years rolled by and nothing happened.* He was strong in his spirit and held on tightly to the promise of his inheritance. He never wavered, never doubted and did not allow the passage of time to dim his hope or his vision. Dear one, we can trust all of our promises into the capable hand and wisdom of our Loving Father.

August 16

Go Get Your Promise!

Joshua 14:12 "Now therefore give me this mountain, whereof the LORD spake in that day; for thou heardest in that day how the Anakims were there, and that the cities were great and fenced: if so be the LORD will be with me, then I shall be able to drive them out, as the LORD said."

God is a great Promise-Keeper! His very Word is filled with promises for all of us...promises of blessings, promises of a good future, promises of salvation for our family, promises of health and healing! Never forfeit the promises of God, for they are just waiting to manifest to a child of faith!

Caleb got his mountain because he was willing to be different! He trusted in the Lord and believed what God promised! He was willing to wait for the promise, knowing that strength and blessings come to those who wait on God. But most important of all, Caleb wholly followed the Lord all of his life! He knew what was promised and purposed in his heart that he was going after his promise! *He had purpose and knew how to claim God's promises.* He did not allow the passage of time to rob him of his inheritance and would not settle for anything less than what was promised to him!

We can be encouraged to know that God has many promises and blessings awaiting us, and like Caleb, we can rightfully claim those promises! We can put God in remembrance of His Word and boldly claim our mountains! Let's use our faith...and go get our promises!

August 17

The Edge of Greatness

Numbers 13: 27, 30 "And they told him, and said, We came unto the land whither thou sentest us, and surely it floweth with milk and honey; and this is the fruit of it. And Caleb stilled the people before Moses, and said, Let us go up at once, and possess it; for we are well able to overcome it."

We hunger for it. We chase it. We desire it. We dream of it.

So, what is *"it"*? *"It"* is the desire to be great or to do great things, especially if we have been called and chosen by God to make a difference in this world. Sadly, many of us come to the edge of greatness...and give up or hesitate by allowing the fear of greatness to override our dreams. We become paralyzed and unable to move forward, afraid of the great risks that greatness demands of us. *But some will dare, some will risk all, some will take the plunge into greatness and forever change their course in life.*

There are always going to be challenges when we stretch ourselves *God-ward*! We will have to endure countless bad reports from negative people who see the giants instead of the greatness. We will have to swim against the tide of the majority who won't press onward and upward, content to remain as they are in the land of complacency. We will have to go through the land of Kadesh (holiness or separation unto God) to *see clearly* the promise that is before us. It is at this point where most people stop, allowing their Kadesh to become a place of hesitation and waiting instead of a place of conquest.

We are standing at the edge of our greatest moment, looking over into the promise land of our destiny. We must see, taste and touch the "good" of the land that lies before us, for when we do these things, *nothing can hold us back or stop us from going forward.* Refuse to listen to the negative reports of those who will never see what you see. *Be willing to wait, establishing your faith in patience and hope, knowing that the seeds of greatness take time to produce it's fruit.* When our moment of decision comes, let's decide to go forward and over the edge of greatness with a firm belief that God has called us for this moment in time to do exploits for Him.

August 18

Unstoppable

Numbers 14:8 "If the Lord delight in us, then He will bring us into this land, and give it to us; a land which floweth with milk and honey."

There are always going to be those who oppose the plans of God and do everything in their power to silence the promises of God. You will find these doubters everywhere - on the job, in the families, among friends and even in the Church - critics who find fault with something they don't like or agree with. *They are out of sync with what God is speaking and refuse to participate in what God is doing.* They refuse to see what God has set before us and choose only to see the obstacles and potential for failure.

Caleb and Joshua had to contend with these spirits. *Ten of the men who spied the land with them were dissenters instead of proclaimers.* They were out of sync with God's plan, seeing mountains instead of mole hills. Their prayer rooms became silent as their souls began to wither away with the deaths of their promises. These critics have loud voices who will always try to rally the crowd to be on their side. Their purpose is to sabotage the plans of the Lord and keep us from entering into our destiny. We must refuse to heed their voices, for they speak death and destruction to our futures. Refuse to be silenced by their negative words.

God is on our side and has called us to greatness! We must not let the voices of opposition keep us from receiving those promises. If God gave us a promise, then He also has a plan to make it happen, even in the face of insurmountable obstacles and against all the voices that say it can't be done. Listen to His voice. Purpose to be as Caleb and Joshua, and block out the voices of the critics!

August 19

His Anointed Ones

Psalm 20:6 "Now I know that the LORD saves His anointed; He will answer him from His holy Heaven with the saving strength of His right hand."
2 Corinthians 1:21, 22 "Now He who establishes us with you in Christ and has anointed us is God, Who also has sealed us and given us the Spirit in our hearts as a guarantee."

The line is drawn in the heavenlies as the souls of men choose which side they will be aligned with. There is a great interest in the heavens as God anoints His Church and sets them apart from the world. God does not choose unwisely or as the world would choose, but seeks hearts that are pure, hands that are clean, and spirits that are consumed by the call! *They are His anointed ones!*

To be "anointed" is, among other things, to be made sacred (consecrated); to be set apart and dedicated to serve God; to be imparted with enabling gifts and grace; to be divinely designated, inaugurated, or chosen for some purpose. His anointed ones are sealed with His Holy Spirit and filled with destiny and purpose. They are the Daniels who pray, the Hebrew boys who won't bow! They are the Esthers who are called for such a time as this! They are the Ruths who won't turn back! They are the Marthas who serve Him faithfully, and the Marys who worship Him adoringly! They are the Lazarus' who come forth when He calls! They are the Peters who boldly proclaim His message, and the Pauls who spread the Gospel to Kings and servants!

*They are the ones who have God's ear...*the ones whom He will save with His strong right hand! We are children of a Covenant God! Oh yes, He makes a difference between the children of the world and His children! He is faithful to hear us! He is mighty to save us, *for we are His anointed ones!*

August 20

Where Are The Watchmen?

Isaiah 62:6 "I have set watchmen upon thy walls, O Jerusalem, which shall never hold their peace day nor night: ye that make mention of the LORD, keep not silence."

As I listen to the news reports and see the attacks on our Christian belief and faith, I wonder...*where are the watchmen on the walls?* Hell has declared war against the Saints, and many believers don't know how to defend. But some do..and are willing to do what needs to be done. These faithful servants have heard the call to battle *and are positioning themselves through much prayer to be defenders of the faith!*

Just as some are called to positions of leadership, servanthood and ministries of helps, ***there are those who are called to be watchmen within the Body of Christ.*** Strongs Concordance defines a watchman as: tsaphah *(tsaw-faw'); a primitive root; properly, to lean forward, i.e. to peer into the distance; by implication, to observe, await*: KJV-*behold, espy, look up (well), wait for, (keep the) watch (-man).* Brown Drivers & Briggs *defines watchman as: to look out or about, to spy, to keep watch, to observe, to watch.* The watchmen had a twofold ministry on the wall. The first was to watch for the enemy, providing protection for those asleep or at work. The watchman stood on the wall and notified the gatekeeper of the identity of anyone who was approaching the city. Second, the watchmen were to repair the wall after an attack. The watchmen were present day and night (Isa. 62:6). ***There was never a time when the walls were not secure and the people silent.*** The Lord Jesus also prophesied that the period just before His return would be a time of unprecedented deception. In Matthew 24:24, He says that even the very elect would be deceived if possible. II Thessalonians 2:3 reveals that during this period there would be a great falling away from the faith. It is difficult to comprehend how this could happen, until we understand that the subtle deception sneaks in when we are caught off guard!

It's time for the Watchmen to sound the alarm, to be on guard, and to defend the faith! *Are you one of those commissioned to be a watchman on the wall?* Have you felt compelled to pray and seek the face of God for the Body of Christ, for your country, or for the Nations of the World? Do you have a desire to see our land healed and to be a repairer of the breach? If so, stand and be counted as one of the Watchmen on the Walls!

August 21

Where Are The Lights?

Matthew 5:16 "Let your light shine before men, that they may see your good deeds and praise your Father in Heaven."

While returning from a weekend trip to Kansas City on a Sunday evening, I saw something that made my heart drop. The parking lots were empty. The lights were off. Mile after mile, town after town, it was the same everywhere. Size did not matter - it was the same in the large and in the small. *Most of the Churches we passed were empty and dark, causing me to reflect upon the condition of our souls.*

The thought crossed my mind...Our Church lights are burning very dim! *A little shock wave of reality struck me in the pit of my soul as I saw the symbolic emptiness and darkness of our Church parking lots. Are we lit up and full...or empty and dim?* The lights have gone out in many Churches and, sadly, people don't realize they are walking in the darkness. Blind people can't discern the darkness. The precious oil of the Holy Ghost is slowly leaking out and far too few realize the significance of this loss that leaves them powerless and empty. Souls are lost every day, groping around in the darkness while looking for light. *Christ came to light us up so that we will never walk in darkness again.*

My Friend, we have only one lifetime in which to make an impact on our world. We are given daily opportunities to shine for Jesus and to influence our society. We should not just curse the darkness, but also light the way! We are the lights of the world! We can light the way for others to see clearly. When we shine for Jesus, the Father is glorified! Our lights won't go out or burn dimly when we are filled with the oil of the Holy Ghost. We can shine in the darkness and show others there is light and abundant life in Christ Jesus! **Light your candle in the darkness**, be filled with the oil of the Holy Ghost, and shine brightly for Jesus!

August 22

Ready for Training

Luke 4:1 "And Jesus being full of the Holy Ghost returned from Jordan, and was led by the Spirit into the wilderness."
Matthew26:41 "Watch and pray, so that you will not fall into temptation…"

In the arena of sports all players have practice sessions. These training sessions show the strength and weaknesses of each team player. Great players are birthed from the practice sessions. Great leaders are created from practice sessions. Great communication skills are developed in practice sessions. It is during practice sessions that the team members really get to know each other. They learn to recognize certain looks or a secret signal the quarterback or coach will send. Practice sessions develop the skills, talents, and abilities of each player, and create strong bonds between the players. Practice sessions train the boys to become men, good catchers to become great receivers, and good teams to become great teams. *Most importantly, practice sessions prepare the players to meet their opponents, and hopefully, to achieve championship status.*

Our prayer sessions are like practice sessions. When we are in prayer we learn God's ways and where we develop our strengths and learn our weaknesses. We learn to be led by His Spirit. *Notice in the Gospels how often Jesus had "practice sessions."* He spent forty days preparing Himself for His purpose, His mission, His calling. He used this time to get Himself positioned to hear the voice of His Father and to meet His enemy head on. This word wilderness refers to a *solitary, lonely, isolated, uninhabited* place. Jesus often spent time in prayer during the course of His ministry to recharge and to position himself to hear from the Father. It was in a prayer session that Jesus gained the strength and received special grace to fight the greatest battle in the history of mankind, and was able to conquer death and triumph victoriously in the battle for our souls. ***His training sessions prepared Him for Championship Status.***

We must position ourselves in prayer so we can maximize our full potential. *Until we understand the necessity of prayer, we will underestimate the enemy and become lax in hearing our Captain's voice.* Prayer conditions us to hear from God. Prayer positions us to achieve Championship Status. It is through prayer that we are able to pull down strongholds, defeat giants, and wield weapons that are mighty and powerful. Prayer positions us to receive everything God has for us. The more time we spend in "prayer sessions" or "practice sessions", the better equipped we will be to succeed, impact, influence, and maximize our God-given strengths, talents, and abilities. We, too, will face our adversary without fear and triumph victoriously as we gain strength, wisdom, grace, and insight through our prayer sessions. It is through prayer we conquer enemies, defeat foes, storm the gates of hell. Are *you* ready for training?

August 23

Command the Works

Isaiah 45:11 "...Ask me of things to come concerning my sons, and concerning the work of My Hands, command ye me."

    Whatever happens will happen...that's the mentality of a lot of Christians today. We settle back and accept whatever life throws at us, refusing to take responsibility and action for what happens to *US!* Despondent. Discouraged. Defeated. Hopeless. Helpless. Sick. Troubled. Boy, the devil must be having a party at our expense!

    Christ Jesus gave us the authority to command the works of God! He called us to do His works and greater. A lot of us sit back and watch the world go by, wondering if our day will ever come. Guess what! Our day has come! Our time is here! The time for the Church to rise in power, might and glory is now! The earth has been groaning, waiting for the manifestation of the Sons of God! Isn't it time we start walking in the authority and abundant life that is already ours! Too many of our own are sick, diseased and hurting - *attacked by an enemy that has already been defeated!* Too many of our children have succumbed to the worlds temptations and we have let them go, instead of holding on to the promise that our children and children's children will be saved. It's time to stand up, and take our place! Declare war on the enemy! Receive the mantel of authority that will manifest the Sons of God! Command these works and more: Refuse to accept everything the devil throws at you, but take your authority and command forth the works of His hands! Declare your victory! Arise, Arise, People of the Living God, and declare His glory to this generation!

August 24

Transferring Authority

Acts 1:8 "But you shall receive power, after that the Holy Ghost is come upon you..."

If you are wondering why there has been so much spiritual warfare lately, *may I suggest to you that God is preparing us for greater things.*

There is a shifting taking place in the heavenlies that will manifest in the earthly realm. *It is a new season for the Church.* A new day is dawning, ushering in holiness, purity and authority upon believers. A line is being drawn in the heavenlies, defining who we are in the earth. I believe the Church will be as it was in the early days of Acts, proclaiming Jesus to this world, going forth with might and with power, and the demonstrations of the Holy Ghost.

Every battle, every trail and every testing of our faith was sent to make us strong in our belief. *Faith that is not tested cannot be trusted.* We must be proven and tested before we can be entrusted with the authority that is about to be transferred to us. For those of us who have been in the waiting room, just hold on, for we are about to break forth in a new anointing and strength! Change is coming. Are we ready for it? I believe that the greatest Defining Moment of the Church in this generation is on the horizon. Be patient, establish your hearts in faith, and get ready for God to unveil His power and His glory to His trusted servants!

August 25

Season Your Speech

Colossians 4:6 "Let your speech be always with grace, seasoned with salt, that ye may know how ye ought to answer every man."

I truly enjoy being around people who are uplifting and who talk faith! Several friends come to my mind as I recall different conversations that we have had - conversations where what God said was spoken. How uplifting it is to our spirits to be around such people who speak God's word in *all* situations! When we have the Word hidden in our hearts it will manifest itself in our conversations, and there is nothing more powerful or faith-building than to hear God's world repeated in daily conversations.

We are encouraged through Paul's writings to let our conversation be as it becomes the Gospel of Christ, and to let our speech be seasoned with grace. We would see amazing transformations take place in our lives and circumstances if we would begin to season our speech! We've got to love the Caleb's and Joshua's who said "we are well able to posses our land!" I love 85 year old Caleb's speech, *"I am as strong now as I was 40 years ago. I can still take 'em out!"* We enjoy being around the Paul's who declare, *"I can do all things through Christ"* and *"nothing is impossible with God!"* Elijah boldly declared, *"Put some water on the altar, boys, and see what MY God will do!"* I especially love what Jesus said, *"I will"* and *"I can"* that was followed up with *"suddenlies"*.

Our God is a God of cans, wills and suddenlies! Speaking His Word and believing it thrills His heart because then He can show us (and everyone else) that He is a God of His Word and will do what He said He would do!

August 26

Let Faith Do The Talking

Daniel 3:16 "...We are not careful to answer thee in this matter. If it be so, our God whom we serve is able to deliver us..."
Romans 10:8 "...The word is nigh thee, even in thy mouth..."

People have a lot to say. Everyone has an opinion and loves to share them. And that's okay...

Believers should be distinctly marked by the words of faith we speak and by the way we live our lives. Not everyone is going to love us just because we walk in faith and live pure and holy lives. In fact, we will encounter a lot of opposition from those who hate everything we stand for. Three Hebrew boys felt the wrath of a king when they refused to compromise their faith and bow down to is idol. The king didn't appreciate the stand these boys took for God... and against him. But listen to their response... *"We are not careful to answer thee..."* They had a faith that could not be threatened or intimidated, and would not cave under pressure. *"But if it be so..."* They had faith that stood regardless of the outcomes! Faith that would and could take them to a fiery furnace. It takes stronger faith to go through the fires than it does to escape them. *"But our God is able to deliver us..."* Able means He has the power and can do it if He chooses! They had enough faith to put their lives in His hands...and trust Him with the outcome. *"And will deliver us out of your hand..."* Their faith was talking! Their faith knew that God would deliver them from the hand of their enemy. David, when facing Goliath, spoke these words, *"This servant slew the lion and the bear...and you will be as them, ...for I come in the Name of the Lord."* His faith did the talking!

Faith talk will walk us through the fires! Faith talk gives God the control and releases us from fear! Let our faith do the talking for us! It will take us to places where the faithfulness and the glory of God is revealed!

August 27

Get Out of Neverland

Hebrews 10:1 "The old system under the law of Moses was only a shadow, a dim preview of the good things to come, not the good things themselves..."
James 1:16-18 "So, my very dear friends, don't get thrown off course. Every desirable and beneficial gift comes out of Heaven. The gifts are rivers of light cascading down from the Father of Light. There is nothing deceitful in God, nothing two-faced, nothing fickle. He brought us to life using the true Word, showing us off as the crown of all his creatures."

Neverland! It's no place for Believers, yet how sad to see Children of Light living in the shadows of *"Neverland"*. They simply exist in life, and *never* experience the fullness of life with all it's guts and glory. They are side-liners, living life on the fence, but *never* fully partaking of all the good things of the promises of God. They live under the "shadow of the old system" dimly seeing the good things that God has for His children, but *never* having enough faith to leave the old comfort zone to step into the promises of better things. They *never* experience great defeats...or great victories. They are *"saved just enough"*, but *never* really shine. They remain hidden away in the shadows of the past...past mistakes, past failures, and past fears, and *never* really live.

There is so much more for us! The Father of Light has far more for us than shadows of promises to come! Jesus came to give us Abundant Life! *He wants us to come out of the shadows so He can show us off as the crown of His creation!* Shadows are just images of something, intangible and fleeting. When we step out of the nothing of Neverland to embrace the realness of Him, we become reflections of His light and His glory! We become more alive and more vibrant as the Image of Christ becomes real to us. We experience the "good gifts" that can only come from the Father of Light who dispels the shadows of Neverland.

Embrace His Light and step out of the shadows into the blaze of His glory! Dare to leave the old system behind and walk in the newness of His Light! Once we experience His fullness and greatness, *we'll never be satisfied dwelling in the shadows of Neverland again.*

August 28

No Guts, No Glory

Exodus 24:17, 18 "And the sight of the glory of the Lord was like devouring fire on the top of the mount in the eyes of the children of the Lord. And Moses went into the midst of the cloud, and gat him up into the mount..."

So many folks want the shortcuts to glory *but are unwilling to pay the price.* They want it all...wealth, fame, big ministries, great glory, but how much are they willing to do to get it? At the first sign of discouragement some will give up and call it a day. Others fight many battles, and *just before the greatest moment of their lives,* they give up, forfeiting the sweet taste of victory. Some folks look at the mountain before them *(their mountain of victory...their mountain of glory)*, but all they see is the fire that looks frightening and turn away in fear. We'll never taste glory by standing afar and being a spectator instead of a participant.

Think about Gideon - just a lowly farmer whom God called to be a mighty warrior and a man of valor! It took guts to face an army of thousands with only 300 men whose weapons were lanterns and horns! They are recorded forever in history as men who dared and who received glory! Think about David - a young shepherd boy who dared to fight a giant that an entire army feared! He is remembered a mighty warrior and a great worshiper! And there was Moses, a meek man, but a great deliverer and a man who dared to walk right into the Presence of the Living, Holy God! It took guts to go where no one had ever gone, to do something that had never been done, and to embrace something that was greater than themselves. These men faced their mountain, they had courage to climb it, and dared to walk through fires to enter into the glory!

God has called us to run and not be weary, walk and not be faint, to mount up with eagles' wings, and *to wait upon Him* as He renews our strength. The Bible clearly tells us, *"Having done all... stand!"* Wait! See the Salvation of the Lord! This walk of faith is not for the fainthearted, but for those who are willing to climb the mountain, face the fire, and walk into the clouds, going where others dare not go! *Remember this, God will never call you to do something that you and He, cannot fulfill.* There is a mountain of victory for you! He is calling His Church into the Glory Cloud! Perhaps you have been called to achieve something that is greater than you, to do something that is beyond your ability, or to face a mountain that seems unmovable and fearsome! Be brave, dare to embrace your mission, don't be afraid of the fire, accept the challenge, and be willing to do all for His call!

August 29

Open The Map

Psalm 119:105 "Thy Word is a lamp unto my feet, and a light unto my path."

I love maps and find them fascinating. In fact, I have a large map of the world hanging on the wall in my office, and in a matter of seconds I can quickly locate a specific country or region just by reviewing my map. I returned from a vacation and used a map to guide me to my destination and then back home. Driving in the night was somewhat challenging, and several times we missed our turn and found ourselves headed in another direction. Our map was quickly retrieved as we searched for the right road, and without fail, it would guide us back in the right direction. There were a few anxious moments in what seemed to be an out of the way area. *We held on to our map with both hands and referred to it every minute or so until we were safely guided back onto our right path.* By the time we reached home our map was well-worn and well-used!

Our time on earth is often referred to as a journey! It is easy to get lost, confused, turned around or misguided without a good map. Thankfully, we have an excellent Map that will direct us in the right direction, and when we lose our way, it aides us in returning to the right path. The Bible, our Map, is filled with careful instructions that will lead us to our destination. It holds the secrets to life and has all the answers to our questions. There will be many times in our journey that we will question, *"Where, Why, What, and When?"* The Bible, the Word of God, will give us clear, precise directions that will get us where we need to be.

We should clutch our Map to our hearts and refer to it daily for direction and wisdom. When we don't know what to do or where to go, *Open the Map! Search the Scriptures! Review the Instructions!* It is foul-proof and trustworthy. Our Map, the Living Word of God, will never fail us nor guide us wrong. Open the Map!

August 30

Follow The Guide

John 16:13 "Howbeit when he, the Spirit of truth, is come, he will guide you into all truth: for he shall not speak of himself; but whatsoever he shall hear, [that] shall he speak: and he will shew you things to come."
Romans 8:14 "For as many as are led by the Spirit of God, they are the sons of God."

You are not alone. *You don't have to endure another moment of uncertainty, for you have a Guide who will gently guide you through your storms.* You are not without hope or purpose, for He knows the plans God has for your life. He is very wise and has your best interest in mind. He will guide your every step and take you where you need to go, guiding you through every uncertain moment, and *will bring you to your personal place of victory...if you follow the Guide.*

Jesus has provided a Guide to lead us. *He has sent the Holy Spirit, who is the Spirit of Truth.* He won't lead us wrong and is completely trustworthy. He is intimately familiar with us, our desires, our purpose, and our destiny. He is there to assist us when we come to the "forks in the road" and face the great "unknowns" in our lives. This Amazing Guide will comfort us in our sorrow, heal broken spirits and wounded hearts, correct us when we miss it, soothe every fear and calm every doubt, and will never lead us astray. *He will show us things to come and prepare us for our future.* He will keep our feet from slipping and empower us to overcome sin and the lust of the flesh. His fruits are gentleness, love, peace, joy, and mercy. The great Apostle Paul exhorts us to *"be filled with the Spirit."* *One of the distinctions of being a Child of God is living a Spirit led life.*

Life isn't easy to figure out, and we don't know all the answers. We like to retain control, relying upon our instincts and our own logic that often get us into trouble. **But we have a Guide who is trustworthy, dependable, truthful, and faithful.** He knows things we don't know. He is very knowledgeable of life's circumstances and uncertainties. He will get us to the right places, the right people, and through all our seasons...*if we follow the Guide.*

August 31

Then A Hero Comes Along

Galatians 6:2 "Bear ye one another's burdens, and so fulfill the law of Christ."
Romans 15:1 "Now we who are strong ought to bear the weaknesses of those without strength and not just please ourselves."

Look around you today, and then take a closer look at the faces you see. Do you see the burdens they are carrying? Most are hidden from view, but when you take another look and really see them you will find hidden burdens and heavy loads. Look into their eyes (*Oh, I know this can be uncomfortable for most of us*) and you will see pain, grief, sorrow, and disappointment. Are they carrying burdens too heavy for them to bear? Do they feel they are all alone and no one seems to really care? My friend, you can help lift the heavy load someone is carrying. You have been called to be a burden bearer. *I know this isn't glamorous or exciting, but to the person carrying the load it is nothing short of heroic.*

A burden bearer is someone, who, when they hear of a friend's problems, immediately feels the weight of the burden and carries it as well. He/she is someone who keenly feels the burdens of others and *must do something* to help lift the burden through prayer, wisdom, support, and action. A burden bearer will put aside their own hurt or problems to extend love and mercy to another who is in great need. People who are hurting are drawn to burden bearers and feel comforted when they share things with you. Pain can be debilitating and is heightened when one feels alone. Burden bearers give hope and bring peace through their gentle touch and kind words. *They reach into places of the hearts where no one else seems to be able to go.* They impart kindness and reflect the love of a gracious, compassionate Savior who operates through their hands, their heart, their eyes and their lips.

What is your burden today? They come in countless shapes and sizes, from lonely sorrow to crushing cares. But one thing's for sure: there is a great Hero, our own personal Burden Bearer, who will carry us when others have failed us. *He has borne us since*

***before we knew Him. He carried us from the womb and will not
stop even when we are old and bent and gray.*** He alone has borne
the full weight of our sin, and He alone can bear the burdens of life
in a sinful world. He is there, everyday, to help us with our burdens,
caring for us as no one else can. As He lifts our loads and burdens,
let us also extend the same kindness and love to others by taking time
in our busy lives to help bear someone else's burden.

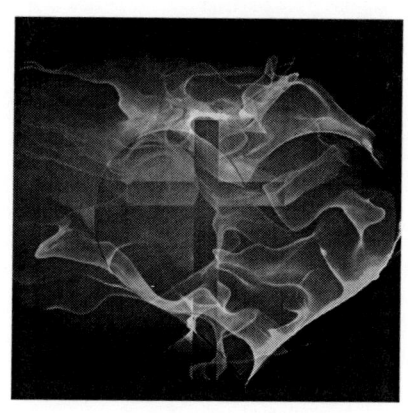

September

By Faith...

subdued kingdoms, wrought righteousness, obtained promises, stopped the mouths of lions. Quenched the violence of fire, escaped the edge of the sword, out of weakness were made strong, waxed valiant in fight, turned to flight the armies of the aliens. (Hebrews 11)

September 1

What Heroes Are Made Of

Hebrews 11:32-34 "And what more shall I say? For the time would fail me to tell of Gideon and Barak and Samson and Jephthah, also of David and Samuel and the prophets: who through faith subdued kingdoms, worked righteousness, obtained promises, stopped the mouths of lions, quenched the violence of fire, escaped the edge of the sword, out of weakness were made strong, became valiant in battle, turned to flight the armies of the aliens."

For years Hollywood has portrayed heroes as tough, untouchable, unstoppable, macho guys who can take out small armies alone, defeat all the bad guys, and hold a machine gun in one hand, a grenade in the other, and has a knife clinched between his teeth. They are *"Faster than a speeding bullet. More powerful than a locomotive. Able to leap tall buildings in a single bound."* They are "supermen"... heroes that are conjured up by imaginative souls who have no clue what real heroes are made of.

There are heroes who walk among us everyday who go unnoticed and seek no recognition. They are the "burden bearers" and "good Samaritans" who inspire us all to be more like Christ. A hero can come from anywhere and anyone can be one. *You'll find them when disaster hits, ministering hope and courage* as they help rebuild lives that have been torn apart. *They are the nameless faces who spend countless hours distributing food to the hungry and stability in unstable conditions. You'll find them in homes, raising children they didn't give birth to, but love them as though they did.* You can see the glimmer of a hero in the eyes of a father who chooses to live a godly life and be the right kind of example for his children to follow; and in the heart of a mother who makes countless sacrifices so her children can have a better life than she did. *Walk down the corridors of any Veteran's Hospital or Medical Facility and you will see the faces of untold heroes* who answered the call to serve their country, willing to make the ultimate sacrifice. Then, there are the heroes of faith who stand guard against the enemy of our souls, *Pastors* who watch over their flocks and keep the wolves at bay and spend untold hours in prayer standing guard for one lost soul; *Evangelists* whose feet carry the Good News to places few dare to go; *Teachers* who guide little hearts though kindness and wisdom. *Heroes give generously of themselves.*

Heroes are made of faith, love, and courage, and are clothed with kindness, mercy, and caring. Not much like the Hollywood versions, but they are heroic and brave, and have a place of honor in God's Hall of Heroes.

September 2

Soldiers of the Cross

Romans 1:16 "For I am not ashamed of the gospel of Christ: for it is the power of God unto salvation to every one that believeth; to the Jew first, and also to the Greek."
Ephesians 4:1-3 "I, therefore, the prisoner of the Lord, beseech you to walk worthy of the calling with which you were called, with all lowliness and gentleness, with longsuffering, bearing with one another in love, endeavoring to keep the unity of the Spirit in the bond of peace."

      The trials you have endured have served to strengthen your faith and give you His heart. You are stronger, wiser, and more trustworthy. The Captain of the Army has great need of you. The Spirit of the Lord is raising up soldiers for this time and season - soldiers who are brave and true. The Captain of the Army is calling forth His Generals...His Chosen Ones *for such a time as this!*
      He is calling for the Abrahams' to stand and be counted... His Spirit is compelling the Esthers' to come forth and intercede on behalf of a nation! He is raising up Daniels' and Pauls' who will not bow down to the idols of this world! He is speaking to the Peters' to boldly proclaim His Word without compromise! The Spirit of Unity is now at work in the Body of Christ, bringing the elect together in harmony and one accord! The Spirit of Wisdom and Grace is manifesting through us! He is giving Divine revelations and Godly solutions to men and women who are honorable, faithful, and committed to the Cross! He is sending orders to those who have an ear to hear! *It is time to take our stand for Jesus Christ!*
      Walk worthy of His calling as a true Soldier of the Cross. Make the great commitment to follow Him and Him alone. Refuse to be hindered by those who won't go, or won't hear what He is speaking to His Beloved Body! God is personally involved in this war we are fighting - and will give us wise strategies that will ensure our victory in Him! *God's plan will not fail!* Trust Him! You are a Soldier of the Cross, and have received the greatest honor anyone can be given! Walk worthy of that great commission!

September 3

The Commission Still Stands

II Timothy 2:3 "Thou therefore endure hardness, as a good soldier of Jesus Christ."

There is a changing of the guard every hour on the hour at the tomb of the unknown soldier. *These men train for six months before assuming guard duty at this tomb, and learn discipline, loyalty, obedience and diligence.* They are undeterred in the duties to guard the tomb and refuse to allow any distractions to hinder their performance. Upon the changing of the guard, the new guard receives these instructions from the departing guard, ***"Orders Remain Unchanged."*** Keep guarding, keep due diligence and keep watch.

Dear One, the orders Christ gave to the Church over 2000 years ago *remain unchanged.* They are just as important now as they ever were...heal the sick...raise the dead...do my works until I come again. We must not let deterrents keep us from remaining on guard, on watch and diligent in the faith! We must not give way to slumber while on guard, but keep alert and attentive. Let us exercise diligence, be patient and wait upon Him! The orders He gave us when He called us are still the same! Soldier of the Lord, be diligent and watchful! Stand strong and firm! *Our orders remain unchanged!* Stay true to the call and don't quit! The Commission given so many years ago has not changed.

September 4

Lest We Forget

Philippians 1:3, 4 "I thank God every time I remember you. In all my prayers for all of you, I always pray with joy."

He is 84 years of age and has spent over 60 of those years bound to a wheel chair. You see, his leg was taken from him just days after he turned 21 while fighting for the freedoms and liberties that we enjoy today. His shoulders are horribly crippled with arthritis from having to use his arms to replace the leg that he lost. Yet, *he is proud of the sacrifice he made and would not change what he did.* Upon awakening from the surgery that was required to remove the destroyed limb, Mr. Moore remarked to his nurse, *"Oh no, I have lost my leg."* She responded to him, *"Don't think of it that way - that you have lost your leg. Think of it as you gave your leg for your country."* Amazingly, this gave him a deep, strong sense of patriotic pride. He considers it a great honor to have given his leg for his country.

Only 17, Jim signed a release statement acknowledging a bad left eye so that he, too, could fight for his country in WWII. Shipped off to countries he had only heard of, he left family and friends behind to join the ranks of men who became heroes before his young eyes. He saw things that no young man should ever see, things that are forever indelible on his mind. With pride in his country, he left his boyhood behind and joined the ranks of manhood.

We have wonderful liberties in America that few nations enjoy. We can still worship freely, without fear that anti-Christians will attack our churches and worship services, and demand that we forfeit our lives for our faith. We still can see the inscription that says, *"In God We Trust"* on our coins and dollars. We still, as of today, can preach against sin without fear of retribution. We still have the freedom to choose how we want to live our lives and how we raise our children.

Mr. Moore, we thank you for your sacrifice. To the Jim's who enlisted at young ages to defend our country, thank you! *To every solider who fought for this country,* **thank you.** To the families of those who made the ultimate sacrifice of loved ones who never came back, our most heartfelt and sincerest appreciation and gratitude. Because of you America is still the land of the free and the home of the brave! We remember and pay tribute to the fallen soldiers and to the ones who so bravely opposed the enemies of our nation. *The next time you see an old solider or a warrior who fought for us, express your gratitude and appreciation. Let them know you appreciate their obedience to the call to... "Let freedom ring!"*

September 5

The Standard of the Lord

Isaiah 59:19 "...When the enemy shall come in like a flood, the Spirit of the Lord shall lift up a standard against him."

The Lord will fight our battles for us! He allows the enemy to only go so far and then He says enough is enough! It is then that we see His salvation and the Horn of the Lord standing strong. All that He requires of us at this point is to trust Him and simply stand in faith, knowing that we, and our victory, are in His hands!

One of the definitions of a standard is this, *"An emblem or flag of an army, raised on a pole to indicate the rallying point in battle."* There is a critical point in the battle when the Spirit of the Lord raises His emblem and rallies His armies to fight on our behalf! It is the pivotal point in the storm when He changes the circumstances. When it seems that all hell has been released against us, God will stand in our defense. He will personally take on the enemy that is trying to wipe us out and destroy our future. *If God be for us then who can be against us!* No weapon formed against can prosper and every tongue that speaks against us will be condemned. This is our heritage! Be encouraged in knowing that God is raising the standard against our enemy - He has taken on your battles and victory is guaranteed!

September 6

One Essential Ingredient

Psalms 27:13, 14 "I had fainted, unless I had believed to see the goodness of the LORD in the land of the living. Wait on the LORD: be of good courage, and he shall strengthen thine heart: wait, I say, on the LORD."

Can I say something very gently to you on this day*? God can work it out.* God in His unbelievable power can work everything out for your good. What Satan meant for evil, God will use it to our benefit. *Just don't lose hope.* In our struggles with circumstances that are beyond our control, hopelessness will strike and try to find in us a target to launch a plan of defeat. But, *we are not defeated* and our weapons of warfare are strong and mighty through Jesus Christ!

We may be looking down on the face of a dream that is now lying lifeless, but don't lose hope. We might be looking at the remnants of a vision that is now lying dormant, but don't give up on the vision. What seems impossible with men is quite possible with God. When we realize that pain was a part of His plan, we can endure the hardness as a good soldier of Jesus Christ. We can look past the mountains of despair...*and see God!* We can look beyond the giants of obstruction *and see the Giant-Slayer!* We can look past the death sentence of doom *and see Resurrection!* We have the capacity to leap into the air, grab the ball on the rebound, and slam-dunk the winning basket. We can survive the lion's dens, the fiery furnaces and the gallows of Haman. With undaunted courage we can go through seasons of setbacks, financial reversals, domestic disappointments, unemployment, and the death of someone dear to us. We can live weeks without food, days without water, and even several minutes without air, but take away our hope and our dreams and purposes will wither away and dry up. Hold on to hope when the situation seems hopeless.

Just don't lose hope. It's the one essential ingredient.

September 7

The Gift of Compassion

Lamentations 3:22 "It is of the Lord's mercies that we are not consumed, because His compassions fail not."

She was found on the side of the highway leading into the countryside, her white hair matted and dirty with a look of pleading and eternal hope and trust in her eyes. She had been abandoned by her family who no longer wanted her. Perhaps she had become too much of a burden for them. Something about her struck a deep chord of compassion in my daughter, who pulled over to the side of the road to see about her. *She went home with my daughter...this rejected, thrown away, big, sweet dog.* Yesterday we found out that this unwanted and abandoned dog was very valuable and of great worth.

She is only a dog, *but how many people do we encounter every day who are like this dog?* They have been wounded by someone they trusted. Rejected and disappointed, they wander aimlessly on the highways of life in hopes that someone might stop and show them some compassion. They might not be much too look at, and perhaps might even smell different, *yet on the inside of them there is a flicker...a little flame of hope that someone might see their worth.* Beloved, the love of Christ that dwells in the heart of every Believer should be moved with compassion for these unlovely, rejected souls who desperately need kindness and compassion. It is the Love of Christ that drew us to Him when we were unworthy and unlovely. This same love will reach out to them and draw them to Him! He found great worth in us and paid a great price to buy us from the clutches of sin and hopelessness.

Look around you...and you will see them. Let Love be your compass and it will guide you straight into the path of someone who needs what you have to give. *Be ruled by compassion...not judgment*. Extend this wonderful gift of compassion to someone around you, for after all, it's about reaching out to those who most need His love.

September 8

You Have God's Attention

Genesis 29:31, 32 "And when the LORD saw that Leah was hated, he opened her womb: but Rachel was barren. And Leah conceived, and bare a son, and she called his name Reuben: for she said, Surely the LORD hath looked upon my affliction..."

Have you ever tried to get someone's attention, but no matter how hard you tried, they just seemed uninterested in what you had to say? No matter what you did or said, you just couldn't seem to get their attention. This is especially true if you are like me and not very forward or pushy. Someone jokingly said *"There are over six billion people in the world, but only eight of them are supermodels."* Many of us go unnoticed in the crowds and are not recognized for the gifts and the talents we have.

Leah felt unnoticed. She was, in a word, ugly. To make matters worse, she had a sister who was a true beauty. Forced upon a man who didn't want her, she was in a losing battle for the attention of her husband. He was simply uninterested in her. But Leah got the attention of someone who literally changed her world - God! *He saw in her what Jacob did not see...the makings of a mother whose children would be the heirs of Abraham. He saw in her the seed of Praise - Judah.* He gave her what Jacob could not give Rachel...a son whom she named Reuben. It means "Behold, a son!", or in other words..."You have my attention and I am noticing you!" God gave her a second son whom she named "Simeon" which means "God has heard!" Somewhere between the third and fourth child Leah began to see that all the love she needed was already available through God. She was loved! Even if nobody else on earth even cared if she was alive, God loved her. In that, she could praise God!

Do you sometimes feel that nobody cares for you? *Maybe you are struggling to find a reason to even continue trying. You are significant in God's eyes*. He is watching when no one else is. He has spared no expense to secure your eternal preservation in His presence. Beloved, God hears you. *You have His attention*, and He will do for you what He did for Leah.. He will change the unbearable circumstances in your life when you call out to Him. *He will seed in you great things that you will give birth to...and out of this Praise will be birthed!* You have His attention and He has taken great notice of you! The fact that the LORD noticed Leah ought to give us cause to praise Him. For if He saw Leah, we can know He sees us! And if he sees us, we can also be recipients of His favor.

September 9

Guard Your Heart

Proverbs 4:23 "Keep your heart with all diligence, for from it flow the issues of life."

What is in our hearts will come out! It doesn't take long to know what is in a person's heart...just let them talk and they will reveal the things that are most important to them! You can tell where a persons' interests lie if you listen to them long enough.

The world has a long list of things that would love to set up house in our hearts. We are to be extra mindful of those things that will try to invade our deepest, innermost recesses of our hearts. 1 John 2:16 says this..."*For all that is in the world, the lust of the flesh, and the lust of the eyes, and the pride of life, is not of the Father, but is of the world.*" Our eyes and ears are often the channels that allow these things access into our hearts. One glance at something we should not see can be disastrous, as the image slowly weaves a web of lust, seduction, and desire that begins to consume us. Satan knows if he can just get us to see it, hear it, or want it, he can gain access into our hearts. If he can plant a tiny little seed of bitterness or unforgiveness, he can stunt our growth and render us powerless. Pride, fear, unforgiveness, and love of the world make their entrance into our hearts when we are caught off guard. Make sure nothing is allowed entrance into your heart through the eye gates, the ear gates, or through pride *except that is passes by the Guard of the Holy Ghost!* Give Him permission to stand guard over your heart! Fully submit to His gentle warnings when anything destructive or unlike Christ tries to enter.

The Message Bible says it like this..."Keep vigilant watch over your heart; that's where life starts." Be vigilant and be diligent over your heart, for from it flow the issues of life!

September 10

Guard Your Time

Jeremiah 8:20 "The harvest is past, the summer is ended, and we are not saved."
John 9:4 "We must work the works of Him Who sent Me and be busy with His business while it is daylight; night is coming on, when no man can work."

Where does the time go...and what are we doing with the time allotted to us? Are we focused on the right things...the things that will last, or are we allowing time to march on with little being accomplished? The cry of the Heart of God could well be this... *"The harvest is past, the summer is ended...and so many are not saved!"* When projects consume us more than people...when people consume us more than His Presence...*then time has lost its value.*

A wise and loving Pastor friend wrote, *"I was called out late last night to the hospital for a friend who had a heart attack; and as I drove back a few hours ago, **the important from incidental was easy to distinguish**. I just don't have time to suffer fools gladly. I just don't have time to joust with theologians counting the number of angels on a pinhead. I just don't have time for folks who act out what they don't believe. **But I have all of the time entrusted to me by Him for folks who have real issues requiring the only real answer: Jesus.**"* I, like him, have little time for playing the games so many people play, for my time is far to valuable to throw away on things that will pass away quicker than last year's hot, top ten list. I, too, must learn to discern the times, and focus on those things that are eternal. I, too, must learn to guard my time and protect it from thieves that come to distract and steal the precious moments that can't be replaced.

We must be on guard to protect the precious from the common, and use our time wisely and in such a way that we are effective instead of adequate. These "little foxes" can invade even the most guarded areas if we are not careful. We used to sing an old spiritual song, *"Time, Lord, Time...Time is winding up."* The Words of Jesus can be heard amongst the busyness..."*Work while it is still day, for the night is coming when no man can work."*

September 11

A Door of Hope

Hosea 2:14, 15 "Therefore, behold, I will allure her, and bring her into the wilderness, and speak tenderly to her. And there I will give her vineyards and make the Valley of Achor a door of hope. And there she shall answer as in the days of her youth, as at the time when she came out of the land of Egypt."

This Amazing God we serve knows how to turn our nothing into something, our sorrows into joy, our fears into faith, and our troubles into hope. We live in troubled times and many are looking for answers, solutions, and hope. Fears fill the hearts of many who don't know where to turn or what to do. There is only One solution....*Jesus is our door of hope when there is no hope.*

Achor means "trouble", and was the place where Joshua asked Achan, *"Why have you brought this trouble upon us because of your disobedience to God's command?"* We still have a lot of Achans, today who are rebellious and disobedient, bringing trouble to our families, our Churches, and even our Nation. Yet, God who is full of mercy and compassion offers us a *"door of hope"* in the midst of our troubles. In Isaiah 65:10, He proclaims a blessing of prosperity and rest to the place that was once "trouble". He tells us in Hosea, *"Yes, you will go through the wilderness, but in the midst of your troubles, I will be your door of hope. You may be in the valley of trouble, but it will not overtake you. You are not as the world that has no hope, but you are a Child of God and an heir of promise. **I am your door of hope**."*

The hope spoken here is not just wishful thinking, but means confident expectation, solid certainty. It means we know God is not going to leave us troubled, distressed, or defeated. It means He will show up in the midst of trouble to defend us. He is our hope...He is our future, and in Him will I trust because He has set His love upon us! I earnestly wait and expect in quiet confidence that God is with me. And, while we may not understand why He draws us into the wilderness, we can know this - *a door of hope is provided for us.* Walk through that door of hope and leave behind the despair and the doubt. God has good things ahead for you!

September 12

Be Willing to Trust Him

Psalm 9:10 "And they that know thy name will put their trust in thee: for thou, LORD, hast not forsaken them that seek thee."

The most beautiful gift we can give to God is our trust that is born out of love! Without trust, no relationship will work out, including our relationship with Him. *Lack of trust will cause us to limp through life,* forfeiting the peace and joy that the Lord gives to all who trust in His name. Many say they love the Lord, but do they trust Him?

Love requires trust, even when we don't have all the answers. God does not always show us His complete plan, but will show us in bits and parts. *He requires trust from us...*trust that He knows what He is doing and is capable of working everything out for our good. When He says He is the Alpha and the Omega...the Beginning and the End...He is telling us that He is completely capable of not only giving us a word and a promise, but is capable of walking us through it to completion. He might not do it the way we would, but He will do it! We might as well relax and enjoy the journey that takes us to our destination and trust Him to do everything He promises. We shouldn't fret because it's not going according to our plans and our timing, but simply trust that GOD KNOWS WHAT HE IS DOING!!! It is easy to trust the Lord, for He cannot fail! We can't allow our insecurities to obscure the blessings and promises of God. Commit to trusting Him...no matter how it looks and especially how it feels.

When the world is turned upside down, we can trust Him! When everything that can go wrong has gone wrong, trust Him! When others have failed us, we can still trust Him! When nothing is working out like we hoped, trust Him! Feelings come and go, but God remains faithful and true. *May God give us hearts that trust!*

September 13

Take It To Jesus

Hebrews 4:14-16 "Therefore, since we have a great high priest who has passed through the heavens, Jesus the Son of God, let us hold fast our confession. For we do not have a high priest who cannot sympathize with our weaknesses, but One who has been tempted in all things as we are, yet without sin. Therefore let us draw near with confidence to the throne of grace, so that we may receive mercy and find grace to help in time of need."

You have a Great High Priest who welcomes you with open arms to come to sit at His feet, and enjoy His Presence. In His Presence we will find fullness of joy and pleasures that satisfy us like nothing else can. He restores our souls and loves on our wounded, tender spirits, and gives rest to our weary hearts.

The world around us is in a state of emergency and few know what to do about it. People are so distressed and anxious, and simply don't know where, or who, to turn to. *Point them to Jesus!* Our leaders are struggling to find answers that can heal this land and mend the divisions. *Point them to Jesus!* Our children walk into war zones when they enter the classroom as educators are scratching their heads to find a remedy for the violence. *Point them to Jesus!* Our Churches are looking for the new "edge" that will attract restless worshippers and satisfy the longing hearts. *Point them to Jesus!* Businessmen are searching for the "right contact", the "new deal" and the "best connection" to secure their businesses. *Point them to Jesus!* Disease stricken souls are waiting for the new medical breakthrough that will give them new hope and new life. *Point them to Jesus!* There is a cry of sorrow and a wail of heartache that screams in the silence of lonely hearts who feel there is no one to understand. *Point them to Jesus!*

We know the remedy and Who the cure is! ***Shouldn't more of us be running to Him and not away from Him?*** We don't have to carry the weight of the world on our shoulders, for He tells us to cast our cares upon Him! We don't have to walk in fear, for He is love and perfect love casts out fear! Everything we need, desire, long for can be found in His Presence. Come boldly into His throne room and there you will find your loving, caring, High Priest who knows what you need! He will ease your mind and give you perfect peace. Talk to Him and tell Him all that is on your hearts. He understands, He hears, and He cares.

September 14

What Do YOU See?

2 Corinthians 5:7 "For we walk by faith and not by sight."

We must walk by faith and not by sight. Faith, the evidence of things hoped for and the substance of things unseen! Faith is not a mere feeling...*it is simply trusting God to do what He said He would do.* Faith is seeing what God sees! **So how do we see things?**

A shoe manufacturer who decided to open the Congo market sent two salesmen to the undeveloped territory. One salesman cabled back: *"Prospect here nil. No one wears shoes."* The other salesman reported enthusiastically, *"Market potential terrific! Everyone is barefooted."* Get God's perspective. When Goliath came against the Israelites, the soldiers all thought, *"He's so big we can never kill him."* David looked at the same giant and thought, *"He's so big I can't miss."* Ten spies came back and said, *"We are like grasshoppers in their sight...they are too big for us."* Two came back and said, *"Man, take a look at this fruit that is growing on our land that God gave us, now let's get rid of these trespassers!"*

See yourself in partnership with God...*and you will triumph over the giant.* The giants in our lives may be bigger than us sometimes, but thankfully we are in a partnership with God who is bigger than our giants! It's only a matter of getting the right perspective!

September 15

Mountain Top Bound

Genesis 8:5 "...In the tenth month, on the first day of the month, were the tops of the mountains seen."

Just as God remembered Noah, He will also remember us! He has not forgotten about us during the storms and turmoil's, but rides with us through every wind and wave. He holds us safely in the palms of His great hands! *Our boats may rock for a while and we might feel the turbulence of the winds, but it will not last forever.* The storms will cease and the flood waters will abate. Mountain Tops await us!

Noah, too, entered an ark of safety, and when the flood came, *Noah and his family rode on top of the storm!* They were held in the palms of God's hands during the worst storm the earth has ever seen. These obedient, faithful, and God-fearing men and women were hidden away in an ark of safety. When destruction and chaos hit, they were safe, protected, and sheltered from the devastation. Noah had no other place to go, and had to stay where he was until the turmoil was over. *One day the waters abated and the mountain tops were in plain sight!* A sealed promise from a covenant God awaited Noah and his family as God placed His beautiful rainbow in the sky.

There is a rainbow promise awaiting those who endure the storms. God has heard and God remembers you. He is not a God to forget...and He will let you see the mountain tops just when you think He has forgotten about you. Your prayers and alms have come up before Him...and you are Mountain Top Bound!

September 16

I Call Him Lord

Acts 10:36 "...He is Lord of all."

Miriam-Webster's dictionary gives the following definition of Lord: *1: one having power and authority over others. a. a ruler by hereditary right or preeminence to whom service and obedience are due. b. one of whom a fee or estate is held in feudal tenure. c. an owner of land or other real property.*

Born-again believers call Him Savior! Without Him there is no salvation for mankind. And, oh what a Savior He is! Some who know Him as Savior have not yet walked on into the "Lordship" level with Him. They know Him only as Savior, there is so much more to Him! Everyone wants and needs a Savior, but many don't want a Lord. *He is Lord of Lords and King of Kings, and has full power and authority over powers and principalities!*

Those who know Him as Lord have surrendered full control to Him, confident that He is Lord of All, and Lord of every problem we face! He has full control on earth and in heaven! Our service and full obedience are due to Him! *We call Him Lord*! Our lives are wrapped up in His...His purpose, His desires, His will...and His plans for our destiny! He, as our Lord, is privy to every thought and desire that abides within us. He, as Lord, supplies every need that we have, for it is in our place of surrender and submission, that He can become the Supplier of all we need, want and desire. We rely completely upon Him, for without Him, we can do nothing! He is our everything...*He is Lord!*

September 17

He Sings Over You

Zephaniah 3:17 "The Lord thy God in the midst of thee is mighty; He will save, he will rejoice over thee with joy; He will rest in His love, He will joy over thee with singing."

I love this scripture...it speaks of God being in our midst and of His might! It tells us that He will save us...from our sins, from our enemies, from our troubles. *But it also declares that He rejoices over us with joy and He will joy over us with singing!* He finds great pleasure in our joy! To think that God loves us so much that He sings over us! There is something so wonderful and divine about a child of God that it causes heaven to dance with joy!

There is a return of joy for God's little ones! Just to know we have been redeemed by the Blood of Jesus and Heaven knows who we are is great cause to rejoice and be glad! We'll see more unexpected blessings and divine interventions as we delight in Him and seek His Kingdom! He is in our midst...He is mighty...He will save...and He rejoices over us! His love is sure and steadfast, unshakeable and nothing can separate us from His love!

Do we "tickle His heart" when we express our delight and glee in the blessings He sends our way? I pray that I will never allow anything to overshadow the blessings He sends! May I never fail to express my joy and delight in His wondrous love and unmerited favor that is showered upon me each day. We can find joy in the blessings we have instead of complaining about what we don't have. Look for the blessings in the small things, *think about His goodness*, and find some time today to "tickle His heart" by expressing your joy in the small things!

September 18

Leave Them Singing

Revelation 14:3 "They sang as it were a new song before the throne..."
Ephesians 5:19 "Speaking to one another in psalms and hymns and spiritual songs, singing and making melody in your heart to the Lord."

They gathered in my home, these eighteen friends and family who had fled from the path of Hurricane Gustav. The concern and worry was evident on their faces as they anxiously awaited reports of how their homes and properties withstood the storm. They seemed to not know what to do, and weren't really up to any sightseeing, or even a trip to the zoo with the children. I decided we'd do something for them to uplift their spirits.

The following evening I prepared a big pot of gumbo for them and invited them over to our Church fellowship hall to enjoy a hot meal with the promise of some singing to follow. Two of my daughters and my oldest granddaughter sang and played music for them. It wasn't long before two of the men and one of the mothers walked upon the stage, took the microphone and began belting out, *"I'll Fly Away"*! The children joined them on the stage and began singing one of their favorites with much gusto. Smiles replaced weariness and laughter rang out as the music filled the air. Cares and worries were vanquished immediately. They didn't want to leave, and kept requesting *"one more song"*! They left changed...different from when they arrived. Heaviness was gone and their steps seemed lighter. *They left laughing...they left singing.*

One of my favorite things about going to my Father's House is the singing. You can always tell when the people have been lifted up and encouraged, because they usually leave with a smile on their face, a song on their lips, and a little tap of their feet. Isn't that how we should leave Our Father's House...singing!? I think that's how we should leave each other...with gladness in our hearts and songs upon our lips. Cares and worries can't stay where there's lots of singing! We should sing more...and laugh more! *We'd all feel a lot better if we did!*

318

September 19

Seek Him and You'll Find Him

Luke 2:46 "And it came to pass, that after three days they found Him in the temple..."
Jeremiah 29:13 "And ye shall seek me, and find me, when ye shall search for me with all your heart."

Years ago when my children were small, my husband I took a group of teens to a youth function that was several hours away. We had to take two vehicles – he drove one, and I drove the other. After the event we decided to stop along the way only to discover that my daughter, Myra, was missing. Her father thought she was with me...and I thought she was with him. Panic-stricken, we hastened back to the Church, only to find that she had caught a ride home with someone else!

Mary and Joseph had a similar experience when Jesus was 12. They had already gone a day's journey when they realized young Jesus was not with them. How could they lose God's Son - His plan for mankind's salvation? *Panic-stricken, they hurried back to the temple...and it was there they found Him!* I know well the relief that filled their souls!

So many are seeking Him today as the raw truth of their emptiness hits them in the depths of their lonely hearts. Panic stricken souls can still find Him in the temple today! But, not only can He be found in the temple, but *He can be found walking on the stormy waters* to calm His beloved disciples! *He can be found at the tomb of dead hopes and buried dreams* to speak resurrection life into hearts that have given up. *We will find Him on the Mountain of Transfiguration, showing the Glory of God* to those who believe on Him. *He will be found in a group of two or three* as they call upon His Name. *He will be found in the multitudes,* and can still be seen taking the time to heal a blind man or a woman bent over in pain. *He will be found where worship is poured on Him* like the oil in Mary's box. *He will be found in a garden of prayer,* destroying strongholds and conquering powers of darkness. *Sinners can still find Him at the foot of the cross,* where His Blood will cleanse the vilest heart and transform a life into His image. The only place He cannot be found is the empty tomb of unbelief, but to those who seek Him...*He will be found!*

September 20

Today We Taste Victory

Psalm 118:24 "This is the day the Lord has made; we will rejoice and be glad in it."
Jeremiah 1:10 "See, I have this day set thee over the nations and over the kingdoms to root out, and to pull down, and to destroy, and to throw down, to build, and to plant."
Joshua 10:14 "And there was no day like that before it or after it, that the Lord harkened unto the voice of a man: for the Lord fought for Israel."

We awoke this morning to a new day to do whatever we choose with it. For some it will be just another day that has slipped through our fingers, another day that was like yesterday, but *for some of us it will be a day of hope, a day of rejoicing and a day of victory!*

This is one more day to praise the Lord! This is one more day to face Goliath and defeat him! This is the day for those who have stumbled or failed to get up one more time! *Today offers one more opportunity for the sinner to come to Christ!* Today offers us one more chance to share the good news of Jesus Christ to someone who needs Him. This could be the day of your greatest victory yet, for *who knows what God will do on this day!* This could be the day when God turns everything around for you! This day is a day of great potential and full of promise! It is a day of new opportunities and new beginnings! We should take advantage of one more day to lift up our voices in worship and praise...to forgive someone who has hurt us...to reconcile a brother or sister back to the Household of Faith...to visit someone who is shut in...to pull down strongholds...to destroy the works of Satan...to subdue kings and kingdoms for Christ...to preach this gospel to every part of the world.

Who knows but today might hold the breakthrough you have so desperately waited for! Who knows but today salvation will come to your household! Who knows what great things we will accomplish through our faith! Who knows but that today will be our day of great victory! *When we wake up with the Lord on our side, who knows what He will do for us this day!*

September 21

For The Sake of the Call

Mark 1:17 "And Jesus said unto them, Come ye after me, and I will make you to become fishers of men."

When I gave my life to Jesus many years ago, *I gave all of myself to Him.* I gave up the wrong for the right and have lived my life to please Him. It was a complete and whole hearted surrender! When He called me to carry His Name and His Message I did not question it - *I just obeyed and submitted to His Call!*

There were others who followed the Master - they came from every walk of life. Some where humble fishermen who laid down their nets to follow someone who told them He would make them fishers of men. They abandoned their careers, their families, and their futures to follow Jesus. All because Jesus said, *Follow Me.* Jesus said, *"Whoever loses his life for My sake will find* it." Whoever abandons his life will live it to the fullest. *Abandonment to God is dangerous. Serving God to the fullest extent is not a safe and quiet life. It is war. It is sweat, hard work, toil and sometimes heartbreak.* It can even lead to death. Yet it is only when we completely surrender and abandon all for the sake of the call that we can live our life to its greatest potential! It is an adventurous life that will take us many places where we will meet all kinds of people. Some will receive our message of hope and truth, while others will scorn and reject us. *But, it is well worth the surrender, for it is a life lived filled with purpose, passion, and power!*

We cannot be anemic Christians any longer! If we are not completely surrendered to Him, then we are not truly surrendered. We must make it all about Jesus and stop making it about our personal desires, wants and wishes. It's not about fame or wealth, but about souls and eternity. *It's about believing in Him so much that nothing can separate us from His truth.*

September 22

God Uses Basket Cases

Acts 9:25 "Then the disciples took him by night, and let him down by the wall in a basket."

Have you ever felt that you were a "basket case" and not much good for anything? Perhaps it was something you were going through that left you feeling helpless. Well...the good news today is this...*God uses basket cases!*

Rahab had a horrible past and had little to offer anyone. Everyone knew her lifestyle and had labeled her as unworthy and not much good. Yet, God took this unworthy basket case and used her to help take out a city! When the men of God came into the city to spy it out, she used her basket to hide them from the hands of their enemies, earning her a place in the lineage of David! Moses was born a basket case, yet his little basket took him straight to the Pharaoh's palace and into the arms of the Princess. This little basket case became one of Israel's greatest leaders, taking them out of slavery and moving them towards their promise land! Paul, the great apostle of faith and courage, also became a "basket case" escaping from those who sought to kill him. This basket case wrote most of the New Testament, leaving us a legacy of truth, faith and bravery that compares to none!

The enemy might try to come into our lives and mess us up, but *God will send us a basket of salvation!* Satan might wage war against us and try to capture our minds and thoughts, but in the heat of the battle *God sends us a basket of victory!* The deceiver can try to get us off track and make us think we are on the run, but he is just a pawn used to propel us to *our Basket of Destiny!* He will try to rob us of everything great and good, but God sends baskets of provision in our hour of need! When we feel that we are just another basket case, we can rejoice, because we are in the company of great men and women whose courage and bravery took them to great places!

September 23

Spend Time With a Faithwalker

Hebrews 10:38 "Now the just shall live by faith..."

One of things that pleases the Father the most is to *believe Him*...not just believe in Him or on Him, *but believe what He says!* It's called faith, and we all have a measure of it. I have found that spending time with those who walk by faith will always increase my faith!

If your faith needs to be increased or strengthened, may I suggest spending time with a Faithwalker! Many can talk it, but look for those who truly walk in faith. You will begin to see things on a new level, and your spiritual eyes will become keen to what God is doing, and what He can do! Find someone who lives the faith life, and sit with them for a while. *You will see and hear things that will amaze you and build your faith.* You will soar to some pretty high places as faith takes you to new dimensions! Your journey of faith will go from boring to soaring! You will live out your greatest, God-given dreams!

We all need to be inspired and encouraged to step out on faith. Spending time with a faith walker will give you the courage you need to take that first leap of faith!

September 24

You Have Been Found

Psalm 89:20 "I have found David my servant; with my holy oil have I anointed him."

The eyes of the Lord are upon you today, for He is searching for those that He can trust with His precious treasures. He is searching for someone who will stand in the gap and pick up the sword of truth... someone He can entrust with His vision and anoint for His purposes. He carefully examines those whom He calls, searching the inward parts to see what is in the heart. *The Lord hath sought a man.* The Spirit of God is passing your way today, seeking for precious vessels and beautiful pearls.

There is excitement in the voice that is calling out to you, much like that of the Shepherd who found the lost sheep. There is joy in the voice, like that of the Widow who found the lost coin. There is ecstasy in the voice, like that of the Father of the Prodigal. It is the voice of God in Psalm 89, *"I HAVE FOUND DAVID MY SERVANT!!!!"* David had long been found before Samuel had ever sent for him. The eyes of the Lord had already been upon David before the oil of anointing ever touched his head. His eyes were upon the shepherd boy in the early dawn, when in the first flicker of daylight the young lad led his flock from the fold out into the damp pasture. They were watching David when in an outburst of heroic faith he rescued a trembling lamb from the jaws of a lion and a bear. His ears heard the sweet songs as the Psalmist poured out his great love for the one he called his Lord. It was in those long days where only the eyes of the Lord the character and spirit of a King being developed in a young Shepherd boy!

God sees in you the makings of a Priest or a Priestess! He sees what is hidden from the eyes of man...the character, the faith and the spirit of a King! *He is there in the lonely days and nights when no one else is around...watching you develop!* He hears the songs of midnight and the prayers for the saints that no other ears have heard. He receives the worship and adoration that can only come from pure hearts that worship freely and joyously. 2 Timothy 2:19, *"The Lord knows them that are his..."*

September 25

I Can't Give Up Now

Hebrews 10:23 "Let us hold fast the confession of our hope without wavering, for He who promised is faithful."

Growing up in the Bayou land of Louisiana with a Father who was a fisherman, we were exposed to a lot of wildlife. One of the most common species was the turtle. I remember my mother cautioning us... *"Don't let a turtle bite your finger, for if he does, he will never let it go until he hears the thunder! He is tenacious and nothing and no one can make him let go!"* I'm not sure how true that is, however, it did give me a very healthy respect for the lowly turtle.

Too many people today *"let go."* They let go of the truth instead of binding it upon the tabernacles of their hearts. They let go of the principles of God's Word and adopt a watered down version that appeases the flesh, but makes the spirit weak. *Sadly, some folks just give up, not realizing that today's battles are tomorrow's victories.* Someone hurt them or offended them...and they walk away from the Only One who loves them enough to die for them. Beloved, nothing and no one can ever justify us giving up! As Peter said, *"To whom shall we turn?"* Instead of walking away from the One who loves us, we should run to Him with our hurts, concerns, offenses and disappointments, and release them into His protective care. He knows what to do and what we need better than anyone else! Why give up when He has so much going for us? Why allow anyone to rob us of our crown? I refuse to give up now when tomorrow might just be the day of my greatest victory!

September 26

The 'Staying Power' of God

Jude 1:24 "Now unto him that is able to keep you from falling, and to present you faultless before the presence of his glory with exceeding joy."

"*Staying power! The power to finish what you start!*" The ability to commit yourself to something without giving up or moving on when the results are slow in coming! We don't see too much of this these days.

But God gives us sustaining power! We have been endued with power from on high to stay the course and finish the race! God, in His amazing wisdom, gave us the Holy Ghost to keep us true, on course, and on track! This power of the Holy Ghost gives us "*staying power*"! God knows that without the power of the Holy Spirit we would fail, or give up, or move on! He knows that in our own ability and strength, we are insufficient to finish the course. We have been given a holy sustenance that gives us the strength to endure to the end - the Holy Spirit! We fail because we have not been endued with that power, or when we rely on our own strength and wisdom instead of that of the Comfort and Guide!

The race is not given to the swift nor is the battle given to the strong...but it is given to those who refuse to give up and go under! Victory belongs to those who put their trust in the arm of the Lord and who won't give up! Look to Him for He is the Author and Finisher of our faith! He will keep us and give us "*staying power.*"

September 27

You Matter

Isaiah 49:16 "Behold, I have engraved thee upon the palms of my hands; thy walls are continually before me."

You are not alone. You are not forsaken. You are not forgotten, nor are you a mistake. *You are not a failure.*

The One who guides this universe with His breath has formed you and designed you in such a way that there is no one else like you on earth! You were created to Conqueror. You were set up to Win! You are remembered by the One who forms time and creates destinies. He is on YOUR side! He will never walk away from you, but remains closer than a brother. He is the hand that guides you continually. *His voice is the voice that you hear in the depths of your soul urging you on, and compelling you upward.* He knows your name...and calls on you frequently! He knows all of your secrets and can be trusted with those dreams that are too precious to share with others. He knows your thoughts and has forgotten all about your sinful past, and has given you a great future. He is there with you through every storm, every fiery trial, and every valley that you walk through. He is there with you for every win, every victory, and every challenge. You are loved unconditionally by Him. He clothes you each day with His kind favor, mercy and grace.

You are not alone, nor can He ever forget you, for you see, you are engraved on the palms of His hands.

September 28

If Only We Knew

Ephesians 1:3, 4 "Blessed be the God and Father of our Lord Jesus Christ, who has blessed us with every spiritual blessing in the heavenly places in Christ, Just as He chose us in Him before the foundation of the world, that we should be holy and without blame before Him in love."

If you only knew! If you only knew how greatly you are loved! If only you knew how many times the hand of the Loving Father kept harm and evil from coming near you! If only you knew of the many times His mercy and grace surrounded you and covered you.

How very quick the enemy is to accuse, blame, and attack! How devious are Satan's attempts to convince us that God is against us or, or angry with us. How subtle he can be as he tries to sell us the lie that bad things happen because we deserve them. We must be armed with the truth of God's Word! *God is not against us because of our sin. He is with us against our sin*! He is FOR us! He is for US! HE is for us! He wants us to be victors, not victims; to soar, not sink; to overcome and not be overwhelmed! He has made all of His wisdom, strength, and might available to us through the Blood of Jesus Christ! All we need has already been provided for by Him!

If only....we could realize what a *lover of mercy* He is! If only we could grasp the truth that *we are so abundantly loved*! If only we could receive the knowledge that we are never alone and our purpose is found in Him! He chose us to be His!

September 29

Handle With Care

Micah 6:8 "He has shewed thee, O man, what is good; and what doth the Lord require of thee, but to do justly, and to love mercy, and to walk humbly with thy God."

In our Wednesday Night Bible Study we are learning about our personality types and spiritual gifts. It's amazing (and amusing) to see the responses of everyone as we learn about our particular personality strengths and weaknesses. Eyes widen, expressions of amazement or dismay flit across our faces as our character traits are opened up to us. Not only do we see our own strengths and weaknesses, but we also see each others.

Many of us strive for perfection in our walk with God, trying to please Him with acts, deeds and things that will get us noticed. Sometimes I think we are very critical and hard on ourselves when we need to just take a breath, sit back, give ourselves (and each other) a break. Life is very short and people are very fragile - handle with care! People are the only eternal things on the planet and cannot be replaced. We only have one life to live - live it with purpose. Allow the Blood of Christ to cleanse and forgive us of every sin, and fill us with Agape' love! Love one another...*if we don't love each other, who will*? Be tender and kind hearted to each other, especially those of the household of faith.

I'd like to challenge us today to handle this day with care! Don't be so hard on yourself (or someone else), *but handle with care*! Make the most of this day - not by being so busy and consumed with things - but by taking the time to appreciate each other...and Him.

September 30

Do It God's Way

John 5:30 "I can of mine own self do nothing: as I hear, I judge: and my judgment is just; because I seek not mine own will, but the will of the Father which hath sent me."

I learned a fascinating fact about the Monarch Butterflies... they each have these solar cells on their wings that receive warmth from the sun that causes their wings and muscles to be flexible so they can fly. They are cold-blooded insects who have all of the right equipment to allow them to soar, *but they can only soar if they have received solar power from the sun.* They are totally dependent upon the solar power of the sun to give them the warmth and strength to fly and how much solar warmth they receive determines how high and how far they will soar!

We are stronger and wiser once we realize that we are totally dependent upon Him. On our own we are limited and powerless, full of dead dreams and hollow religion, but *once the rays of His love touch us, we become empowered to soar and to be what we were designed to be.* Many times we will try to circumvent His way by taking short cuts and doing things our way, but we will eventually find out that our ways lead to heartache and emptiness. Without Him we can do nothing. Without Him, there is nothing! When we look to Him that we are able to see clearly. Often He will take us on out of the way paths to teach us that it is not at all about us, our sufficiency, our talent, our charisma, and our independence, but it is all about Him, His glory, His Power and His Church!

Jesus, the Lamb of God, laid aside His own will and surrendered His Father. He came not to do His own will, but the will of His Father who sent Him. He was the example for us to follow, teaching us that in our own selves we are limited and powerless, but in Him *we live, we move and we have our being.* Our ways lead to pain, sorrow, defeat and death, but doing things His way, the righteous way, will lead us to the paths of everlasting life, blessings untold and heavenly places to soar in. *There will always be wrong ways, our ways, right ways and God's ways!* Let's do things God's way for they are perfect and prosperous!

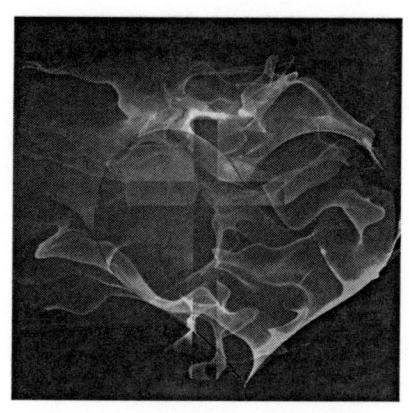

October

"*Life is not measured by the
number of breaths we take,
but by the moments that take our breath away.*"
-Anonymous

October 1

The Testing Place

Psalm 66:10-12 "For you, O God, tested us; you refined us like silver. You brought us into prison and laid burdens on our backs. You let men ride over our heads; we went through fire and water, but you brought us to a place of abundance."

I heard the story about the Pastor who was given too much change after paying the trolley driver his fare. He sat there debating on what to do. Times were tough and he could really use the extra change. As the trolley came to his stop, the Pastor reached in his pocket and pulled out the extra change. *"You have given me too much change,"* he told the driver. *"You made a mistake." "No, I made no mistake,"* said the driver. *"I deliberately gave you too much change. See, I was in the service last Sunday and heard you preach on honesty and integrity, and I just wanted to see if you could live up to what you preached. You passed the test."*

Count on it! ***You are going to be tested!*** The tests will come in unexpected places from unexpected sources, and it is in the small things that we are often tested. Great doors swing on small hinges in comparison to the door. *Great character reaches it's height by progressive development. Great victories often are achieved through many small steps.* Our commitment to Him will be tested. Our faithfulness will be tested. Our integrity will be tested. Our works will be tested. Our strength to stand and endure will be tested. Our very faith, the foundation of truth on which we stand, will be tested. We will be tested in our weak areas as well as our strengths. Someone will be watching us to see if we have what we say we have. Character has to be worked into the soul by the testing ground of life. Before we can soar to the next level we will be tested where we are today. Testing always comes before promotion! Although the arrow may now rest in the quiver or remain in the shadow of His hand, *at the precise moment when it will accomplish it's greatest effect*, it will be produced and launched in the air.

Untested people cannot be trusted, for they have no experiences to strengthen their faith. It is those who receive the testing and make the grade that will be chosen by the Hand of God to greatly impact the world around them. *Embrace your place of testing, for God will use everything in your test to promote you to your next place of destiny.* The testing place is not meant to be a place of defeat, but a place of great victory!

October 2

Rejoice Anyway

Habakkuk 3:18, 19 "Yet I will rejoice in the Lord; I will exult in the [victorious] God of my salvation! The Lord God is my Strength, my personal bravery, and my invincible army; He makes my feet like hinds' feet and will make me to walk [not to stand still in terror, but to walk] and make [spiritual] progress upon my high places [of trouble, suffering, or responsibility]!"

It is not what we go through but how we go through it that determines our failure or our success. We don't get to choose our trials or tests, but we do get to choose our attitude while we are in the refiners' fire. *I may not like the test, but I trust the One who is holding my hand,* and I choose to go though my tests rejoicing!

Things will not always work out like we had hoped. Bad things will happen to good people. We, as Children of God, will go through the refiners purging fire so we can become more like Him. He wants us to be steadfast and unmovable, with a faith that has been tested and is unshakable. It's how we go through these testings that reveal what is in our hearts. We're going to go through them, so we might as well go through them rejoicing...*rejoicing that He believes in us enough to put us through the fire.* We rejoice because He is our strength...our personal bravery and our invincible army! He gives us hinds' feet so we can make it to the high places! We can be complainers or we can be praisers! We can turn away or we can keep pressing on! We can suck on sour grapes or we can feast on joy and gladness! *Our attitude determines our altitude!*

Though the fig tree shall not blossom, though the barns be empty, though the times are tough and the righteous are overturned by wicked rule...*the Lord is still in His holy place* and *I will still rejoice* in the God of my salvation!

October 3

God, Are You With Me?

Isaiah 43:1-3, 5, 10 "...Fear not, for I have redeemed you; I have called you by your name; You are Mine. When you pass through the waters, I will be with you; And through the rivers, they shall not overflow you. When you walk through the fire, you shall not be burned, Nor shall the flame scorch you. For I am the LORD your God, The Holy One of Israel, your Savior; Fear not, for I am with you; You are My witnesses, says the LORD, And My servant whom I have chosen, That you may know and believe Me, And understand that I am He..."

A few nights ago my daughter couldn't sleep and was very heavy in her spirit. She began to pray in the late hours of the night. She cried out to the Lord, *"God, are you with me? I need to hear from you now. I need some answers."* She got her Bible and it opened to Isaiah 43 & 44. There she found exactly the answers she needed to hear, **"I am with thee, you are My Witness".**

It is certainly no secret that many of us are in the heat of great battles. I want to suggest to you that *God is going to use you to do great things...*if you stay true to Him and don't cave under the pressure of the enemy. We are called for HIS purposes to be HIS witnesses, and are singled out by HIM! Satan sees this and will do everything he can to stop us, using intimidation, fear, delusions, and lies, but look at what God says.... *"FEAR NOT...YOU ARE MINE! I will be with you WHEN you go through the waters, and the rivers and the fires!"* Yes, we will go through tests, but if we hold on to His Word, we will come through triumphantly! Hold fast the Word of faith, refuse to give in to the adversary and know that this trial is sent by God to reveal HIS Nature and HIS purpose in you! God uses people He can trust, and trust is perfected in the trials. Don't let these trial be in vain, but allow them to make you trustworthy!

Hold on, dear one! Don't bow under pressure, but seek the Lord, for only HE has the answers.

October 4

Held By God

Psalm 46:1 "God is our refuge and strength, a very present help in trouble."

Our steps can become unsteady and the difficulties of life can seem overwhelming. There are moments when we need to stop struggling and *just rest in the Arms of our Savior.* We need to be held...and to know love that heals.

I stood beside a young mother and father who held and rocked their baby girl for the last time. I heard this mother sing one last lullaby to her baby daughter before releasing her into the arms of Jesus. I saw this father gently kiss her cheek and caress her little cheek one final time. But then, I saw something in their eyes that would astound many...a *simple but profound trust in Jesus that He has a wonderful purpose in the life and death of their precious baby girl.* They allowed Him to hold them in their deep sorrow and great mystery of life. *They resisted the struggle and accepted His peace and great love.*

God will do the very same thing for us. *When we can trust Him enough to stop struggling against the things that are sent to test our faith, we will find peace that surpasses our understanding, and the deep abiding rest and love of a Savior who knows what we are feeling.* He will hold us, comfort us, and give us assurance that He knows what is best. He will gently and tenderly lift us above the shadows and hold us until the storm passes. He will soothe our hurting hearts and give us His strong shoulder to lean on. His peace fills our hearts and minds until we can smile again. To be in the hands of God means His divine assistance is evidenced over and over again in our times of need and desperation. His powerful hands created worlds, and yet they were gentle enough to bless the little children. This *is what it's like to be Held by Him.*

October 5

Tears That Move God

Psalm 56:8 "Thou tells my wanderings: put thou my tears into thy bottle: are they not in thy book?"

Sounds of weeping and lamenting can be heard all over the world, especially during calamities, wars, and destruction. The world seemingly has hardened its heart to those cries and mourning, and is back to business as usual. But there is one sound of weeping that has the attention of God. There are tears that are so precious to Him that He puts them in a bottle...*they are the tears of the Saints.*

The sound of weeping can be heard in the Father's House as the Priests and the Saints weep for what once was and is now lost, and cry out for restoration and mercy. *Tears that will never be shed in public are being shed in private prayer closets from prayer warriors who sense the impending warfare in the heavenlies.* There are tears soaking the altars of prayer, pleading with God to save a nation who has lost her way. Pastors are crying out for revival fires to burn again in cold, dead hearts and churches. Ministers called to carry this precious Gospel are interceding on behalf of nations who desperately need saving. There are the cries and tears of parents who weep for the future of their children, a Godless future that calls good evil. There are the broken-hearted souls who have no one to turn to or lean on, whose sorrow is so grievous that no one can understand the pain and emptiness. He may be raising you up to intercede for a nation, or for a people, and prayer is your source for strength as you weep for those you are called to. Someone must cry out for the children. Someone will weep for the innocent. Someone must intercede as Abraham did for Lot. *These tears are not in vain, for these are the prayers that will demand answers and avail much!*

God sees your tears today. He is very aware of your burden, your pain, your hurt, your sorrow, your loss, your disappointments, and your grief. *Your tears have His attention as you pour out your heart upon the altar of prayer.* Your tears matter to Him. Your tender heart is a gentle reflection of His heart... a heart that is moved with compassion and yearning. He will heal your hurt. He will answer the prayers of the saints. And one day, when we stand in the Presence of Our King, He will wipe every tear from our eyes and say, "Well done!"

October 6

None of These Things Move Me

Job 42:2 "I know that You can do everything, And that no purpose of Yours can be withheld from You."
Acts 20:24 "But none of these things move me, neither count I my life dear unto myself, so that I might finish my course with joy, and the ministry, which I have received of the Lord Jesus, to testify the gospel of the grace of God."

God does not want us to be moved by what we see, feel, think, hear, taste, or touch. He wants us to trust Him wholeheartedly and to believe that He will fulfill His purpose in us. We are sometimes too quick to respond emotionally or fearfully when things don't go as we had hoped, *but God is looking for people who choose to trust Him* in spite of everything that is going wrong. Our best response in times such as these is to simply trust Him and refuse to be moved by conditions and situations that are beyond our control.

Paul was not moved by bad circumstances, or the beatings he received on his back for preaching Jesus, or by the terrible things many people said about him. He knew that God had a purpose and a plan for his life, and nothing and no one could withhold that purpose from being fulfilled. *He determined in his heart that he would finish his course with joy.* He was determined that everything he had gone through would be used to testify of God's grace. He wasn't going to let all the bad experiences, the beatings and the hardships he endured go to waste, *but used them all to declare God's goodness, His faithfulness and His grace.*

What are you moved by today? What circumstances are you facing that seem to shake your trust and faith? Can we say as Paul said, *"None of these things move me"*? Beloved, whatever you are going through, choose to trust God with it. We can trust Him just as Job trusted God with everything he had gone through by saying, *"God, I know you can do anything, and your purpose will be done."* We can trust God today just as Paul did by refusing to be moved by what we see and believe God will work out everything in the end for our good.

October 7

Strength for Today

2 Samuel 22:33, 34 "God is my strength and power: and He maketh my way perfect. He maketh my feet like hinds feet; and setteth me upon my high places."

Jesus has strength for you today!

It doesn't matter what you are going through or what you are facing, *there is strength for you.* Jesus has just what we need, and if we will turn to Him, He will graciously give us our portion for today. The beauty of God's goodness is this...He already knows what we need today and has made full provision for us! He tells us to not worry about tomorrow, but to focus on this gift of today and trust Him to take care of all of our tomorrows.

We become depleted of our energy, strength, wisdom and even our hope because of the necessities, demands and pressures that are made on us. It is when we are depleted and empty that Satan tries to discourage us, but it is also during this time when the Lord of Glory desires to impart His strength and peace into us. It is important to begin each day anew with Him, allowing Him to fill us with His strength so we can run our race in confidence and assurance. We need to have enough of Him to take us through today. Find a quiet place to be alone with Him to receive from Him. There is wisdom and insight that He longs to impart to us. He has strength and hope for us. There are instructions that He wants to speak to us. There are high places that He has prepared for us to dwell in. He has what we need...we only need to go to Him to receive it!

October 8

Hope for Tomorrow

Romans 5:5 "And hope maketh not ashamed..."

Christ gives us hope for our tomorrows!

We are pressing on to bigger and greater things in Christ, knowing that He has already planned our today and secured our tomorrow. We have great promises awaiting us, and for many of us, those promises are woven into the things, places and people we encounter today in anticipation of completion on the morrow! How we handle today determines what we receive tomorrow! *Our now determines our next*!

Wrap up every promise with faith and tie the loose ends with hope! It is by faith that we receive. It is with hope that we press on! Hope gives wings to our faith. *Hope prepares our hearts to receive in faith the future that God has planned for us*. Hope rescues us from the elements of despairs and failures! Don't despair, but hope! Don't give up, keep hoping!

October 9

Perfect Peace

Isaiah 26:3 "Thou will keep him in perfect peace, whose mind is stayed on thee: because he trusts in thee."

Peace is not the absence of trouble, turmoil or pain, but it is the confidence that God is with me in all things. It is trusting in the One who, at a pivitol point in my storm, is able to change my circumstances. Having lost my father, my husband, and my only son within a two year span, *I know very well the importance of the need for peace.* I know the importance of keeping my mind upon the Lord when loneliness and hopelessness try to invade my heart.

There is a great need for peace in these trying times. We live in such a fast paced world that we sometimes leave little room for peace. With all of the distractions and clamor, it is sometimes hard to keep our minds upon the Lord, yet when we do, He is ever faithful to fill us with perfect peace. Peace that soothes the pain, peace that brings light into the darkness of not understanding the 'whys'. *Peace is the evidence that we have placed our complete trust and confidence in the God of yesterday, today and tomorrow.* It is knowing that our paths are ordered by Him, and nothing can touch us without His permission, and knowing He is more than able to handle everything we face. As we walk into our today, walk knowing that He is the God of peace, and as we meditate upon Him, He will impart that perfect peace to us.

October 10

Looking Unto Jesus

Revelation 1:8 "I am the Alpha and the Omega, the Beginning and the End…"
Hebrews 12:2 "Looking unto Jesus, the author and finisher of our faith…"

It's wonderful to start our day out with Jesus!

Many times distractions beset us during the day to take us in different directions than we had planned. Tasks get unfinished, business doesn't get conducted, and needs go unmet - *all because we don't always finish what we start*. Many times people give up too soon, not realizing that the prize is within reach. I often see those who begin this walk with Christ get distracted and never complete their course. But…when we start everything with Him, and we keep Him involved in all that we face, He will help keep us focused on the important things. He is a finisher of what He begins. The key is this… *"Looking unto Jesus"*. He always finishes what He starts!

October 11

He Is Strong Enough

Ephesians 3:20 "Now unto Him that is able to do exceeding abundantly above all that we ask or think, according to the power that worketh in us."
2 Corinthians 12:9 "...My grace is sufficient for thee: for my strength is made perfect in weakness..."

He is strong enough...
>To carry your load
>To lift your sorrow
>To remove your burden
>To direct your paths.

He is wise enough...
>To guide you through safely
>To give you clear direction
>To trust Him with your dream
>To divinely connect you.

He simply asks that we trust Him. He will get us there. He will see us through. He has already prepared blessings for us on the other side of this test of faith. He will not let go of us, leaving us to fend for ourselves. Trust Him. Let the power of faith that is in you be His conduit to work His greatness and excellency in your life. He is strong enough to carry you from testing to victory. Trust in His strength...His might...His power...His love. He will never fail us!

October 12

A Sound Mind

2 Timothy 1:7 "For God has not given us the spirit of fear; but of power, and of love, and of a sound mind."

How reassuring it is to know that we have soundness of mind through Christ Jesus!

Several years ago there was a phenomena that was sweeping the country in which members of high school bands were having fainting spells. I remember seeing these events on the TV where one band member would faint and a wave of other members followed suite. For a while no one could diagnosis the cause until someone figured out that the first band member had his knees locked, which caused him to faint. The other members were "monkey see, monkey do." ***Their minds were open to the power of suggestion.***

The mind is a wonderful, amazing, powerful and fragile enigma with a network of memories, ideas, thoughts and creativity. No man-made computer will ever be able to duplicate the power of the human mind. We see, hear, touch and smell things that send powerful messages to our minds which determine what we will say and do. No wonder the scripture tell us, *"Let this mind be in you which was in Christ Jesus."* He gives us soundness and clarity in our minds. Worries, fears and troubled thoughts flee when we put on His mind. Peace and soundness of mind - how precious these are to us in the times that we live in today. In the midst of a world filled with instability, insanity and troubled minds, we can walk with power, love and a sound mind, thanks to Christ Jesus.

October 13

There Is Peace For Us

John 14:27 "Peace I leave with you, My peace I give to you; not as the world gives do I give to you. Let not your heart be troubled, neither let it be afraid."

There is no need to be troubled or afraid! Jesus, the Prince of Peace, gives peace that will calm our hearts and spirits. There is a better way for us to walk because of Jesus - *it is a path of peace.* All over the world people are searching for peace and comfort - give it to them! Comfort those who are hurting and speak peace to those who are troubled in their minds and hearts. His peace can bring healing and wholeness to those who are broken and afraid.

Share His peace with someone today - make a difference in their life. Touch them with gentleness and kind words, and bring light to their darkened world. Jesus makes all the difference for us! Pray for their peace and for the peace of Jerusalem today. It is in our power to minister to someone needing peace - do it!

October 14

Seek God First

Matthew 6:33 "But seek ye first the kingdom of God, and His righteousness; and all these things shall be added unto you."
Psalm 37:4 "Delight thyself also in the Lord; and He shall give thee the desires of thine heart."

It is so amazing how God speaks to us and then confirms His Word through others! For the past several days we have heard the Lord saying to seek Him first and to delight ourselves in Him... and everything else would be added. He spoke this to us first through prayer, and then confirmed it Sunday through a precious minister friend, and then again last night after prayer...and then again later last night through a minister friend who came by to visit! For the past week we have heard this over and over..."*Seek me first*!"

God *must* have first place in our hearts. He is sounding the call to those who will hear Him, "*Seek Me, delight in Me, and I will give you the desires of your heart.*" Too often we come to Him, seeking Him for what He can give us instead of seeking Him for the pure delight of being in His presence. We are in such a hurry for God to do something for us NOW, *that we forego the pleasure of walking with Him* and talking with Him, and listening as He whispers His secrets, His desires, His plans to us. If we could only understand that *the best place to spend our time is with Him,* in His presence! There we will find fullness of joy and pleasures evermore!

We all have difficulties that we face, problems for which there seems to be no solutions, and cares that are too heavy for us to carry. We all have schedules that are so demanding that too often leave us offering Him the crumbs left over from our busy day. We want so much, dream great dreams, and desire to live the best life we can, but is only through our longings for Him that all this can ever be complete. When we seek Him first, He will add everything we need to fulfill our hearts desires. Seek Him first...delight yourself in Him! He'll do the rest!

October 15

A Dose of Good Medicine

Proverbs 17:22 "A merry heart does good like a medicine..."

They came down the center aisle, giggling and walking very proud, carrying a sign that said, *"We love you"* that was full of tiny handprints. These, the youngest members of our church, brought smiles to the faces of all who saw them. With much pride and dignity the three year old girl handed me a beautiful and colorful elephant bank and said, *"This is for you!"* The little boys dug deep into their pockets and pulled out some bright shiny new gold dollar coins. Each one plopped their dollar into the elephant bank and giggled even more. It was pure joy watching these little ones as they loved on me...their Pastor.

But...it wasn't quite over yet! There was one more thing that *they simply had to do!* They showered love and joy upon us by performing the *"chicken dance"* for me! When the clapping part came they would call out loudly...*"We love you!"* Before they were finished the entire church was laughing and giggling and enjoying the performance of these littlest ones. Their simple gestures delighted all of us and brought much joy. I wish you could have been there! I am sure that I am the only Pastor on the planet who had the chicken dance performed as part of a tribute! And, I wouldn't trade it for anything!

It's no wonder that Jesus Himself loved being around the children. They can lift the heaviest heart with only a smile and a heartfelt hug (they give great hugs)! They love generously and without motive (they could also teach us how to love better)! Perhaps, for a moment today, we can step outside of our adult mindsets, and once again capture the delightful joy that these innocent souls find so easily. Perhaps today, if only for a moment, we can once again see the world...and each other...through the eyes of a child! Perhaps today we can laugh uninhibitedly and give someone else a dose of good medicine!

October 16

Reel 'Em In

Matthew 4:19 "...Follow me and I will make you fishers of men."

I did not know how it would be possible for our littlest members to outdo what they did last year in their tribute to their Pastor, but they did...

They came down the aisle one by one in single file with fishing hats and fishing poles, their faces lit up with happy grins and big smiles that lit up the entire church! They perched on the edge of the stage to do some serious fishing. My daughter sang, *"Going Fishing"*...and my, how our little ones fished! They cast their lines and reeled in like they had the biggest fish on their hooks. They fished with zeal and enthusiasm, and were very serious about their fishing. I am sure that in their little minds, they were reeling in boat loads of fish!

If we fished for men with the enthusiasm and zeal these little ones had, we would reel in a "fish" every time! We just need to have the right "bait." So today, I'm going to visit the "bait shop" and get some love, joy, enthusiasm, and peace. I'll go to Ephesians 6 and get the right "gear" so that I can be prepared to catch some fish. And just maybe...I, too, can reel in a catch...and share Jesus with my fish!

October 17

My Aaron and Hur

Exodus 17:12 "But Moses' hands were heavy;...and Aaron and Hur stayed up his hands, the one on the one side, and the other on the other side, and his hands were steady until the going down of the sun."

There are times when we all need someone to strengthen us and hold up our hands. Ministers, especially, need such reinforcement, for the battles are often fierce and the tasks demanding. *Little can be achieved when battle-fatigue and weariness set in, draining us of our strength.* One of the keys to a thriving ministry is to have people surrounding you that will lift up your hands when the battles wage hot. I am thankful to have such people reinforcing me - some who are part of my family and congregation, and others who are partners with me in ministry.

Yesterday my Church honored me with a special service and beautiful dinner. As I looked into the eyes of church members, I saw their faces alight with love as tears flowed freely down their cheeks! I saw generous hearts and big spirits! I saw those who have spent many hours over the past years with me in prayer and travail...and my heart whispered, *"Thank you."* I looked at my daughters who have always been involved in my ministry, and who worked especially hard to make this a memorable event...and I thanked God for their wholehearted support. I listened to my son-in-law as he delivered a message about the role and love of a Shepherd, and thanked God for such a man whose support has been so God-sent. He has one of the purest spirits and greatest hearts of any man I have ever met. *These are my Aaron's and Hur's*!

The Pastor Appreciation Service was beautiful, but the greatest tribute they gave is their belief in me and in the Church. What more could a Pastor ask for than to have members who see the vision and work together to accomplish it. What more could a Minister ask for than for the belief and support of his/her family? In my book, there is no greater compliment a Minister can receive than to have your family believe in you and in your calling!

353

October 18

Chosen, Not Cast Away

Isaiah 41:9 "You whom I have taken from the ends of the earth, And called from its farthest regions, and said to you, You are My servant, I have chosen you and have not cast you away."

Have you ever felt forsaken and cast aside? Does the enemy of your soul make you feel that you are a "has been", "used up" and "forgotten" soul? Listen to what God says to you today, *"I have chosen you, I have called you by name...you are mine and I will never forsake you."*

You are a chosen child of God and *He has NOT cast you away*! Be fully assured that God is very much aware of what you are going through and He has not left you alone. Just because others reject you doesn't mean that God has. Just because some of your brethren won't accept you doesn't mean God has rejected you. And just because you walk through wilderness places doesn't mean God isn't there with you. In fact, I find that He specifically chooses wilderness places for us so He can be God to us! He is glorified in our wilderness experiences because it is there *"The Sharon Plain will be a pasture for flocks. The Achor Valley will be a resting place for cattle and for my people who search for me."* (Isa 65:10) Because you are HIS, He will cause the desert to bloom - just for you! Because you are His chosen, He will give you a "resting place" in the times of trouble...a mountain top experience when you are in the valley.

A castaway is something or someone that is discarded and thrown away...a shipwrecked person or a person who has been rejected. *We are NONE of these things!* God tells us in His Word...*I have not cast you away! Look for the Rose of Sharon to bloom for you! Look for His hand of provision in the pit! Look for His protection while in the danger zone, and His peace while in the storm. Look for the beauty of the Lord in the wilderness, for He is there to bless you in spite of everything the enemy has thrown at you. You are His!*

October 19

Remembered By The King

II Samuel 9:1 "And David said, Is there yet any that is left of the house of Saul, that I may shew him kindness for Jonathan's sake?"

Once there was a young boy who was the grandson of a king and lived in the finest palaces and had servants who waited on him day and night. When only five years of age, his grandfathers' kingdom was overthrown and the boy was carried away by his servant from the life of luxury he had known. While carrying him away, the servant dropped him, resigning him to the life of a crippled fugitive. Many years later, after spending all of his life wearing the rotten rags of a beggar and living in fear, he was summoned by the new King who offered him a place at his table and a home in the palace for the rest of his life. What brought this about? *The king remembered a blood covenant made years ago between himself and the boy's father.* Because of that covenant, kindness was shown to the son of Jonathan by David the King.

Many times we feel forgotten and lonely, and wonder if anyone really knows or understands what we are going through. We know that we were born for better things and destined for more, yet we are held back by circumstances that are beyond our control. We sense that we are more than what we appear to be, but go unrecognized and unacknowledged. If this speaks to you, let me say that you are remembered today by the King of Kings. *It is because of His blood covenant that the Father asks, "Is there anyone that I may show my kindness to?"* He sees and recognizes you as His child, bought by the blood of His own Son, and desires to bestow upon you all the gifts of royalty, seating you in high places with Him. He has all of the "right connections" and the authority to change your circumstances!

Dear One, if it seems that your labor of love has gone unnoticed and you have been forgotten by people that you have poured yourself into, know that our Father has taken notice of these things and will reward you accordingly. *He sees you and remembers you, and has prepared a special place for you at His table!* We must never grow weary of well doing because we feel unappreciated and unrewarded by others. Our labors of love are remembered by the One who matters the most! We are not forgotten, but remembered by Him.

October 20

The Tender Heart of God

Psalms 91:1 "He that dwells under the secret place of the Most High shall abide under the shadow of the Almighty."

The Lord's heart is so tender towards us, and He longs to bring fulfillment and peace to our busy, hectic lives. He sees the struggles, feels our pain, and yearns with all of His great, big Father's Heart to fulfill us and make us complete.

His heart cries out for us just as it did when Jesus, overlooking Jerusalem, wept and said, *"How I would have gathered thee to me like a mother hen does her chicks."* His eyes are upon the hearts of men and women, and yearns to be Lord, Savior and "Friend" to them. Like the people of Jerusalem, He desires to gather the poor, the disheartened, the weak, the lonely and outcast, the needy, and the lost to Himself. Like the gentle clucking of a Mother Hen, the Spirit of the Lord is bidding us to come under the shelter of His wings and find comfort, healing and security. He is gently drawing *"whosoever will"* to come to Him, and find the peace and safety they seek.

Jesus loves us, this we know! We can be assured that His heart is full of tender and loving thoughts for us today.

October 21

You Are On God's Mind

Jeremiah 29:11 "For I know my thoughts that I think toward you, saith the Lord..."
Psalm 40:17 "For I am poor and needy; the Lord thinketh upon me..."

Contrary to Eleanor Roosevelt who said, *"God is too busy with the affairs of this world to care about the details of life"*, Jesus tells us that God sees the sparrow that falls, and clothes the fields with lilies, and He also cares so much for us that He has numbered the hairs on our head. You are on His heart and mind, and He is thinking of you today. He does indeed care about every single detail of your life.

His eye is focused upon you...your cares, your struggles, your needs and your hurts. He is aware of the lies of the enemy, telling you that God is not with you, that you have failed, or that you are unworthy. God has heard your cry and your prayer, and is speaking to you today..."*I am with you always...*" (Matthew 28:20) He sees what is in your heart and knows the plans He has for you. Give your battles to the Lord, for your battles are His, and He will fight for you. Perhaps you have felt the intensity of the battle growing stronger as the war wages on, but know this...the battle is not yours, but belongs to God! He will not fail you!

You are on His mind! He is always thinking of His children. He is very concerned about the state of this world, but He is also concerned about you, His little One, and the struggles and battles you are going through. You are dearly loved, and you are needed. Trust Him with your life, for you are on His mind!

October 22

What Does God Say?

As I was meditating upon His Word and pondering the events and tragedies taking place in our world I thought, *"What would God say to you and these little ones who are going through so much turmoil, sorrow, suffering, and loneliness?"* This is what I believe He would say to encourage our hearts:

To those who are displaced because of hurricanes, floods, tornadoes, and earthquakes, He would say, *"When you go through the waters, the rivers and the fires, I am with you."* Isaiah 43:2

To those who feel alone and lonely, and whose lonely pain is as a sharp knife cutting deeply into their hearts and souls, He would say, *"I love you with an everlasting love. So I will continue to show you my kindness."* Jeremiah 31:3

To those who are fighting sickness and disease, He would say, *"I will restore health unto you, I will heal you of your wounds."* Jeremiah 30:17

To those who are unjustly and relentlessly attacked, He would say, *"No weapon formed against you will prosper."* Isaiah 54:17; and *"If I am for you, who can be against you?"* Romans 8:31

To those who are struggling with guilt and stains of sin, He would say, *"I am faithful and just to forgive you of all your sins"* 1 John 1:9; and *"Neither do I condemn you; go your way; from now on sin no more"* John 8:11; and *"I demonstrated my own love toward you, in that while you were a sinner, Christ died for you."* Romans 5:8

And to the Church who is experiencing division because of politics, worldliness, and the fall from grace by some Spiritual Leaders, He would say, *"A fountain cannot produce bitter and sweet water, and where there is envying and strife, there is confusion and every evil work, but seek wisdom that is pure, peaceable, gentle and easy to be intreated, full of mercy and good fruits.."* James 3:11,17; and, *"Many who once walked with Christ are now enemies of the cross, so stand fast in the Lord. Don't be moved by division, fear, strife or failures, but become unshakable in your faith and your love."* Philippians 3:18, 4:1

He would say to us to look to Him, for He is the Author and Finisher of our faith. *"Don't be troubled by the things of this world, for they are only temporal, and they, too, will pass. Don't get so caught up in the affairs of this world, but think upon Me and My Word. Don't defile yourself with unholy things, but walk in truth and light. Put your faith and trust in me, and know that I am with you always. My love covers you and my peace guides you. I have hidden you under the shadows of my wings and have set my banner of love over you. You are Mine, I have chosen you, and I will take care of you."*

October 23

It's God's Turn

Revelation 2:7 "He who has an ear, let him hear what the Spirit says to the churches..."

In the art of great conversation there is a time to speak and a time to allow the other person to have their say. A good conversationalist knows that it's not just what he says that is important, *but also knowing how to listen.* We are great at speaking out what is on our hearts and minds, but we can sometimes be very poor listeners. Once our turn to speak is over, our minds begin to wander and we don't really hear what the other person is saying.

I think **it's time for the Church to let God have His turn to speak**! We've heard a lot of what man has had to say - some of it good and some of it has only brought confusion. If we can learn the art of listening, God will speak things in our ears that will confound us, instruct us, promote us, and direct us. *He has much to say to His Bride, things that eyes have not seen, nor have our ears heard!* In the Book of Revelation, the Spirit cautions us several times to *hear* what the Spirit has to say. For after all, when it's all said and done, **it's only what He says that really matters**! His Word will stand forever! It's wonderful to hear uplifting sermons and messages designed to self-help us. But, Friend, *when God speaks a Word to us, it is a Word that is in due season* and will cut through all the smoke screens that we sometimes put up, bringing illumination and revelation.

I am ready to hear His anointed Word! Word of God speak! God, it's your turn now...for we have had our say and now we will hear what You will speak to us!

October 24

In Christ I Stand

2 Chronicles 20:17 "Ye shall not need to fight in this battle: set yourselves, stand ye still, and see the salvation of the LORD with you, O Judah and Jerusalem: fear not, nor be dismayed; to morrow go out against them: for the LORD will be with you."

There are some battles we will not fight. *There are some battles that only He can fight.* There are some times when we can do nothing except trust Him. When we look at everything going on in our world, it looks hopeless - economic failures and stock market crashes. Natural disasters and human tragedies. Corrupt politicians and messianic "wanna be's." False prophets and compromised shepherds. Failed governments and falling churches. It's no wonder people are confused, angry, and mixed up.

Paul said, "We are troubled on every side, *but not distressed*; we are perplexed, *but not* in *despair*; persecuted, *but not forsaken*, cast down, *but not destroyed.*" There are some questions that will never be answered, but we trust Him. There are some things that will happen that will shake us to the core, but we have a foundation that remains unshaken. There are some things we will never agree with or on, but we agree with Him...His Word. And then, there are some times when He just says, *"Stand still and see my salvation. This battle is mine and I will fight it for you. Just stand."*

When troubles seem unrelenting and our tests of faith seem hard, we will say like Paul, *"but not..."* as long as we stand in Christ Jesus. I don't know the how's, the why's, or the when's, but this one thing I know for sure...In Christ I stand.

October 25

Let God Be God

Psalms 62:11 "God hath spoken once; twice have I heard this; that power belongeth unto God."

It is a part of our human nature to try to hold on to what power we have, for after all, God gave us the power of choice and free will. We don't like it very much when things happen that are beyond our control and power. Yet, there will always be things and people that we will never be able to control. We can't control what people do to us or what they say about us, but *we can control how we respond and put them in God's care.* We can't control the weather, *but we can trust the One who IS in control*! We are much better off relinquishing our power and our will to Him, and giving Him full control of everything in our lives. *We are limited - He is unlimited! We are small - He is great! We are weak - He is strong!*

There is a rest and a peace that can only be found when we turn everything over to the Lord and surrender our wills, our thoughts and our ways to Him. We are filled with anxiety and unrest when we wrestle against things that we have no control over, but when we trust in the arm of the Lord, we are filled with quiet confidence and strength. I have learned that when I am struggling with things that are beyond my control to give it to the Lord and allow Him to be God! He does a much better job than I can, for He truly does have the power to take care of it all! Let God be God!

October 26

Who Is On The Throne?

Isaiah 6:1 "In the year that king Uzziah died I saw also the LORD sitting upon a throne, high and lifted up, and his train filled the temple."

There is a vast difference between sitting in a chair and sitting upon a throne! Anyone can sit on a chair but only Sovereign Kings sit on thrones. Many people deny the Throne and all it stands for... and the One who sits upon it. Atheism believes there is no throne; there is no seat of authority or power all the universe must answer to. Humanism believes there is a throne that is occupied by man. The Bible makes it clear that there is a throne in heaven, and no fallen man sits on the throne, but the Lord God is enthroned in Heaven. Isaiah saw the Lord *sitting upon His Throne and ruling creation in His Sovereignty!*

Isaiah might have felt like we sometimes feel, especially during the electing of a new President, or the passing of a well loved and respected leader. We feel unsettled and anxious, not knowing who or what the new ruler may be like. Here, God is showing His Majesty and Supremacy to Isaiah. Leaders may come and go, but God remains seated upon His throne and will rule forever. His throne is high and lifted up...a place of majesty and exaltation.

There is another throne that God desires to occupy. It is found in the heart of man. So often we resign the Lord to a chair instead of giving Him the throne! However, once we can see Him in His Sovereignty and Majesty, there is only one place that is worthy enough for Him...the throne of our hearts! He only is worthy enough to occupy this holy and sacred place...why should we allow any other person or thing to take what belongs to Him? May we give God our thrones...and not just a chair. May He be Lord and not only Savior.

October 27

I Know Him

Philippians 3:10 "That I may know him, and the power of his resurrection, and the fellowship of his sufferings, being made conformable unto his death."

I am often asked if I know different ministers or people. Many times my response is, *"I know* **of** *him or her, but I don't know them personally."* Then there are times when a name is mentioned in a conversation and I can say, *"I know him or her."* What a difference that one little word *"of"* can make! Who we know can make great impressions on others.

Some people claim to know of Christ, and *then some know Him!* It is the difference between light and darkness, sunshine and rain and day and night. We have been called into a glorious fellowship with Christ Jesus and are no longer called servants, but friends, heirs and joint-heirs with Christ. We are now in the *"inner circle",* born again into the family of God through the righteousness of Christ! **Knowing Him** is what makes the difference between intimate relationship and religious rituals! Those of us who are intimate with the Lord are familiar not only with His blessings, but also His sufferings... His very heartbeat and we feel what He feels...see what He sees... and loves with His love. Paul could never be content with knowing Him casually, but wanted to know Him intimately, as only friends can. Islam knows of Jesus Christ as a prophet and teacher. Religion recognizes Him as One who contributed great truth to the world. But those of us who are washed in His blood know Him as Savior, Redeemer, Counselor, Friend...and our Big Brother!

If anyone were to ask me today, "Do you know Jesus?" I can truthfully say, *"Oh yes, I know Him!" I know Him in all of His blessings...and in some of His sufferings. I know Him as the beginner of beginnings and as the ending of all stories! I know Him as the King of Kings and as my personal Savior!"* What a great honor to know Him in these precious and sacred ways!

October 28

Covenant Keeper

Psalm 89:34 "My covenant will I not break, nor alter the thing that is gone out of my lips."

She is still there each night, hanging on nothing but His Word... and as I gaze upon her beauty, I can see reflections of my Covenant God! The awesome, majestic moon reminds me of the eternal things of God and of His faithfulness to one such as I. I am reminded that the God I love and serve is a ***Covenant Keeping God!***

As I was meditating upon the Word, these words in Hebrews 13:5 leapt out to me..."*I will never leave thee nor forsake thee*", reminding me again that *He is a Covenant God!* I am comforted to know that God will never alter His Word, nor will He break any of His covenants...and He will never forsake me. What a beautiful promise from our great Covenant-Keeper! How reassuring to know that He is incapable of failing me and to know that I can trust in Jesus to work out everything for my good! "But ye are come unto Mount Sion and unto the city of the living God, the heavenly Jerusalem...and to Jesus the Mediator of the new Covenant, and to the blood of sprinkling, that speaketh better things than that of Abel." Hebrews.12.:22, 24. C.I. Scofield said this, "*The covenants of God are a sovereign pronouncement normally unconditional in the sense that God obligates Himself in grace, by the unrestricted declaration, "I will" to accomplish certain announced purposes. While we are responsible for obedience to the covenant in order to receive the blessings, human failure is never permitted to abrogate the covenant or block its ultimate fulfillment.*"

Wow! God's Covenants will forever remain unbroken and intact...fulfilling their purpose and achieving their goals. We, as Covenant Children, can walk in the blessings of obedience to His Covenants, being fully assured that God will perform what He promises!

October 29

I See VICTORY!

1 Corinthians 15:57 "Thanks be to God who gives us the victory through our Lord Jesus Christ!"

A few days ago the sky was filled with dark, black clouds that echoed my feelings about a lot of things that day. All of a sudden I saw a brilliant blue sky peeping through the blackness that startled me in its intensity and instantly lifted the heaviness of my heart! It was as if the Lord was saying, *"Things are not as dark as they appear, but behind every storm and behind every cloud is the bright hope and victory I give to my people... hope that says I am a God of victory and not defeat, purpose and not complacency, restoration and not destruction. I am your Victory!"*

Look beyond what you see...*and there you will see God!* Today Abraham is childless, but *tomorrow he has offspring too numerous to be counted!* Today Joseph is in the prison, but *tomorrow he will be in the palace, ruling and governing a nation!* On Friday we see a cross and a tomb, *but three days later we see resurrection power!* Yesterday seemed like a day of defeat when Satan stole what was yours, but *tomorrow is the day he returns it plus seven-fold!* You might hear lots of "no's" today, but just wait...*God has a "yes" for you in His perfect timing.* Today you see dark clouds obscuring your view, but keep looking up! *You will see the brilliant promise of victory!*

I keep hearing His voice whispering these words to my spirit..."*have hope, trust me, believe what I say, put your faith in Me. I never fail.*" Look beyond what you see and behold the victory behind the clouds!

October 30

Agree With God

Proverbs 18:21 "Death and life are in the power of the tongue..."
John 1:1 "In the beginning was the Word, and the Word was with
God, and the Word was God."

If we would only agree with God and say what He says
we would be so much better off! The words that we use and the
conversations we have with ourselves have creative power. They can
create positive things or negative things. It is our choice. The tongue
has the power of life and death. This is why it is so important to be
diligent in using the power of the tongue to create a positive force in
our lives.

One way to stay out of trouble is to simply say what God says!
Get in agreement with Him. Stop defeating yourself with negative
words such as *"I can't", "I'm sick," and "I'm not good enough."*
Instead, use the Word, *"I can do all things through Christ." "I am*
more than a conquorer!" "I am healed by His stripes." "I am blessed
beyond measure." "I am made righteous through the Blood of Jesus
Christ." "I am chosen and redeemed!"

What we say has the ability to create situations, emotions,
and thoughts in others. A kind word helps people, but negative words
hurt - sometimes for a very long time. The words we speak leave a
lasting impact on others. Choose words that agree with His Word!
Speak blessings and life instead of curses and death! Simply agree
with God and watch the creative Word come alive in your heart!

October 31

If There Be Any Praise

Philippians 4:8 "Finally, brethren, whatsoever things are true, whatsoever things are honest, whatsoever things are just, whatsoever things are pure, whatsoever things are lovely, whatsoever things are of good report; if there be any virtue, and if there be any praise, think on these things."

"If there be any praise...think upon these things!"
Some of the greatest battles we fight are fought on the battlegrounds of our minds. One thought can completely turn everything around for the day...either for good or for bad. No wonder Paul exhorted us to "think upon the lovely things, the good things, the things that bring praise and glory!" He knew that if he didn't take control of his thoughts, someone or something else would, and *there was simply too much at stake to allow any negative or condemning thoughts to control his day*!

Satan tries to keep us chained to the past through thoughts of guilt and condemnation that are focused on our failures and mistakes, *but God has great plans for our future, and His thoughts towards us are exciting and good*! Let's bring our thoughts into agreement with God's thoughts and as we do, we will find those things that bring Him praise and glory! God wants us moving forward, not dwelling in the past! So, we made mistakes yesterday - *get over it!* God does every time we go to Him and ask Him to forgive us! He is not thinking about yesterdays' mistakes or sins, in fact, *He says He doesn't even remember them! Why should we?* Refuse to be held hostage by negative thoughts from yesterday! Step into the world of praise and excellent thinking! Today, go forward with a new beginning, for this is a new day! He has good plans for you, so forget about yesterday! Think upon those things that bring hope, encouragement, peace...and glory! Bring every thought into the obedience of Christ...and *agree with God's way of thinking*! There you will find praise and glory!

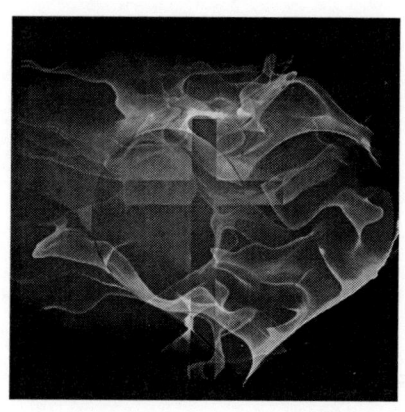

November

Count your blessings like children count the stars.

-Anonymous

November 1

The Power of Praise

Psalm 149:6 "Let the high praises of God be in their mouth, and a two-edged sword in their hand."

There is tremendous power in our praise! Our praise delights His heart and He finds pleasure in people who worship Him - people who can worship Him through the storms, through the trials, through the upsets and in the victories. Often we don't feel like praising Him - *praise Him anyway!* Sometimes burdens overwhelm us - *praise Him anyway!* Sometimes worry, fears or doubt surround us - *praise Him until peace and faith prevail!*

God loves our praise! There is something about praise that gets God's attention - every time! He dwells and inhabits praise! Praise is His habitation! I find that God lives in hearts that are brimming with praise! Praise will put the enemy on the run! When he comes to you with his condemnation and lies, begin to praise the Lord and watch how fast your foe will flee! He cannot dwell in the place of praise. Put him on the run with your praise. Praise is a powerful weapon when wielded in love, adoration, and truth.

As you enter into the courts of the Lord, enter with praise, for praise will open the doors and unlock the gates the lead into the Presence of Almighty God!

November 2

Break Forth In Praise

Galatians 4:27 "...Rejoice, O barren, you who did not bear. Break forth and shout..."

Did you know that your praise will bring your breakthroughs? Your praise will produce some powerful manifestations of God's Glory?

There are some things that praise in itself will produce in our lives. One of those things is a *"breaking forth"* into a *place of victory.* Many times I have observed people who came to Church filled with distress, discouragement and pain, but as they began to worship and praise the Lord, they were uplifted, encouraged and healed. Our release and breakthrough is tied to our praise. If we want God to touch us, then we must touch Him, and we do that by giving Him praise. *When praise goes up, His Presence and His power will come down!*

When we break through in praise, God will break forth in glory. In Matthew 23, Jesus rebuked the Pharisees, calling them a den of vipers. These Pharisees had structure, self-righteousness, laws and rules, but there was no praise or worship in their hearts. There is a spirit in our churches and in our country that wants to keep us quiet in praise. Hands that used to go up in worship now hang down in defeat. Voices that once shouted in praise are now silenced by a religious spirit that demands that we act dignified. The dance that brought us victory has now diminished into a form of entertainment that produces lifeless worship. But, when praise breaks forth, amazing things happen. When we offer up praise, God will send breakthrough! Sarah offered her dried up, elderly body and a son broke forth! Moses offered a rod and a serpent broke forth! Gideon offered 300 men and victory broke forth! Break forth and shout unto the Lord...and watch those chains fall off, the burdens removed, and freedom to live victoriously be rendered unto us!

November 3

The Provision in Praise

Daniel 3:25 "Look, he answered, I see four men loose, walking in the midst of the fire; and they are not hurt, and the form of the fourth man is like the Son of God."

What we perceive as a place of danger will be a place of protection when we praise Him. God always shows up when people praise Him - He just can't stay away! Praise produces powerful protection.

Three brave boys would not bow to the demands of the spirit of silence, but boldly and courageously praised the living God! Praise protected them in a fiery furnace! Daniel would not succumb to the spirit of silence that tried to shut up his praise, and took a stand for the right over the wrong. His praise protected him from hungry lions.

Your praise will bring supernatural protection. Your enemy would love to silence the voice of praise, for if he can do this, then he has you in his clutches. He cannot stay where praise is, for Praise ushers in the Presence of the Living God…the God who will defend you against every evil attack…the God who will protect you in the pavilion of His safety and hide you under the shadows of His wings.

November 4

The Place of Miracles

Psalm 147:12-14 "Praise your God, O Zion. For He has strengthened the bars of your gates; He has blessed your children within you. He makes peace in your borders, and fills you with the finest wheat." Luke 18:39 "And they which went before rebuked him, that he should hold his peace: but he cried so much the more, Thou son of David, have mercy on me."

Praise will take us to the place of miracles!

The blind man worshipped Jesus...and was healed! Praise took him to his miracle. Many around him tried to silence him, but he cried out even louder! They said to him, *"Be quiet! Shut up! You are making a spectacle of yourself! Where is your pride...your dignity!"* He refused to be silenced by the crowd of mockers and hushers! He praised through his blindness...and got the attention of Jesus! Praise was the birthing place of his miracle.

The same spirit that tried to shut up Blind Bartimaius tries to silence us. The enemy of our miracle knows that if he can silence our praise, he can hinder the miraculous! He knows that our praise will get God's attention, so he will do everything in his power to get us to shut up. He will employ pride and dignity as weapons to silence us. He will use those around us to hush us. We need to catch what Bartimaius had...praise that takes us to the place of miracles! Praise that refuses to be silenced by the hushers and pride! Praise that gets the attention of the One who is drawn to praise and who can give us our miracle!

November 5

Shut Up The Hushers

2 Samuel 6:16 "As the ark of the Lord came into the City of David, Michal, Saul's daughter [David's wife], looked out of the window and saw King David leaping and dancing before the Lord, and she despised him in her heart."

The 'hushers' of this world will always criticize our devotion to God. They will try to shut down our praise and demand that our worship be a form or ritual instead of passionate adoration. The 'hushers' will come out in full force to silence the voice of praise and prayer. Sadly, even our churches have 'hushers' who stand on alert, waiting to silence the passionate praise from a child in need of a miracle. But, even the 'hushers' can't stop praise from coming forth from those who are passionately in love with Jesus!

'Hushers' despise and scorn praise, especially passionate, fervent praise. They don't understand it and become critical of those who worship without restraint. Because of her critical spirit, God shut up the womb of Michal and she was unable to bear children. The spirit of the 'husher' wants us to remain barren and unfulfilled. He knows that praise will usher in the Presence and Power of the Living God. He knows that praise is the birthing place of miracles.

'Hushers' can't stand praise...and the power it evokes. They hate hearts that are filled with praise and love for a Soverign God. We must never allow our spirits to become critical of our worship and praise, lest we become spiritually barren and unfruitful. Criticism will rob us of the purity in our praise and will open doors for religious spirits to enter in our hearts, producing a form of godliness but denying the power of God. But, He that the Son has set free is free indeed! Praise is liberating, freeing us from the hostile influence of demonic forces. Praise brings the presence of God into our lives. Today we can praise Him with purity and holiness and with passion and adoration.

November 6

The Place of Overflow

Joel 2:23, 24 "Be glad then, ye children of Zion, and rejoice in the Lord your God: for He hath given you the former rain moderately, and He will cause to come down for you the rain, the former rain, and the latter rain in the first month. And the floors shall be full of wheat, and the fats shall overflow with wine and oil."
John 4:23 "But the hour cometh now, and now is, when the true worshipers shall worship the Father in spirit and in truth: for the Father seeketh such to worship Him."

Our praise will bring us to a place of overflow.

There is a place of praise that will usher in the overflow blessings! *This place of overflow is a place where the latter rain and the former rain meet in the streams of glad hearts.* It is the place of abundance and of blessings, and where the Spirit of Praise flourishes. Hell fears a praying and praising church. Satan's worst enemy is a saint that can touch God with prayer and praise. A church where there is a lot of prayer and praise going up threatens him. We need to realize that Satan does not want us to break free and the last thing he wants is for us to live in the place of overflow. *To live in the place of overflow is to constantly have a flow of the anointing of the Holy Ghost.* We can't allow the enemy to take our praise from us, but we must determine that our praise will go forth and nothing will hinder us.

We praise God because He is worthy to be praised. We praise Him for the mighty things He has done for us. We praise God for eternal salvation that now belongs to us. We praise Him because He loved us when no one else would, and blessed us beyond measure. He is surely worthy to be praised today. *He is a generous Father who deserves generous praise!*

November 7

The Goodness of God

Psalms 107:8 "Oh that men would praise the Lord for his goodness, and for his wonderful works to the children of men!"

The Psalmist David put it this way..."*Goodness and Mercy shall follow me all the days of my life.*"

Truly, God is good to us. We might not have everything we want, or sometimes what we think we need, but God is *still* good to us. *He gives us mercy when we are deserving of judgment.* He extends grace when we struggle in our faith. He is compassionate. He offers love instead of condemnation. He gives hope when everyone else has turned against us. He is forever faithful to pick us up when we fall or stumble, and love us back into His family. *He is the Father to the prodigals, and the forgiving Savior to the sinners.* He is our great Intercessor, praying for us in the garden. He is our gracious King, extending His unmerited favor towards us. God is RICH in goodness, kindness, and patience. He is so very, very, very generous – even with those who least deserve it. The more we come to know the Lord, the more we recognize His extreme generosity with us in every area of our lives!

Last night I took a moment to enjoy His handiwork in the darkened skies. The moon was full and bright, with a beautiful, soft, luminous glow all around it. As I gazed upon the lovely sight, I thought, "*How could anyone looking at this magnificent moon deny that there is a God.*" Yet, they do, and yes, God is still trying to get their attention with His goodness and love. 'God is good, God is great' is the little prayer of grace we learned in elementary school. God is Good!

November 8

Yet

Habakkuk 3:17-19 "Although the fig tree shall not blossom, neither shall fruit be in the vines; the labor of the olive tree shall fail, and the fields shall yield no meat; the flock shall be cut off from the fold, and there shall be no herd in the stalls; YET I will rejoice in the Lord, I will joy in the God of my salvation, The Lord God is my strength, and he will make my feet like hinds' feet, and He will make me to walk upon mine high places."

We have a reason to sing and rejoice, for the Lord is Our God and our strength! He knows us by name and has called us to walk in high places with Him!

I love the heart of this prophet of old...he did not allow circumstances, victories or failures to dictate his worship or diminish his loyalty to his God! He lived in one of the most troubled times in Israel. Times were hard and Israel was in despair. Promises were unfulfilled, victory was fleeting, and struggles were a way of life. Sounds a lot like our times, doesn't it?! However, Habakkuk had a relationship with God, and it was his love for the Lord that would not allow him to give up. He determined he would praise God no matter how it looked! He had decided to trust God all the way, knowing that it is only through trials and testings that faith can be made stronger and more perfect. The future looked unpromising - YET, he praised God! The crops had failed - YET, He rejoiced in the Lord. *He might have woke up not knowing if he would have food in his mouth, but he still had praise in his mouth!* Habakkuk knew God was greater than the trials, greater than the famine, and greater than the circumstances that offered no hope! YET, he joyed in his salvation, and knew God would give him hinds' feet that would take him to higher places than where he was walking then.

I, too, will praise the God of my salvation! He's my rock, my sword, my shield! He is my Comforter and my strength! YET, I will rejoice in Him, for I know my Redeemer lives, and He will give me hinds' feet, too!

November 9

Summum Bonum...the Chiefest Good

Psalm 52:1 "...The goodness of God endureth continually."
Nahum 1:7 "The Lord is good, a stronghold in the day of trouble, and He knoweth them that trust in Him."
Romans 2:4 "...The goodness of God leadeth thee to repentance."

We awoke this morning to God's goodness and faithfulness. Each morning as He kisses the grass with dew, He is thinking of ways He can show us His love and His goodness. As I performed my morning tasks and prepared for my day I sensed the quiet love and tenderness of God. It is a stillness - a quiet strength - that He has graced me with, reminding me that He is so very, very good.

The original Saxon meaning of our English word "God" is *"The Good."* God is *summum bonum*, the chiefest good. Even when we don't understand the workings of God, He is still good. His goodness shows up through the hard times and the best of times, and is everlasting. His goodness is a stronghold for us in our troubled days.

It is this goodness of God that leads men to repentance. It is this goodness that causes us to trust Him again and again. It is this goodness of God that gives us the strength to continue on in this life of faith. May you feel His great love for you and His goodness embracing you today. He is good...all the time.

November 10

Give God A Party

2 Samuel 6:14 "And David danced before the Lord with all his might..."
Psalm 96:11 "Let the heavens rejoice, and let the earth be glad..."
Psalm 9:1 "I will praise thee, O Lord..."

Today, I will praise the Lord!

Today I will celebrate God in every way I can, and if I could throw Him a party, I would invite you to the celebration! I would have lots of singing, rejoicing, and all of His favorite things and His favorite people. Since some of this isn't possible, I've decided to have a party for God in my heart!

I will sing to Him today! My songs will come from my heart as I rejoice in His goodness to me. I will pray tribute to Him by acknowledging His Sovereignty and Holiness. I will honor Him with gifts of praise and adoration from a heart that is truly thankful and grateful. I will dedicate this day wholly unto Him and heap upon Him my declarations of love. *I will show Him how much I love Him by keeping His commandments and obeying His Word.* I will not withhold anything from Him, but with pure, unadulterated joy offer Him wholeheartedly everything I am, everything I have, and everything I desire. I offer Him the very best I have to give. I will laugh with Him today. My heart will leap and dance for sheer joy as I celebrate this *wonderful, amazing, awesome, merciful, gracious, lovely, righteous, and holy Savior*! I will weep with tears of gratitude as I remember His goodness to me. *I will spend this day honoring Him.*

I invite you to join me in celebrating Jesus, and the amazing, unfathomable love of our Heavenly Father who gives His very best blessings and gifts to us. This is His day...the day He has made...and I will be glad in it!

November 11

Think About His Goodness

Psalm 103:4, 11 "Who redeems thy life from destruction; Who crowns thee with lovingkindness and tender mercies...For as the heaven is high above the earth, so great is the mercy toward them that fear him."

Last week I spent an entire day celebrating Jesus. I did this by acknowledging His blessings, His creative handiwork, and with songs from my heart. It was an amazing day as I thanked Him for paying the price for my salvation, for redeeming me from destruction, and for blessing me with countless blessings. The joy and peace that flowed was indescribable. The atmosphere was filled with a sweet aroma of His tender Presence. *It was a day that bears repeating over and over again.* It was a day that I cherished and desire to relive.

So, today I will mediate on His goodness to me. I will cast down negative thoughts and imaginations, and think only upon things that are lovely and pure; things that are of a good report. I will dwell upon thoughts of His greatness and of His great favor. I will rejoice in the truth of His Word and in the Power of His Might. I will believe that all things are possible with Him. I will accept the Crown of Favor and tender mercy He offers, and walk befitting a child of God. My actions and words will proclaim His goodness to me, and to all who honor Him. This will a day of Praise, Worship and Adoration.

It will be a great day...a blessed day. I will soak in the rays of His love. I will rest in quiet confidence, fully assured of His love and mercy. This will be a good day...a great day!

November 12

Graciously Graced

Hebrews 4:16 "Let us then fearlessly and confidently and boldly draw near to the throne of grace (the throne of God's unmerited favor to us sinners), that we may receive mercy [for our failures] and find grace to help in good time for every need [appropriate help and well-timed help, coming just when we need it."

You are graciously graced today! The deep love of our Heavenly Father is poured upon you without measure. *He has placed a crown of favor upon your brow and clothed you in mercy and loving-kindness.* Like the beautiful Queen Esther who found favor in the King's eyes, so also has the King of Kings extended His favor and grace to you!

The Grace of God covers you. You may be facing some giants right now, or in the midst of a heated battle, but grace has been appointed for you today. The fiery darts of an angry enemy cannot penetrate His grace that abounds in you. You may wonder why the enemy has targeted you and singled you out, but know this, God's grace will get you through this also. It does not matter what the world thinks of you, or what is being said against you. What does matter is you have found favor in the eyes of the Most High God, and He has chosen you to shine through. You are graciously graced! His divine favor rests upon you, so hold your head up high!

You are graciously graced to enter the Presence of the King to find help and wisdom in times of trouble and need. His favor rests upon you. Come boldly to His throne, for you have found grace in His sight.

November 13

The Blessings of Obedience

Deuteronomy 28: 1-6 "If you listen obediently to the Voice of God, your God, and heartily obey all his commandments that I command you today, God, your God, will place you on high, high above all the nations of the world. All these blessings will come down on you and spread out beyond you because you have responded to the Voice of God, your God."

The Good News today is this...the blessings of the Lord will follow those who obey His Word! The Bible is simple in it's teachings of how to be blessed by God! Today we can be partakers of the Covenant blessings and the benefits of our Covenant God because of the Blood Covenant of Jesus Christ! *Just obey what God's Word says*!

These incredible blessings come through obedience to His Word and when we respond as Sons and Daughters of God...

- *God's blessing inside the city, God's blessing in the country;*
- *God's blessing on your children, the crops of your land,*
- *The young of your livestock, the calves of your herds, the lambs of your flocks.*
- *God's blessing on your basket and bread bowl;*
- *God's blessing in your coming in, God's blessing in your going out.*

"God will defeat your enemies who attack you. They'll come at you on one road and run away on seven roads. God will order a blessing on your barns and workplaces; He'll bless you in the land that God, your God, is giving you. God will form you as a people holy to Him, just as He promised you, if you keep the commandments of God, your God, and live the way He has shown you. All the peoples on Earth will see you living under the Name of God and hold you in respectful awe. God will lavish you with good things: children from your womb, offspring from your animals, and crops from your land, the land that God promised your ancestors that He would give you. God will throw open the doors of His sky vaults and pour rain on your land on schedule and bless the work you take in hand. You will lend to many nations but you yourself won't have to take out a loan. God will make you the head, not the tail; you'll always be the top dog, never the bottom dog, as you obediently listen to and diligently keep the commands of God, your God, that I am commanding you today. Don't swerve an inch to the right or left from the words that I command you today by going off following and worshiping other gods." (The Message Bible - Deuteronomy 28:7-14)

Need a blessing? Just believe God's Word, apply it, obey it... and stand on it! It's just that simple!

November 14

Seasons of Blessings

Ezekiel 34:26 "And I will make them and the places round about my hill a blessing; and I will cause the showers to come down in his season; there shall be showers of blessings."

"*I am greatly blessed and highly favored of the Lord!*" is a statement often made by believers. He calls us blessed and greatly favored!

God's hill (the place where He is set up as Lord and King) is the source of blessing to all who dwell there and to those who dwell in the surrounding areas. He will cause them and the places surrounding His hill to be named in blessings. Life can bring us through many "dry" places and through many trials, but it is the blessings of the Lord that refresh and revive our spirits! It is out of the goodness of His heart that He blesses us! It is during our seasons of blessings that we experience blessings on every hand! Every way we turn we run into blessings! Blessings overtake us and produce a great overflow. His favor shines upon us like a neon light. He will bless our faithfulness! He will bless our giving! He will bless our seed! When the seasons of blessings come, they will fall upon us as showers of blessings that cannot be numbered! And, not only are we blessed, but everyone around us will be blessed. He blesses us so we can bless those around us! I have found the closer I stay to Him, the greater the blessings flow in my life. The more I celebrate Him the more He blesses me! His blessings make us rich and add no sorrow!

It is out of the goodness of God's heart that He sends us seasons of blessings. He loves on us through others by showering us with blessings that brighten our days. His love for us is revealed by showing us unmerited favor and kindness, even in the small things. He has ordained certain seasons of blessings for us...seasons that bring us great refreshing, and make us secure in the knowledge that we are deeply loved and favored by Him. He knows our desires and longings. We all need to be loved and acknowledged, and no one does it better than Jesus! He will shower us with blessings just to show us how much He loves us.

November 15

Blessings In Disguise

Proverbs 10:22 "The blessing of the LORD, it maketh rich, and He addeth no sorrow with it."

Blessings often come in the form of disguises, surprising us unexpectedly. What may seem like a detour or a set-back will often result in some of our greatest blessings.

No one could see blessings coming from an elderly couple who were barren and childless, yet all the nations of the earth are blessed from a womb thought barren and dry. No one expected anything good to come out of a slave boy who spent years in a dark prison, but God saw trustworthiness and faith in him that He could use to bless and preserve a Nation. Who, but God, can see blessings disguised in delays, trials, dungeons, and set-backs? Think of those times when a red light delayed you, but you saw the provision of God down the road as you passed an accident that could have been you. Or, perhaps you have been laid off only to be promoted elsewhere to the position you dreamed of having.

There are no greater riches than those God gives, even when we can't see the blessings hidden in our times of testing and waiting. Be encouraged and know that we can trust Him to bless us with all good things, and the true riches of Christ Jesus bring us no sorrow, but makes glad our hearts!

November 16

He Has Blessed

Numbers 23:20 "Behold I have received commandments to bless: and He has blessed; and I cannot reverse it."

God has commanded His blessings to us this day! We are blessed beyond measure because of the blessings of the Lord! His blessings will always overtake us when our ways are pleasing to the Lord!

When God speaks a blessing over us *it cannot be reversed!* It is important to remember when we are in the heat of a battle that the Lord is with us and has commanded the blessing of victory over us. No matter how hard Satan tries, he cannot reverse the blessings God speaks over us! Regardless of who Satan uses to try to negate our blessings, they cannot be reversed! He can pull out every trick known in his little bag, but none of them can reverse the commanded blessings of the Lord! *Only we* can stay the hand of blessings by acts of disobedience to the commandments of the Lord! *But when our ways are pleasing unto Him, nothing or no one can stay the blessings!* No one can curse what God has blessed! He will curse everyone who curses His blessed ones and will bless everyone who blesses His blessed ones!

We are blessed of the Lord and must learn how to walk in those blessings! We are blessed when we walk through the valleys of the shadows of death! We are blessed when we go through the fires and floods! We are blessed when facing giants of opposition! We are blessed without measure! Everything that our hands touch is blessed! Every place that our feet tread is a blessed place! We are blessed because we are His!

November 17

Forget Not His Benefits

Psalms 103:1-5 "Bless the Lord, O My Soul, and all that is within me, bless His holy name! Bless the Lord, O my soul, and forget not all His benefits: Who forgives all your iniquities, Who heals all your diseases, Who redeems your life from destruction, and Who crowns you with loving-kindness and tender mercies, Who satisfies your mouth with good things, so that your youth is renewed like the eagle's."

Sometimes God just wows me! To think that everything I need for today has already been provided for by my Father is so amazing! I can't help but bless Him! He has given us some amazing benefits to enjoy today - how can we forget them! He forgives us of all our iniquities! He heals us of ALL our diseases. He redeems our lives from destruction, and crowns us with loving-kindness and mercies! He fills our mouths with GOOD things and RENEWS our youth! WOW!

By receiving this Word, we give God total access and all legal rights into our lives to bless us and to keep us from destruction! As heirs to His kingdom, we wear crowns of mercy and loving-kindness. We are healed of any and all diseases that try to invade us. I love this - He redeems our lives from destruction! We know that Satan came to kill, steal and destroy, but Praise God, we are redeemed from his evil intents! What Satan means for evil - God turns for our good. And Ladies - He renews our youth! These are some pretty amazing benefits that we have, all because we belong to Him. It is no wonder that David blessed the Lord, and loved to praise Him! Remember today, the benefits that you have as a Child of the King! They are truly glorious!

November 18

Only The Best For His Children

Luke 15:22 "But the father said to his servants, Bring out the best robe and put it on him, and put a ring on his hand and sandals on his feet."

Sometimes people can make some pretty good messes of their lives, can't they?! They make bad decisions, wrong choices and poor judgments, leaving them feeling worthless and shamed. It is in those moments of solitude, loneliness and abandonment that they can still find a loving Father, who not only sees the faults, imperfections, defects and blemishes, but He also sees great value!

This young man who once enjoyed Sonship made bad choices. He wanted to "sow his oats" and make his own way. When all his wealth and friends were gone, he found that the only dining companions were pigs, and the only food around was hog food. He remembered the life he once led...and shame and dismay filled him. He remembered how well the servants had it in his father's house and purposed that he would go back there...not as a son, but as a servant. When his father saw him coming home, his heart rejoiced and flowed with love for his wayward son. *He brought out the best* that he had and gave it to his son. No servants robe for his son! He restored him to his place of Sonship and placed his ring on his son's finger. See...he knew about those flaws in his son, but he also saw the worth in him. Was the son worthy of restoration? Most people would say, *"Probably not."* Yet to this father, His son was worthy of only the best!

It is the same with our heavenly Father. He doesn't judge or condemn us when we make mistakes, but keeps on loving us. He sees value in us where others only see flaws. He sees us as a great treasure. He sees great worth in us. He sees awesome potential in us and opens up to us his storehouse of blessings! He gives us His best! He calls us His Sons and Daughters!

November 19

Perfect Conditions Not Necessary

Acts 16: 23-26 "And when they had laid many stripes upon them, they cast them into prison, and made their feet fast in the stocks. And at midnight Paul and Silas prayed, and sang praises unto God: and the prisoners heard them. And suddenly there was a great earthquake, so that the foundations of the prison were open: and immediately all the doors were opened, and every one's bands were loosed."

Perfect conditions are not necessary to praise the Lord! True worship and praise cannot be locked up, chained up, bound up, or shut up. Even the very forces of hell cannot extinguish the fire that burns in a soul that is ablaze with love for the Savior. Praise cannot be stolen from a true heart of worship. Unfavorable conditions don't lessen who God is, for He is God of the valley as well as God of the mountains.

You've heard the saying that it's easy to praise God when things are going well, but I have found that those who don't praise Him in imperfect conditions won't praise Him when everything is great. Give me hearts who will worship God in spite of storms, setbacks, lashings, disappointments, and failures and I will show you someone who knows the Risen Savior in all of His might, power, and victory. God is looking for people who will praise Him in the victories *and* in the battles, in the storms *and* in the blessings, in the abundance *and* in the lack. If we want to live the life that Paul spoke of, the life of an overcomer and more than a conqueror, we must realize that God is worthy of our praise and worship, regardless of imperfect conditions. *Trials will come and go, but Jesus is Lord over all.* Offering Him praise will assure us of His Presence in our lives, for He inhabits the praises of His people. Not only do I need Him in my trials, but I need Him in my victories, for not only is He with us in our trials, but *He ordains victory for His people!* And there is one little nugget here...*our praise holds the key to unlocking prison door not only ourselves, but for those around us.*

The Psalmist, a man with a heart for God, said it like this, *"Oh that men would praise the Lord."* Paul and Silas lived the "in all these things we are more than conquerors" life...and so can we.

November 20

No Complaints Allowed

Psalms 92:1, 2 "It is a good thing to give thanks unto the Lord, and to sing praises unto thy Name, O most High: to shew forth thy loving-kindness in the morning, and thy faithfulness every night."

What if on our National Day of Thanksgiving we decided to place a restriction over our mouths and hearts that said, *"No Complaints Allowed."* When asked, *"How are you"*, what if our response was, *"I am blessed and I have no complaints whatsoever!"* What if we used our words to bless the Lord and each other instead of criticizing and finding faults. What if we took the time to give thanks unto our Gracious Heavenly Father for kindnesses forgotten and blessings we took for granted. What if we saw only the good in our loved ones instead of faults. What if today we said *"Thank You"* to those who bless us and who love us unconditionally.

The highest form of prayer is gratitude. Instead of asking God for more, perhaps we can begin by thanking Him for everything He has already given us. Perhaps we will see the blessings we overlooked. Perhaps today we will see that we have much to be thankful for!

November 21

Counting My Blessings

James 1:17 "Every good and perfect gift is from above, and comes down from the Father of lights, with whom there is no variation or shadow of turning."

There are a lot of things in this world that are designed to bring worry, fear, anxiety and doubt, and if we focus on those things we will never have a moment of rest and peace. Bad news and negative influences are all around us...the planet is on meltdown, the economy is bad, the bills are unpaid, crime is getting worse...the list could go on forever. Thankfully, we have a Savior, a Great God who has better things for us. We can see hope, beauty, blessings and the faithfulness of a loving and caring Savior! Oh, how He loves us! He has opened up His treasury to give us all of His very best gifts - mercy, compassion, peace, kindness, joy, hope, grace...*the list could go on forever*!

Dear one, if there is one thing He would speak to us today that would quiet our troubled minds and bring rest to our weary minds, I believe it would be this, *"I will take care of You! I am faithful to meet all of your needs. Trust Me!"*

I like this old song that Bing Crosby sang...It reminds me that when we count our blessings we will be too busy to look at the negative things.

> *When I'm worried and I can't sleep*
> *I count my blessings instead of sheep*
> *And I fall asleep counting my blessings*
> *When my bankroll is getting small*
> *I think of when I had none at all*
> *And I fall asleep counting my blessings*

May you find many blessings to count and to give Him thanks for!

November 22

In All Things Give Thanks

1 Thessalonians 5:18 "In everything give thanks: for this is the will of God in Christ Jesus concerning you."

Sometimes we wonder how we can give thanks to God for the bad things that happen to us, or how can this possibly be the will of God, until we take another look at what Paul says. *This is the will of God...to give thanks.*

Does that mean that everything that happens to us is God's will? No, I don't think so, for it is not God's will that we make bad choices and go back into lifestyles that He redeemed us from. However, God can use our mistakes, our mess-ups, and the bad things that happen, to work good in our lives. Romans 8:28 says, *"All things work together for good to those who love God."* Those who love Him learn how to praise Him, regardless of situations, circumstances, and our own weaknesses! We praise Him because He is God, He loves us, and has redeemed us! It is God's will for His children to give Him thanks in all things, all circumstances, and in all situations! How can we do this? Because He loves us...and we love and trust Him!

It's so much easier to give thanks when we trust in His love for us! We, too, can say as Paul, *"I will give Him thanks in everything!"* It is the "giving thanks" that is His will!

November 23

Five Kernels of Corn

2 Chronicles 20:21 "Give thanks to the Lord, for his steadfast love endures forever."

I shared a brief but poignant story yesterday in our Thanksgiving Service of how the pilgrims gave thanks for five kernels of corn. Times were very tough and there were seven times as many graves needed as there were homes built. Many of the pilgrims did not survive in the harsh wilderness of the new land. The ones who survived were diligent and faithful in giving thanks to the Almighty for His provision...despite of the hunger and lack of food, for His Divine guidance...despite of the hand of death that swept through their humble abodes, and for His unfailing love...despite of the sorrow and grief that met them each day. Food was so scarce that they were only allowed five little grains of corn for each person each day. As the years went by and the land began to produce bountiful harvests, they continued this tradition each year by giving each person five kernels of corn as a remembrance to give thanks to the God who brought them through some of the most horrific and inhumane conditions they would ever face. Those five little kernels of corn represented something that was bigger than their poverty, hunger, loneliness, despair and neediness...they represented the hand of the Almighty God and the blessings that He holds in His hands.

Sunday morning service was a bit different yesterday. There was a very sweet spirit as our congregation reflected upon the blessings of the Lord. Each of us found reasons to be grateful and thankful, and shared thoughts that were mingled with tears of appreciation with each other. Perhaps one of the most meaningful words of gratitude I heard was the one from a young woman who had gone through many trials over the past couple of years. She said, *"I am thankful for my past because it gives me a future."* Someone once said, *"Some people complain because God put thorns on roses, while others praise Him for putting roses among thorns."* Our attitude of gratitude will cause us to see the good side, the God side, of everything. God has brought us through many things, and will continue to be there for us. That is worth thanking Him for!

November 24

Come To His Table

Psalm 23:5 "Thou preparest a table before me in the presence of mine enemies, thou anointest my head with oil, my cup runneth over."

The Father has spread the table for you! You have been given a *"By Invitation Only"* to sit at His table and in His presence.

Dear One, we are no longer confined to living a life in the lower elements of this world, but have been called into heavenly places with the King of Kings. We do not have to resign ourselves to eating crumbs today, for we have been given a feast at the Master's table. We no longer have to hide in darkness for fear of our lives, but a place at the Royal table has been reserved for us! He has chosen us, not because of our abilities, talents and skills, but because of unmerited favor and grace. It is because of the Blood Covenant of Jesus Christ that we are made worthy! All that He has is now at our disposal!

The same Heavenly Father that prepared a table for David in the presence of his enemies has prepared a table for us! *Even in the presence of our enemies.* How great is the Father's love for us. He has anointed our heads with the oil of the Holy Spirit! Our cups overflow with living water that only He can give! *Come! S*it at the Royal table today to partake of His blessings that He has prepared just for us!

November 25

Give Us Our Daily Bread

Matthew 6:11 "Give us this day our daily Bread."

God knows what we have need of today, and is very faithful to provide us with fresh bread. I am thankful that we don't have to eat leftovers or stale bread when we dine at His table, but everything is fresh and applicable for this day.

When Israel journeyed through the desert, the Lord provided them with fresh manna every day, except for the Sabbath. They would get a double portion of food the day before the Sabbath that would be enough for both days. He called forth water out of the rock to quench their thirst and cool their hot and tired bodies.

He knows what we have need of today! He has what we need to sustain us this day! His words are Spirit and Life, and can satisfy even the hungriest of souls. His Words bring heath to our bones and joy to our hearts. As we set this day aside to worship Him, be mindful that all that we need can be found in His House at His table, and He will not deny us!

November 26

A Slice of Gratefulness

Isaiah 25:1 "O Lord, thou art my God; I will exalt thee, I will praise thy name; for thou hast done wonderful things; thy counsels of old are faithfulness and truth."

Have you ever received a note or a card from someone who expressed their sincere appreciation for something you did? If you are like most of us, you probably kept that note. One such person has held on to a note for over forty years, and when asked if he remembered what it said, the man pulled the note from his wallet. Forty years after receiving the note, he still considered it one of his most valued possessions and carried it with everywhere he went. Words of appreciation, thankfulness and gratitude for things we do for others mean a lot to us when they are meant.

I looked up the meaning of gratitude - *The state of being grateful; warm and friendly feeling toward a benefactor; kindness awakened by a favor received; thankfulness."* The ability and willingness to express sincere appreciation is one of our most endearing qualities. It sounds simple, yet the expression of sincere gratitude is rare. It is not easy, and frequently not considered important to convey real appreciation in our world where convention rather than authenticity rules most of our communication. Yet it remains one of the most treasured and cherished gifts we can receive - that of sincere gratitude and heartfelt thanks.

As we prepare to gather around family tables to celebrate our National Day of Thanksgiving, let us serve up a huge slice of gratefulness for all the blessings that our Father has bestowed upon us and for those we can call family and friends. I am grateful for His blessings that overtake me every day, for the Blood of Jesus that still has the power to forgive and cleanse us of our sins, for the gift of eternal life, and for my most treasured earthly possessions...my children, grandchildren, family and friends.

November 27

The Lord is Good to Us

Nahum 1:7 "The Lord is good, a stronghold in the day of trouble; and He knows those who trust in Him."

What a good God! What a great God! Wisdom and power, glory and might all belong to Him!

Some people think that when they serve Christ, all their troubles will come to an end - no more valleys and no more storms. However, God doesn't promise an easy path, but He does give us something more wonderful and more powerful - He gives us His love and help! When things don't go our way, He steps in and says, *"My ways are higher than yours - Let me show you the better way!"* When people disappoint and hurt us, He comes to us and says, *"I will never disappoint you."* When we fall short of the mark, He bestows on us the gifts of mercy and forgiveness. When we go through the trials, His grace is there, leading us through. Yes, God is good!

His blessings overtake us! His love sustains us! His strength picks us up! His compassion heals us! His mercy forgives us! His lovingkindness remembers us! His glory transforms us! His wisdom guides us! He is a good God...all the time, every day, every hour! It is the goodness of God that brings men to repentance! Let Him show you just how good He can be! Taste and see that the Lord is good!

November 28

In The Presence of My Enemies

Psalm 23:5, 6 "Thou preparest a table before me in the presence of mine enemies: thou anointest my head with oil; my cup runneth over. Surely goodness and mercy shall follow me all the days of my life: and I will dwell in the house of the LORD for ever."

There is a cloud of fear and uncertainty covering the earth today. Nations are paralyzed by this fear and have no answers to offer to people. Economical hardships and financial setbacks strike fear deep into the hearts of many who once knew prosperity and success. The world would say that it's only going to get worse...but *they don't know the One we serve!* Thank God we don't live by the world's standards, but we live and abide by His standards...and *He has better things for those who love and serve Him!*

The Lord is our Shepherd...we shall not want! He prepares a table for us, not in the absence of the enemy, but in the presence of our enemies, and says His people will never be ashamed! He calls us to victory, not defeat; to peace, not fear! He anoints our heads with the oil of special blessings and the favor of God! Our cups run over with abundant drink that refreshes and revives us during the dry seasons. His goodness and His mercy assure us we can receive His love, His help, His strength, and His provision in our times of need.

Whatever you are facing today, know that He is with you. You may be facing the enemy of lack, or the enemy of hurt, but a table is spread just for you by the Hand of the Lord! He is there to calmly and gently guide you. Your steps are ordered by Him. Trust the Hand that is guiding you, He will not lead you wrong. He cares for you and your needs, especially when forces of evil rise up against you, and *in the presence of the enemy, He prepares a table of plenty...a table of hope...just for you!*

November 29

He Will Look For You

Luke 15:4 "What man of you, having a hundred sheep, if he loses one of them, does not leave the ninety-nine in the wilderness, and go after the one which is lost until he finds it?"

The nights are getting quite cold as winter approaches. My house cat, Socks, often wanders and I become quite concerned when he doesn't come in on the cold days and evenings. I become concerned about him in the cold and what he might encounter while exploring the wooded area behind our home. I call him and *go looking for him until I see him running towards me*, ready to come in to the warmth and safety. Once he is in, I can relax knowing he is safe and warm.

How much more our Heavenly Father is concerned about us! Socks is only a cat...a pet to enjoy, but you and I are so much more to God! We are created in His image. We are as lambs among wolves sent out into the world, and when we wander or lose our way, He will tirelessly search and call for His little lambs by name. He knows that it is imperative to find us quickly due to impending dangers of the cold, the unseen predators, and being away from the safety of His care. He won't quit searching for us until we are safe in His shelter. Even when we stubbornly resist His calling, He is patient and loving with us in our cold, frightened pain, and will keep searching, keep looking, and keep calling until we walk through His doors into safety, warmth, and love.

Perhaps you know someone who has lost their way. Let God use you to remind them He hasn't forgotten them, but is still calling their name. Maybe you have wandered from the fold and aren't sure if there would be a warm welcome awaiting you if you returned. Our Father, like the father of the prodigal, has a warm welcome awaiting you. He is looking for His little lost ones, He is calling out their names beckoning them to come in from the cold, the dark, and the danger.

November 30

Be Still And Know

Psalm 46:10 "Be still, and know that I am God; I will be exalted among the nations, I will be exalted in the earth!"

Then, there is God! In the stillness of the night and in the quiet rising of the sun, God is there, bringing peace to a heart that is hurting. He can be found in the wee hours of the morning writing a song upon the lips of a saint who has known suffering and sorrow. He is there in the busy hours of the day guiding one lost soul back to safe shores.

He is there, when all other help is reduced to nothing and we've reached the limitations of what man can do. He steps into the stillness...and *we suddenly know He is God!* When our glory has faded and our power has become useless, He shows us what a loving, caring God can do. His wisdom supersedes our understanding and knowledge, and we learn to trust Him even when it looks hopeless. And, when our steps falter and become a little slower under the weight of heavy cares, He gently scoops us up and carries us until we are strong again. He exalts Himself among the nations and declares Himself to those who search for Him.

Then, there is God! You are not alone, *but you are accompanied by One who is greater than any mountain in your path.* He fights for you and defends you against your enemies. He vindicates His little ones and empowers His people to rise up from the ashes of defeat and to step into His glory! Yes, when man has reached his limits, and all that can be done has been done...there is God! Be still...and know!

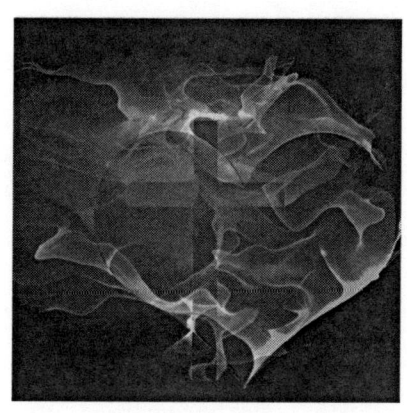

December

Christmas signifies God's purest, boldest,
most over-the-top show of love for the world.
- Ella Jane Coley

December 1

The Miracle Landing

"The ship is anchored safe and sound..." Walt Whitman in "O Captain My Captain"
Hebrews 7:25 "Therefore He is able to save completely those who come to God through Him, because He always lives to intercede for them."
Isaiah 25:9 "Surely this is our God; we trusted in Him, and He saved us. This is the LORD, we trusted in Him; let us rejoice and be glad in His salvation."

Everyone is still talking about the Miracle Landing on the Hudson River, and how the calm attitude of the pilot saved the lives of every passenger on board. He was Captain in every sense...skilled, professional, trained, and experienced. One hundred and fifty-four lives depended on him...and he did not fail them. His training on the battlefields of the Air Force prepared him for this one moment in time...a moment when the eyes of the world would look on him and see the character, the strength, the experience, and the great love he had for those entrusted in his care. A true Captain, he would not leave the plane until he had walked it twice in search of someone that might have been left behind. Only then did this brave hero abandon the downed plane.

We also have a Pilot...a Captain...who will make sure we safely land! Engines may blow and power may fail, but He has the experience, the training, the knowledge, and the skill to land us safely! He, too, is prepared for each crisis we might encounter, for He engaged in the battle for our souls...and won! He won't abandon the ship when times get tough. He's not afraid of adversity, but remains calm under pressure. His attributes are clearly visible for all to see and prove He is quite capable of mastering every situation. His orders are clear and precise, and when we obey His command, we are assured safe passage and a smooth, miracle landing. It may seem as though our plane is crashing and our ship is sinking, but our Captain will not fail in His mission. There will be no wounded, no one overlooked, and no passenger left behind on His watch. He will not rest until we are anchored safe and sound.

December 2

He Guides My Ship

Psalm 48:14 "For this is God, our God forever and ever; He will be our guide even to death."

     In prayer this morning the Lord quietly spoke this to my heart..."*Just tell them I am at the helm. Remind them that I am still in command."* As He spoke, I could see His hand upon the helm, strong, full of strength and confidence, the hand of One who is not afraid of storms. His hand formed the worlds and rules the universe. His hand...the hand that scooped up dirt to make man in His image... is the Hand of grace and guidance. His hands...that made a paste of spit and dust for a blind man's eyes...still gives comfort and healing. His hands...that bear the prints of old, rusty nails...are the Hands that hold our salvation and our hope. His hands guide this ship of mine and lead me to safe harbors.

     It does not matter what storms we face or how choppy the waters become, for what really matters is ***He is at the helm***, guiding us safely through. He is in full command, in charge of every situation. And as the old song goes, *"Storms may come and winds may blow and rock this ship of mine. But the reason my ship has never sank... is Jesus pilots my boat."*

December 3

Wait For The Promise

Genesis 18:14 "Is any thing too hard for the Lord? At the time appointed I will return unto thee according to the time of life, and Sarah shall have a son."

The promises of God are *"Yea and Amen!"* Has He not spoken and will He not do it? *God is not a man that He should lie.* Perhaps you, like me, are waiting for a promise to be fulfilled. Can God still do it? Oh Yes, if He said, He will perform it!

Sara and Abraham were up in age when God told them to go to a place they knew not of. God gave them exceeding great promises…promises that His seed would produce great nations and bless the nations of the world. *But, how could this be?* They were barren and past the child bearing age. I can imagine that Abraham's heart beat a little faster, his eyes lit up, and he probably danced quite a jig! Genesis 15:6 tells us that Abraham believed the promise! ***And at age One Hundred…Abraham got his promise!*** The Promised Heir had come after years and years of waiting!

Wait for your promise! God will send it at the appointed time! *Is anything too hard for your God?* No! There is a promise waiting to be birthed and a dream waiting to be lived! So, hold on tightly to your promise and refuse to give it up! Wait until it comes!

December 4

Trust the Promise Giver

Genesis 22:2 "And He said, take now thy son, thine only son Isaac, whom thou lovest, and get thee into the Land of Moriah; and offer him there for a burnt offering upon one of the mountains which I will tell thee of."

The greatest and final test was now upon Abraham! What started years ago with a command from God to leave his land was ending with another word...*go sacrifice your Son of Promise*! This was His son that he loved more than anyone, except God.

But, Abraham was deeply intimate with the voice that was now demanding this sacrifice...it was the voice of the One who had called him friend for the past thirty years. We will not find in this story where Abraham questioned God, nor did he try to make a bargain with Him. Immediately he quietly began the journey of sacrifice. He didn't tell his wife, his servants, or his son anything other than he was going to offer a sacrifice to the Lord. "*Where is the lamb?*" asks young Isaac. Abraham showed no doubt, no fear, or no sorrow as he answered the boy, "*God will provide.*" Abraham built the altar and laid his precious boy upon it. As he raised the knife to slay his son, that Voice called out and said, "*For now I know that thou fearest God, seeing thou hast not withheld thy son, thine only son from me.*"

What is going on here? Most of us would have called every Pastor and prayer line we could find to pray that God would change His mind. Many of us would have bargained with God or denied that it was His voice speaking to us. After all, what kind of God would demand such a thing? God wants to bless us with all good things and to prosper us, however ***God never intends for the blessings to take His place in our hearts***. Many times He will test us to see if we can handle the promise! Abraham passed the test because he knew His God; he had a long term relationship with Him; he valued the covenants of God; and he knew God could be trusted with the promise! We, too, can trust God with our promises. God wants our complete love and trust. We can be like Abraham, who trusted the Promise-Giver more than he loved the promise!

December 5

His Divine Purposes

Job 23:14 "For He performeth the thing that is appointed for me..."

Romans 8:28 says, *"All things work together for good to them that love God..."* As believers and Children of God, we can be assured of this - God has a Divine plan for our lives. As we walk with Him, He will perform those things that He has appointed for us! *When He speaks something into motion, there is no power on earth that can stop His plans from unfolding!*

In spite of everything that Job was going through, he knew God wasn't finished with him yet! He had lost his children, his wealth, and his social standing. But Job held on to the most important thing...the only thing that would bring out of his despair...*his faith!* As we read the end of Job's story we find that God gave him double for his trouble!

Everything that touches us is used by God for His Divine purpose. Every sorrow, every pain, every disappointment, every struggle, every victory, every dream, every blessing are tools used by the Master Potter to perfect His plan in our lives. What the devil means for evil, God turns for our good! His plans for us are good, and He gives us a future and something to look forward to. God *will* perform those things He has appointed for us.

December 6

Hidden Treasure

Matthew 6:21 "For where your treasure is, there will your heart be also."

For every valley, there is a mountaintop! For every storm, there is a rainbow! For every battle there is victory decreed for those who trust in the Lord! For every need, there is provision. *He is Jehovah -Jireh, Our Provider!*

We can learn how to turn our pain into our gain! Even our failures can be stepping stones towards our success. There are treasures of darkness and hidden riches in those secret places where trials and tests take place. *He gives us treasures from our trials!*

Some people blame the Lord for the hardships they walk through. They get angry at God when things don't work out the way they had hoped. Some experience bitterness and anger because of trials and tests they faced. In their immature state of mind, they turned from instead of to the One who was there to help them achieve victory. He is the Friend that is closer than a brother, and the One who will never leave us or forsake us! It is in our weaknesses that we can partake of His strength. It is during the testings of our faith that He becomes Lord of All to us. Look for those treasures in the secret place of pain or sorrow. Look for treasures of character that is developed through brokenness. Look for the joy that is set before you…and you will find the treasures that are hidden awaiting you!

December 7

Tidings of Peace

Luke 2: 13, 14 "And suddenly there was with the angel a multitude of the heavenly host praising God, and saying, Glory to God in the highest, and on earth peace, good will toward men."

Oh, the wonderful Peace of God! It sees us through some hard, lonely times, giving us rest and assurance that all is well with God! One of the main reasons many people end their lives is because they have no peace, yet, peace has been provided if only they had sought the Prince of Peace.

Peace came to the earth through a birth announcement carried by angelic messengers! God extended His Hand of goodwill and kind favor to mankind by sending Peace in the form of a little baby. The Prince of Peace came to a world writhing in turmoil, heartache, restlessness...and hopelessness. Peace penetrated the unrest and the shadows of darkness with it's glimmer of hope for all mankind. Tidings of Peace! Good will to all mankind was the message long ago!

Jesus Christ came to bring peace to our anxious hearts and worried minds. His peace covers us like a soft blanket, keeping us warm and secure in the face of turmoil. When He makes His entrance into our lives...He comes in Peace, the kind that passes all our understanding and fills our hearts with an unshakable, unfathomable blanket of pure peace, love, and joy.

December 8

No Other Name

Acts 4:12 "Neither is there salvation in any other: for there is none other name under heaven given among men, whereby we must be saved."

God attaches great significance to names. His own names are powerful testimonials to His great glory and majesty: God Almighty (El-Shaddai), God of Peace (Yahweh-Shalom) and God Our Provider (Yahweh-Jireh), among others. There is a Name that is lovelier than any other name! We have a Name that has been given to us that will quiet our fears, calm our storms, and bring peace to our troubled minds. *That beautiful, life-giving Name is Jesus!*

Jesus! I whispered His Name to my young children as fever burned hotly in their little bodies...and saw the power of His Name bring healing. *Jesus!* I called His Name in times of duress and struggles, and immediately felt peace calm my heart. *Jesus!* I spoke His Name when I drank from the bitter cup of sorrow and gained strength to face another day. *Jesus!* I shouted His Name in the face of my enemy and saw him turn and run! *Jesus*! I embraced His Name in my sin and received forgiveness and new birth! *Jesus!* I shared His Name with sinners and witnessed the transformation as salvation was imparted to them. *Jesus!* I called His Name lovingly in my moments of deep loneliness and was filled with His sweet Presence of love, peace, and joy!

There is no other Name by which we can be saved! *Jesus,* the Name above all names, is given freely to all who believe in that wonderful Name! *Jesus* - God is salvation! *Christ* - the Anointed One! The angel said unto Joseph and Mary, *"You shall call His Name Jesus and He shall save the people from their sins!"*

December 9

The Silent Years

Galatians 4:4 "When the time had fully come, God sent forth his Son, born of woman, born under the law."

Four Hundred and thirty years have passed since the Lord had visited His people! Four hundred thirty years have slowly gone by since the prophet had prophesied! It was a time of great silence in the Temple and apostasy was the order of the day! A great shifting had taken place and Israel was under the domination of the great world power of that day, Persia and the Medio-Persian Empire. In Jerusalem, the temple had been restored, although it was a much smaller building than the one that Solomon had built and decorated in such marvelous glory. The lineage of David had fallen and religion had clasped hands with tyranny. *No one had prophesied! No one had heard from God! No one had received a blessing!*

It's a like that in our time. There is nothing stirring in the Sanctuary! The fires on the altars have died out! We go through the rituals of worship, but it is passionless and cold. We have waited... and waited...and waited upon the Lord, but He has remained strangely quiet. We are diligent in our service to Him, but *we need something more*. Our prayers have gone up continually, yet remain unanswered. We are desperate for a Word from Him and *realize we will die without it*. But **something is happening in the temple!** Something is stirring and fires that have gone out are being rekindled! Our worship suddenly seems more passionate and our praise more joyous! He is walking into dead churches that haven't felt or heard from Him in a long, long time! His entrance is making a statement to those who have waited for His coming...*"I am here and have come to silence the silence! You have waited patiently. You have prayed diligently! Your hunger for me has manifested in my throne room!"*

Light has arrived and darkness is fleeing! Praise and worship now fills the silent temples! The Word of the Lord has come to us in power, in might, and in triumph! The silence is defeated and the Blessings of the Lord are here! He has come and the years of silence are no more!

December 10

The Reproach Is Lifted

Luke 1:25 "Thus hath the Lord dealt with me in the days wherein he looked on me, to take away my reproach among men."

Imagine serving God all of your life, living righteously, and keeping His commandments...but you bear a reproach because you are barren and have no children. Such was the case of Zacharias and Elisabeth. Faithful in the House of God, exemplary leaders of worship and service, but they bore the stigma of being barren. Perhaps they felt as we do sometimes - the more we put into our service to God the less we receive. The world points fingers of blame and wonders why we are unproductive. Criticized by some who enjoy *"the blessed life"*, we ourselves wonder why the blessings pass us by.

God has held back His blessings for *"such a time as this"* in your life - *a time in which your moment has passed you by and your season has come and gone!* He has something far greater in mind for you - something so miraculous that can only be done by God! You have reached this stage in life where you cannot do it on your own power...and *you need a miracle!* You have diligently served the Lord and kept His temple undefiled all these years, but now your moment has arrived! He has come to remove the reproach and take away the stigma that has followed your barren ministry! The miracle you sought has found you...*and you will rejoice and no more bear the reproach*, the blame, the critical pointing fingers! His Word is resonating through the silence, bringing life, hope, and joy!

December 11

The Right Place and Time

Luke 2:36-38 "And there was one Anna, a prophetess, the daughter of Phanuel, of the tribe of Aser: she was of a great age, and had lived with an husband seven years from her virginity; And she was a widow of about fourscore and four years, which departed not from the temple, but served God with fastings and prayers night and day. And she coming in that instant gave thanks likewise unto the Lord, and spake of him to all them that looked for redemption in Jerusalem."

God knows how to place us at the right place...at the right time! How many times can we look back and see blessings that came from being at the right place at the right time! It may be a Divine contact or a Rhema Word that in an instant connects us to our Destiny!

Anna spent her life in the temple. Day in and day out she served in the Temple, performing those same duties day...after day... after day. Faithful, loyal and trustworthy, she gave her all and she gave her best to the Lord. No task was too belittling and no chore was too monotonous. She served the Lord from a heart that was pure and devoted...and God saw her! God saw and God rewarded her! Those old eyes that had seen much grief and sorrow *now gazed into the eyes that would one day cause blind men to see.* Those ears that heard tragic tales and grievous complaints *now heard the cry of the Lamb of God!* Those old, boney hands that performed menial chores in the temple *now held the world's hope and salvation*! That old tired body that had given years of service now felt new life coursing through its veins as she held the Son of God!

Yes, God knows how to put us in the right place at the right time to receive blessings that can only be described as amazing, miraculous, and divine!

December 12

Worth Waiting For

Luke 2:25, 26 "And, behold, there was a man in Jerusalem, whose name was Simeon; and the same man was just and devout, waiting for the consolation of Israel: and the Holy Ghost was upon him. And it was revealed unto him by the Holy Ghost, that he should not see death, before he had seen the Lord's Christ."

Simeon had waited a lifetime to see the Salvation of Israel. How many days did he spend waiting and wondering when, when, when? How many times did he remind God that he wasn't getting any younger and life was going by really fast. *Somehow, I don't believe Simeon ever lost hope that his eyes would behold the salvation of the world.* All we know of this man is that he was just and devout... *and was waiting on a promise given to him by the Holy Ghost.* Can you imagine that day when Mary and Joseph took Baby Jesus to the temple? There was Simeon...waiting eagerly to see this new born Child! He took Him in his arms...*and held salvation!* His eyes looked upon that baby face...*and saw redemption!* He felt His little heart beating...and *felt the hope of the world!* He waited a lifetime for this moment...but it was worth waiting for!

Life does go by quickly, sometimes causing us to wonder if we will ever see those things we desired to see of the Lord. Seems like the older we get, the quicker time flies! Yet, there are precious promises made to us...promises given to us by God that we will see with our own eyes fulfilled! These things are worth waiting for!

December 13

God's Unusual Love

Matthew 1:23 "Behold, the virgin shall be with child, and bear a Son, and they shall call His name Immanuel, which is translated, God with us."

Christmas is almost here...and some of the best music and biggest hearts are being heard and seen. I know that for too many of us, it can be a time of stress, worry, concern, and depression, but for a moment today, I'd like for us to remember, truly remember, what Christmas really means.

Christmas signifies God's purest, boldest, most over-the-top, show of love for the world. The method used to deliver His gift was most unusual - *a young virgin.* The setting was most unlikely - *a smelly stable!* The guest list was unheard of - *shepherds invited to visit a baby King!* The birth announcements - *were simply out of this world.* Angelic Choirs filled the night skies with heavenly lullabies, and the message delivered was unprecedented *"Peace on Earth and Goodwill to Men."* Seems like a strange way to save the world, doesn't it!

Perhaps we need to remind ourselves every day that this is what Christmas is all about - God's unusual love delivered in an unusual way to us. Tell the children and grand children about the miracle of Christmas, and the hope and peace it offers to all who believe! The best Gift has already been given and is worth celebrating! Let Peace fill your hearts and minds...it was given to you 2,000 years ago along with the Gift of love wrapped in flesh and born in a manger.

December 14

There's A Celebration In the Stable

Luke 2:15, 16 "And it came to pass, as the angels were gone away from them into heaven, the shepherds said one to another, Let us now go even unto Bethlehem, and see this thing which is come to pass, which the Lord hath made known unto us. And they came with haste, and found Mary, and Joseph, and the babe lying in a manger."

I love celebrating special events with my family and close friends. Special moments in life deserve to be celebrated. Special people deserve to be acknowledged. Celebrations of such times and people bring us great joy and satisfaction, and create memories that will long be enjoyed after the celebration is over.

I was thinking about this little family who celebrated the birth of God's Son in the manger. There were no balloons, no music, and no fine china to serve delicious food. But, nevertheless, ***there was a celebration going on in the manger!*** God's Son had been born! The guest list included Angelic Visitors, Shepherd Boys, and Wise Men from far away. *The party was on and Heaven was celebrating in great style!* The Messiah had come to save His people! The King had arrived, but not in the splendor and glory that came from being born in a palace! Instead of purple apparel, the Prince of Peace was wrapped in swaddling clothes! His mother sang to Him and was accompanied by the voices of angels!

There was a celebration that took place long ago in the stable in Bethlehem! It was a celebration is still going on!

December 15

Some Unlikely Guests

Luke 2:8-16 "And there were in the same country shepherds abiding in the field, keeping watch over their flock by night. And, lo, the angel of the Lord came upon them...the angel said unto them, Fear not:...for unto you is born this day in the city of David a Saviour, which is Christ the Lord. And it came to pass, as the angels were gone away from them into heaven, the shepherds said one to another, Let us now go even unto Bethlehem, and see this thing which is come to pass, which the Lord hath made known unto us. And they came with haste, and found Mary, and Joseph, and the babe lying in a manger."

They were some of the most unlikely guests to ever receive such an invitation as this! They were divinely invited to see the new born King. Who would have thought that someone such as they would receive heavenly tidings and great honor? What was God thinking?

They probably smelled as bad as the sheep they were watching. Their education most likely lacked things such as proper manners, social graces, and common courtesies. Often ignored and over looked by society, these strong, unlikely guests were in a state of shock at this Royal Invitation. Someone had paid close attention to them, looking past their rough exterior to see hearts that were as tender as the Shepherd Boy of long ago who became a king. Some had observed how kind they were to the sheep and watched how at times they put their own lives in peril to save a lamb that had gone astray. *These unlikely men were found worthy by a Proud Father to celebrate the birth of His newborn Son.*

As unlikely as it seems, we, too, have been given an invitation to enter into the Presence of the King! We are His guests as He prepares a splendid table before us and says, *"Come and Dine."* We, too, have been issued a Royal Invitation to *"go and see"* this King of Kings. Let us, like these unlikely guests of long ago, eagerly and with much haste enter into His Divine Presence!

December 16

Our Finest Gifts

Matthew 2:11 "And when they had come into the house, they saw the young Child with Mary His mother, and fell down and worshiped Him. And when they had opened their treasures, they presented gifts to Him: gold, frankincense, and myrrh."

"*Don't go empty-handed*!" I can still hear my mother telling her children this as we prepared to go to God's House! She instilled in us the importance of bringing gifts, especially to Him. My older sister was a great believer of bringing gifts when she came to visit, and always brought a cake or some baked goodie. These gifts always made the visit special and turned it into a celebration. *Our gifts reflect our hearts*, bringing honor and a spirit of celebration to the person or event.

Three wise men long ago recognized the importance of bringing gifts to the Son of God! They went out of their way, traveling for many, many miles to see the Baby King. Distance was no problem and every inconvenience was minor. Their gifts were the finest they could offer...gold, myrrh, and frankincense, befitting a King! *These gifts reflected their belief in this Baby...a belief that acknowledged Him as a King*! I am reminded of another gift that was lavished on this same King. Costly perfume was lavishly poured from a broken alabaster box upon His feet from the heart of a worshiper! Those who had not yet understood Who He was couldn't understand why such an expensive gift was "thrown away."

Wise people still seek Him and worship Him! They recognize Who He is and lavish on Him their finest gifts! Wise ones see Him as the Son of God and King of Kings, and hold nothing back from Him. Nothing is too good for Him! *Once we really see Him, we, too, will offer Him our finest gifts.*

December 17

Great Things Come In Small Packages

Micah 5:2 "But you, Bethlehem Ephrathah, Though you are little among the thousands of Judah, Yet out of you shall come forth to Me The One to be Ruler in Israel..."

Something tugged at my heartstrings while reading this Scripture. I thought..."*God is really a sentimental God. He favors the little and the humble!*" Our Magnificent Creator chose to bless the Nations of the Earth through a humble, but meaningful City called Bethlehem.

Bethlehem...the *House of Bread*...had some special heartstrings attached to it. It became home to Ruth, whose very name evokes images of loyalty and trust. The great Shepherd Boy who became King was born here*! There was a great love connection to this special place.* No wonder God wanted His Son to be born in Bethlehem. *This beloved "City of David" gained eternal honor and prestige as the Birth City for the Son of God, who also came to us in a "small" package!*

There are a lot of precious people who are overlooked and thought insignificant by society, but *these little ones have a special love connection and Him that command His favor.* There are many ministries that are "invisible" because they are not in the spotlight, but *they have His heart!* Your dream may be only in the seed stage, but give it to Him and it becomes a harvest! Just because something or someone appears insignificant doesn't mean God isn't involved! *Little is much when God has it!* The Scriptures cautions us to not despise small beginnings...some of the greatest things come in small packages!

December 18

The Wisdom of Christmas

Matthew 1:18 "Now the birth of Jesus Christ was on this wise..."

You can still see it, especially in the eyes of the children...the wonder of Christmas! The sparkle in their eyes outshines the bright, colored tree lights as they whisper their little secrets to Moms and Dads. You can hear the excitement in their voices as they belt out one more Christmas Carol. Children seem to understand what we sometimes miss...miracles can be found in the Christmas story.

The world needed a miracle...and found One wrapped in swaddling clothes. It doesn't seem logical that a little baby could be born of a virgin, yet He was. It makes little sense that the hand wrapped around Joseph's finger would rule the world, yet He does. It defies all logic and reason that a baby would be the salvation of mankind. The wisdom of Christmas is this...*to make atonement for the sins of man, Jesus had to be human. To have the authority to forgive sin and the ability to live sinlessly, He had to be God.* Only God could be so wise and loving to deliver such a Perfect Gift!

It is said that wise men still seek Him...and therein lies the Wisdom of Christmas.

December 19

So Be It

Luke 1:38 "And Mary said, Behold the handmaid of the Lord; be it unto me according to thy word."

Sometimes God will speak a word to us that is so profound, so impossible, so unimaginable, and so deep that it leaves us speechless. We know the only way it can be done is for God to do it, for it is so far beyond our abilities that we can only say, *"So be it, Lord, according to Your Word."*

Mary's visitation with the angel even superseded that of Abraham's encounter and promise. Her response was beautiful and wise beyond her years...*"be it unto me according to thy word..."* She knew there was nothing she could do to make this happen except make her body available to the will of God. This young virgin simply accepted God's Word and believed He would perform it.

So be it! That should be our response when the Lord speaks His purpose and plans to our spirits! Our minds may try to reason everything out, but some things are beyond reason and logic, and must be walked out in faith. Leave the impossibilities with Him and simply make yourself available...He'll do the rest!

December 20

What's In Your Womb?

Matthew 1:20 "...Fear not...for that which is conceived in her is of the Holy Ghost."
Luke 1:31 "...Thou shalt conceive in thy womb, and bring forth a son, and shalt call his name JESUS."

What seed lies within your spiritual womb? What dream is waiting to be birthed? What greatness lies hidden from sight, ready to manifest?

The Father had a wonderful, gracious plan to save the world... and *it all started with a dream.* Our Creator penned His destiny long before our Savior was manifested in a borrowed womb. Faith filled the virgin's womb, and the creative Word was seeded in the earthly realm. *Destiny came forth! God always starts with a seed...a plan... and a womb of faith.*

My friend, His children are filled with purpose and destiny! He has great plans that He seeds into the spiritual wombs of believers. ***And when God dreams, He dreams BIG!*** When God's purposes are spoken, provision is made! When God seeds a promise, it will always happen! *What is in your spiritual womb today?* Perhaps you, like Mary, wonder how can this thing be? Be like Mary - receive the seed, believe the message, and trust that God will be revealed.

December 21

Make Room For Him

Luke 2:7 "And she brought forth her firstborn Son, and wrapped Him in swaddling cloths, and laid Him in a manger, because there was no room for them in the inn."

I have never seen people as busy as they are now. There doesn't seem to be enough time to get everything done and it seems we are running on pure adrenalin just to keep up. *If we are not careful, we will get so busy that there will be no room for Him in our lives.*

This is, perhaps, one of the most touching moments since time began - *there was no room for Mary and Joseph in the inn.* It was a "busy" time in the City, and the innkeepers failed to recognize the significance of the couple standing before them requesting a room. It was obvious to all that Mary was going to have a baby, and as the labor pains began, I'm sure that even a blind man could see she needed a nice clean place to have her baby. How many doors did Joseph knock on only to hear, *"No Room!"* How many eyes overlooked Mary's condition because they were too busy to realize the significance of the guests standing before them. The hotel staff were probably too stressed and over-worked to see the obvious...*a Baby was coming!* Finally, one innkeeper took pity on the couple and made room for them in a dark, lowly manger.

Are we too busy to make room for Him? Do we find ourselves rushing around and doing things, all in His Name, but sadly fail to realize that in our busyness, we have left Him behind? *Are our hearts so full of the cares and concerns in this life that there is no room for Him there?* Have bitterness, resentments, jealousy, and offenses displaced Him, leaving no room for His peace, His love, and His joy to fill us? My friend, when we are too busy for Him, we are too busy! Today, take some time to spend with Him! Enjoy being in His Presence! Welcome Him with open arms and hearts into your lives! Allow Him to lift the cares, the sorrows, and the concerns from your heavy shoulders! *Make room for Him, and there will be no room left for any of these other things in your life.* He deserves more than a dark, quiet corner in our hearts and is worthy of the best place in your life.

December 22

A Reason To Rejoice

Matthew 1:23 "...God with us."

Our world is full of Grinches, Scrooges, and Herods who would love nothing more than to assassinate Christmas. If only they knew that *Christmas is far more than another national holiday, but was the day Divine Love stepped from the portals of heaven to walk among men.*

Herod thought he could stop Christmas by slaying every baby boy under the age of two, but even a king could not stop God's greatest gift to this world. God's plan for man's redemption could not be stopped, assassinated, or sabotaged! Christ came...and even Herod could not stop his coming! Emmanuel, God with us, was born on that glorious night, bringing hope to mankind and redemption of sins!

The grinches, scrooges, and Herods of our day still attempt to assassinate Christmas...but they cannot! They sue, steal manger scenes, and try to replace Christmas with Xmas or Holiday...but Christmas remains! And so does our reason to rejoice! *"We can sing with or without the presents, the trees, the feasts, and the trimmings, for Christ remains the reason for rejoicing!* It is He who brought peace to us and goodwill to all! Rejoice, for God has come to us... Emanuel, God with us...*and even hell can't stop this*!

December 23

The Gift

John 3:16 "For God so loved the world that He gave His only begotten Son..."

I am reminded today of how very much the Father loves us and how *He gave His very best gift* to us...His only Son, Jesus! That kind of love can only be described as unfathomable!

Many around the world will soon celebrate Christmas...each in their own way and custom. Some will call it a "holiday season", others will focus on "Santa Claus", *and some us will remember that it is still about the birth of the Savior of the world.* He came to bring peace to troubled hearts and minds. He came to reconcile lost souls back to the Father. He came to show us love in it's purest form, for He is love and only in Him can we find the love that we seek. Angels proclaimed His birth and filled the skies with songs! Shepherds bowed before Him and trembled in His presence. Lowly animals sang Him lullabies as His mother kissed His soft cheeks. He left a royal throne surrounded by angels who worshipped Him without ceasing to come to a world where men would reject Him and curse His beautiful Name. Yes, He came to us to give us hope when there seems to be no hope, to give us peace in a world torn apart by wicked acts of men, and to give us joy, even in our times of sorrow.

Oh, what a Gift! Oh, what a Savior! Oh, what wonderful love!

December 24

The Light Has Come

John 1:1,4, 5 "In the beginning was the Word, and the Word was with God, and the Word was God... In him was life; and the life was the light of men... And the light shineth in darkness; and the darkness comprehended it not."

The world we live in is covered with darkness as men struggle to find their ways. Thankfully, God did not leave us to grope in the dark, but sent His Light to us in the nature of Jesus! Jesus, who existed before creation began was there when God said, *"Let there be Light."* As darkness and evil doings began to cover the earth, God the Creator looked upon the darkness and again sent the "Spoken Word", this time in the form of Jesus who became the Word in flesh and dwelt among men. He came to us, clothed in Light and Holiness, so that we would no longer have to struggle blindly to find our way. He alone is the hope of all mankind and the solution to our blindness! *He is the light and His light is the life of men as it pierces the darkness and lights the way for us!*

There are still many who stumble blindly in the darkness and have lost their way, yet there is hope for them! The Light came to us over 2,000 years ago and still burns brightly, bidding men to come to Him! He is the Savior of the World...and we have this glorious privilege of presenting Jesus to our darkened world once again! Arise and shine, for our Light has come!

December 25

He Is Here!

Luke 1:31-33 "And, behold, thou shalt conceive in thy womb, and bring forth a son, and shalt call his name JESUS. He shall be great, and shall be called the Son of the Highest: and the Lord God shall give unto him the throne of his father David: And he shall reign over the house of Jacob for ever; and of his kingdom there shall be no end."

There is great excitement in our homes today! Parents are waking up to the jubilant cries of children! *"Christmas is here!"* rings out, proclaiming that the long awaited day is finally here! Presents are unwrapped, and the glee and excitement cannot be constrained or contained! Savory smells coming from the kitchens permeate through the homes as the best dishes are offered on this special occasion!

I wonder, however, as we busily go through the celebrations of this day how many of us will remember why we are celebrating. God came to us wrapped in the flesh of a new born babe. The greatest gift ever to be given was born on the Bethlehem morning so long ago. He came, a fresh, newly wrapped present, smelling of pure baby love and innocence to bring us peace, love, and great joy! *He is here! Emmanuel! God is with us!*

Remember Him today as you unwrap the gifts and set up the table. Invite Him to the celebration...and make it a day that is all about...Him!

December 26

God With Us

Matthew 1:23 "Behold, a virgin shall be with child, and shall bring forth a son, and they shall call his name Emmanuel, which being interpreted is, God with us."

God is with us!

We will soon take down the trees and put away the Christmas decorations until next year. Life will resume its normal pace as we put aside the busyness of shopping and parties. For some of us, things will remain unchanged and be as they were before Christmas. But, like those wise men of old, there will be some of us who will forever be changed by the message of Christmas!

We will find Him to be closer than we thought. We will embrace the God who dwelt in the heavens, but now walks among men. He will come and dwell in us and be our God! As He makes His entrance into our hearts, He will dispel darkness with the radiance of His glory! Loneliness and heartache will flee from His Presence. Our carnal minds will begin to comprehend the greatness of His Birth... *He is With Us!*

Yes, the trees, the lights, and the pretty ribbons and packages will be gone, but He remains with us! ***Emmanuel...God is with us!***

December 27

Make Some Exchanges

1 Corinthians 13:13 "And now abideth faith, hope, love, these three; but the greatest of these is love."

The stores will be busy with gift exchanges and returns from people who received Christmas gifts that they didn't like, didn't want or didn't fit. As we wind down this year and enter the New Year, we can make some other kinds of exchanges that will give us peace with God and our fellow mankind. We won't have to wait in long lines, nor will we be waited upon by frustrated and harried store clerks, but by a loving and merciful Father who is delighted to make these exchanges for us! Here are just a few exchanges that will bring joy and delight to our hearts...as well as His!

Trade in loneliness by seeking out a forgotten friend. Trade in suspicion and doubt for trust and faith. Exchange unkind and harsh words for gentler and kinder conversation. Get rid of unbelief and replace it with seeds of faith that you can nurture through God's word. Turn in a heavy heart for the spirit of gladness. Replace those old glasses that discolored your vision for renewed sight that sees only the beauty in the handiwork of God. Then...after you have made a "few exchanges", once again give gifts that are without price and cannot be bought. Encourage a teenager or child. Apologize to someone you hurt or offended. Think of someone else before yourself. Appreciate others more. Laugh often and long. Express your gratitude for every kindness someone has shown you. Gladden the heart of the elderly and shut-ins by phoning them or paying them a visit. *Forgive an enemy and be merciful to the unlovely.* Give the gift of time to your family and Church, for they are far more valuable than the things that rob us of precious and irreplaceable moments with loved ones.

Each of us has something we need to exchange and we all have something to give. Let us give our very best. If we are bringing gifts to the altar of love, nothing less than the best will be acceptable, nothing less than all is enough. For out of this wonderful treasury of riches, the greatest gifts operate in and through us...those of faith, hope and love!

December 28

Make Some Future Investments

Matthew 6:19, 21 "Do not store up for yourselves treasures on earth, where moth and rust destroy, and where thieves break in and steal. For where your treasure is, there will your heart be also."

Who or what holds our hearts also holds our futures. We have the true riches of the Kingdom, and yet we often walk with our heads held low and complain about everything we don't have, wish we had, or what someone else has that we don't. Instead of looking at what I don't have, I am sitting here today counting my many blessings...the kind that can't be stolen, taken away, lost, or replaced!

Jesus tells us to not get caught up with things that can be here today but gone tomorrow. Instead, He tells us to invest in things which cannot be destroyed, things that are eternal. *The greatest investment we can make is to invest in Him...His kingdom, His vision, and His plans.* Paul exhorts us to not be entangled with the affairs of this world, for they distract us from what really matters. John tells us to love not the world, neither the things in the world. *When we realize that we are not of this world, our mindset will change.* Our goals and plans will take on a more eternal perspective. Even the things we value and treasure will change. How we view our lives and ourselves will dramatically change! *We are heirs and joint-heirs with Christ Jesus! Priests and Ministers of the Lord whose Kingdom is great!* Life in Christ Jesus is exciting, promising, and liberating!

Life as we know it now can change in a moment. It only took 24 hours for Joseph to go from the prison pit into the palace. In one night Nebuchadnezzar went from being a respected and feared King to a wild man who ate grass and acted like a beast in the field. *Life can change quickly, dramatically, and suddenly.* It behooves us to invest in something...Someone...who will be there today, tomorrow, and for eternity! What treasures does your heart hold? Are they fleeting and empty...or are they eternal and secure?

December 29

Make It Count

Ecclesiastes 9:10 "Whatsoever thy hand findeth to do, do it with thy might..."

The old year is ending, and as I look back on it, I wonder how much of my time and labor has really counted for something. I'm sure that if I counted them, I would find that the thief of time stole many of my minutes by keeping me busy or sidetracked with minor things that were sent to distract me from time better spent.

We have each been given a great gift...the gift of today. We have been given another 24 hours which consists of 1440 minutes. The questions we should ask ourselves is, *"What will we do in these 1440 minutes that will make a difference?"* How many of these 1440 minutes will we use to glorify our King? How many minutes will we give to someone who needs a little of our time? Of these 24 hours that have been given to us, how many will be productive? How many times have we asked ourselves, *"Where has the time gone?"* Our time is like a bank account - we make withdrawals and deplete precious minutes from our account, or we can make deposits of our time that will be productive. Beloved, the best time spent is time we deposit into God's bank account. Time spent with Him is the most important time we can spend! Without His Divine Presence deposited into each of our moments, our time is in vain and spent foolishly.

Let's not let another day be spent in vain, but live each precious minute and hour with zeal, determination and with purpose! Embrace this day and rejoice that we are called and filled with great purpose! Give God His time with us! Take the time to encourage someone who is heavy-hearted. Use the time wisely and make investments that will pay off! *Make these 1440 minutes count for something!*

December 30

Enter Into Prayer

Mark 14:34, 38 "...Tarry ye here and watch...and pray..."

I have felt an urgency to pray...*pray the old year out and the New Year in.* I have designated the month of December to set aside time to pray morning and evening. As we close out the old year and enter into the new...*it must be entered into prayerfully!* How we leave one place determines how we will enter another place, and what better way than to go prayerfully!

Jesus, entering into His final hour before His death, also felt the urgency to pray, for He realized that the only way to triumph over what lay before Him was to go through it prayerfully. His greatest hour was before Him to bring hope and restoration to mankind. His flesh man had to be surrendered so His spirit man could triumph. He would soon leave one realm to enter into a new realm, but this could only be accomplished through prayer. Prayer equipped Him to face the greatest battle and the greatest victory in the history of all mankind.

Spend some time in prayer for this New Year and ask the Lord to give you the strength, wisdom and grace to embrace all that is set before you in this New Season! Prayer is the passage that will take you out of the old dimension and into the new dimension.

December 31

See That You Get There

Job 14:14 "...All the days of my appointed time will I wait till my change comes."
Exodus 13:3 "...For by strength of hand the Lord brought you out from this place..."

As I was going through old papers and files today, I came across a thought that I had jotted down. It simply said this, *"See that you get there."*

As we enter into a new year, there will be new promises, new hopes and new beginnings for many of us. God is a God of the present, but also of the future! He called us out of "Egypt", *the place were He will often fashion and form His fairest and finest vessels.* Many of us have left the old behind in hopes of seeing better things. We have gone through the fires of afflictions, some have known separation and pain while going through the threshing place, and others of us have come from valleys of humiliation that struck a blow at our pride. We've had to battle fears and doubt, and vanquish pride and self-will. We have encountered resentment, bitterness and self-pity that had to be destroyed. We walked through overwhelming loneliness while entering into the place of complete surrender to Him. We climbed mountains of impossibilities and *are now ready to enter into the high places of the Lord!*

It is there...this place of blessing, where God does the impossible for us, through us and with us! *We must see that we get "there,"* for we have gone through too much and have waited too long, and have fought too hard to languish by the wayside! Friend... *see that you get there,* for God has ordained this place of purpose, favor, change and blessings for us to enjoy!

About the Author

Ella Jane Coley is the Pastor and Founder of Passageway Ministries, Inc. located in the South Tulsa area. She is also the President of The Grace Full Gospel Assembly, a Ministry which oversees several Churches and Ministries in the Southern Region of the United States. She has served the Body of Christ through Evangelism, Missions, Counseling and as Pastor.

Her passion for people is evidenced by the love she has for her Lord and Savior, Jesus Christ. She gives untiringly of her time and resources and always has a word of encouragement to share with those who are going through difficult times. Her personal experiences have served to give her understanding and wisdom that continually ministers to others who are in need of encouragement, strength and wisdom.

Contact Information:

Ella Jane Coley
P.O. Box 549
Glenpool, Oklahoma 74033
918-366-6886
Or
Passageway Ministries, Inc.
P. O. Box 507
Bixby, Oklahoma 74008
918-366-4415
www.passagewaytulsa.org
Email: Passagewaytulsa@aol.com

LaVergne, TN USA
18 May 2010
183007LV00004B/1/P